AMERICAN CATHOLICISM
IN THE 21st CENTURY

AMERICAN CATHOLICISM IN THE 21st CENTURY

Crossroads, Crisis, or Renewal?

Benjamin T. Peters
and Nicholas Rademacher
Editors

**THE ANNUAL PUBLICATION
OF THE COLLEGE THEOLOGY SOCIETY
2017
VOLUME 63**

ORBIS BOOKS
Maryknoll, New York 10545

ORBIS BOOKS
Maryknoll, New York 10545

Fathers and Brothers
MARYKNOLL™

Founded in 1970, Orbis Books endeavors to publish works that enlighten the mind, nourish the spirit, and challenge the conscience. The publishing arm of the Maryknoll Fathers and Brothers, Orbis seeks to explore the global dimensions of the Christian faith and mission, to invite dialogue with diverse cultures and religious traditions, and to serve the cause of reconciliation and peace. The books published reflect the views of their authors and do not represent the official position of the Maryknoll Society. To learn more about Maryknoll and Orbis Books, please visit our website at www.maryknollsociety.org.

Library of Congress Cataloging-in-Publication Data

Names: Peters, Benjamin T. (Benjamin Tyler), 1973- editor.
Title: American Catholicism in the 21st century : crossroads, crisis, or renewal? / Benjamin T. Peters and Nicholas Rademacher, editors.
Other titles: American Catholicism in the twenty-first century
Description: Maryknoll : Orbis Books, 2018. | Series: The annual publication of the College Theology Society ; VOLUME 63 | Includes bibliographical references. |
Identifiers: LCCN 2017054905 (print) | LCCN 2017056501 (ebook) | ISBN 9781608337378 (e-book) | ISBN 9781626982710 (pbk.)
Subjects: LCSH: Catholic Church—United States—History—21st century.
Classification: LCC BX1406.3 (ebook) | LCC BX1406.3 .A49 2018 (print) | DDC 282/.7309051—dc23
LC record available at https://lccn.loc.gov/2017054905

Contents

Part II
Opportunities and Challenges for American Catholicism

Preface

In Retrospect

William L. Portier and Sandra Yocum

1996: Bill Clinton enjoyed a sweeping victory over Bob Dole to begin what proved to be his scandal-ridden second term as President. Papal headlines included John Paul II's affirmation of evolution as more than a hypothesis. In Dayton, Ohio, at the University of Dayton, from May 30 to June 2, the College Theology Society held its forty-second annual meeting, with the theme *American Catholic Traditions: Resources for Renewal*. Admittedly, no major news outlet covered the meeting, but those who attended—including (for the first time) colleagues from the NABPR[1]—enjoyed a wide-ranging exploration of theologies inspired by and responding to the "American context." A few of those "resources for renewal" were gathered into the annual volume, taking its title from the meeting's theme. Among those sighted, cited, and sited were Black Elk; Dorothy Day and Catholic Radicalism; the Grail movement; movie director John Ford; William Lynch, SJ; *American Catholic Arts and Fictions* à la Paul Giles; early twentieth-century scholars; John Montgomery Cooper, cultural anthropologist; and Francis Gigot, biblical scholar; as well as the development of college theology itself. In his brief essay, Roberto Goizueta expanded the site to include peoples and their intellectual traditions within the *ecclesia* in America to whom John Paul II addressed his 1999 apostolic exhortation.

2017: Donald Trump celebrated his election as president to begin what has proven to be a tumultuous first year. Papal headlines included Pope Francis's reiteration of *Laudato Si'* (2015) to care for our common home, accepting the overwhelming scientific evidence of the devastating effects of climate change, with special attention to its effects on the poor. In Newport, Rhode Island, at Salve Regina University, from June 1 to June 4, the College Theology Society held its sixty-third annual meeting, with the theme *American Catholicism in the 21ˢᵗ Century: Crossroads, Crisis, or Renewal*. Happily, our NABPR colleagues continue to join us. In planning the 1996 meeting, the major concern among some members was whether American Catholicism offered any such resources. In 2017, that question seems to have been laid to rest, but our post-colon options—crossroads, crisis, or renewal—seem more ominous. We may have home-grown resources, but how can they guide the *ecclesia* in America called by Francis to build bridges rather than walls, to accompany the least and most vulnerable among us, and to do so with joy—the joy of the Gospel? And how can we as teachers of college theology accompany each other and our students as we navigate our way through these crossroads, respond to the crises of our present day, and return to sources whose offer of renewal seems more tenuous than ever? The answer to such questions comes in the daily task of enacting one's vocation as a college teacher and scholar of theology. We take solace and find inspiration in the company of those who share in this vocation. This volume makes concrete the broad expanse of that company—bishops, sociologists, historians, and theologians—who help us locate crossroads, name crises, and search with unfailing hope for sites and sources of renewal. As a son of immigrants, a son of this continent, America, Pope Francis proves another good companion for this part of the ride through American Catholicism. His remarks before the US Congress offered solace and inspiration to all Americans—a point clearly stated in his conclusion:

> In these remarks I have sought to present some of the richness of your cultural heritage, of the spirit of the American people. It is my desire that this spirit continue to develop and grow, so that as many young people as possible can inherit and dwell in a land which has inspired so many people to dream. God bless America![2]

Notes

[1] National Association of Baptist Professors of Religion.

[2] Pope Francis's Address to US Congress, September 24, 2015, https://w2.vatican.va/.

Introduction

Benjamin T. Peters and Nicholas Rademacher

On September 24, 2015, Pope Francis spoke before a joint session of the US Congress, the first time a Bishop of Rome has ever done so. Francis's speech was not only historic but also important for those who study American Catholicism. Francis, the first American pope, built on his predecessor St. John Paul II's notion of one "America" encompassing both continents, North and South, rather than refer to "the Americas," as if divided up by national borders. The pope placed Thomas Merton and Dorothy Day in the pantheon of "Great Americans"—a gesture that surprised many observers, as Day and Merton have typically been at the margins of American Catholicism, rather than at its center.

A little over a year later, on November 8, 2016, Donald J. Trump was elected president of the United States, ending what (up until that point anyway) had been the most divisive election in recent history. Trump's election, and subsequent turbulent reign as president, has revealed many deep divisions not only within US society and culture but also within the Catholic Church in the United States—divisions that generally break along lines of the Republican and Democratic party platforms or "right-to-life Catholics" versus "social justice Catholics." The 2016 election, along with the decades of culture wars that preceded it, have led many US Catholics to question some of their long-standing beliefs about what "America" means and to rethink the ways in which they engage with "American life."

In the wake of these two moments, the College Theology Society gathered in June of 2017 at Salve Regina University in Newport, Rhode Island, to discuss American Catholicism. The conference theme posed a question: Is American Catholicism in crisis, at a crossroads, or undergoing a renewal? Even the most cursory observation of recent news and op-ed pieces concerning the Catholic Church in the United States could lead one to conclude that it is standing at a crossroads or, worse, in crisis. Such pessimistic indications emerge from multiple sources, including but not limited to publications on sociological data concerning the devotional practices of American Catholics, fracture among US Catholics concerning political and economic issues, and disputes concerning the occasional censorship of one or another American Catholic theologian's scholarship.

The conversations at the 2017 CTS annual meeting occurred at a particularly significant moment in the history of America and American Catholicism. The current political and economic climate in the United States has spurred a reappraisal of what we mean when we talk about "America." The "American consensus" that figures such as John Courtney Murray, SJ, once emphasized appears to be coming apart, if it ever existed. This rending of a purported consensus has led many Catholics to reassess their attitude toward the United States, particularly the long-standing belief that US values and ideals somehow offer a uniquely welcoming milieu for Catholicism. Deep divisions over issues related to economic inequality, racism, immigration, abortion, nationalism, and militarism that have long existed just under the veneer of American civil society have burst to the surface in recent years. Furthermore, debates over freedom of speech and religious freedom—for some, foundational issues in American life—are daily in the national conversation.

Not all is doom and gloom. The enthusiasm and excitement that Pope Francis has brought to many Americans both in and out of the church appears unprecedented and seems to reveal something of the hunger that many American Catholics (along with many of their non-Catholic compatriots) have for a renewal of their faith. The "Great Recession" and never-ending wars that have marked American life in these first years of the twenty-first century call to mind another period in US history, a century ago. It was during the first decades of the twentieth century—also shaped by economic and political hardship—that some of the most creative and inspiring figures and movements in American Catholic history emerged. Perhaps now is the time to encourage, identify, and collaborate with such sources of creative renewal—following the legacy of Dorothy Day, John Hugo, Arthur Falls, Paul Hanly Furfey, or Cesar Chavez, to name a few.

Given the vagaries of the contemporary context, fundamental questions emerged around the theme before and during the conference. What exactly did we mean by "American Catholicism"? Would the terms "US Catholicism" or "Catholicism in the United States" better guide the conversation? A number of scholars directly addressed questions like these at the annual meeting. It was the focal point of William Portier's presidential address, in which he encouraged CTS members to "reimagine" the America in "American Catholicism" in the way that Pope Francis has suggested—less as nationalistic marker and more as a sign of solidarity throughout the hemispheres. In a similar way, many of the papers presented at the conference and included in this volume explore new ways (or perhaps recover forgotten ways) for Catholics to understand America and tell the story of American Catholicism.

In addressing our theme's three-part question head-on, Bishop Stephen E. Blaire opened our conference with a plenary address proclaiming that the answer is not one or the other of the three options, but "yes" to all three. The church is always at a crossroads, always in crisis, and always in the midst of renewal. While critical matters within the church were addressed at the conference and in this volume, we were pleasantly surprised that so much of the discussion at Salve Regina (as well as in the present volume) was notably hopeful about this moment in the history of American Catholicism. This optimism may reflect something of the energy and enthusiasm brought about by Pope Francis. Interestingly, when there was talk of crisis, the focus fell on the present moment in US history, when a feeling of crisis is eminently palpable. This sense of crisis seems to reflect a loss of optimism about what can be expected from US political, economic, and social institutions. Many Catholics thus find themselves at a crossroads, asking how (and even whether) to engage with American society and culture and looking for new models for such engagement. Such a realization signals an important moment in American Catholic history, when long-standing assumptions about the relationship between America and Catholicism are being questioned. Although some

Catholics have been asking such questions for decades, for others, these questions are new, again highlighting the significance of the moment.

The call for papers was conceived and written broadly so as to elicit diverse answers to the conference theme. We anticipated that such a call would provide an important opportunity for members of the College Theology Society to read the signs of the times from their respective social locations as scholars and educators in the theological enterprise. The selection of plenary speakers and papers attempted to represent a broad cross section of scholarly perspectives and methods as important resources for understanding American Catholicism at this moment in history.

Emerging from these considerations, we have divided this annual volume into three parts. The first part, "Reassessing 'American Catholicism,'" includes several papers from scholars who offer new (or renewed) ways to think about America and American Catholicism. In his plenary address, Timothy Matovina argues that a new, more expansive, hemispheric perspective on America can positively reshape our way of doing Catholic theology. Following a similar tack, Paul G. Monson explores ways that a hemispheric reading of American Catholicism can help contemporary students integrate otherwise competing narratives on this topic within the context of a largely post-Christian culture.

Part I also includes a panel discussion on a recent Festschrift that examines the significant contributions that William Portier has made to the study of American Catholicism. Here, Curtis Freeman explains the way Portier has helped Catholics and Protestants better understand US Catholicism, American Evangelical traditions, and catholicity writ large. In her contribution, Margaret McGuinness points to ways that Portier has encouraged scholars to fill out the American Catholic story by nuancing narratives and highlighting often overlooked or forgotten sources, especially the contributions of women. Frederick Bauerschmidt concludes the panel by suggesting that contemporary thinking about the relationship between nature and grace—an issue central to Portier's reading of American Catholicism—would be enhanced with a reexamination of the now much maligned neo-scholastic approach.

The final two papers in the first part of the current volume examine contemporary US Catholicism from the perspective of parish life and culture. Patricia Wittberg presents grim numbers on parish membership and active participation in parish life by parishioners from all walks of life. In light of this reality, she offers a strategy that balances assimilation and pluralism as a way to serve the variety of cultures that inhabit the church. In his essay, William Clark also identifies and addresses a crisis in American parishes. Drawing on Pope Francis's "theology of the people," Clark emphasizes the "face-to-face church community as a primary locus for believers' direct encounter with Jesus's self-revelation."

Part II, "Opportunities and Challenges for American Catholicism," includes papers that address the plurality of contemporary issues facing American Catholics. This section opens with contributions from a plenary panel. As the title of her contribution makes plain, Katharine Mahon identifies a crisis of ritual formation as a significant issue facing the church in the United States, namely, "the exaggeration of intellectual participation in ritual," and identifies the detrimental implications of that crisis. Mary Doak recognizes the polarization and division within the United States as a theological challenge to the Christian community. She calls on the church to offer a witness of reconciliation within the church itself, among Christians, and to seek reconciliation in society and the world. Anthony Godzieba challenges what he sees as an increasing theological pessimism in American Catholicism by emphasizing an incarnational view—one found in the Catholic artistic imagination—of a world that abounds in grace.

The remaining essays in Part II address a range of pressing social issues: race, sexuality and gender, generational differences, and the impact of the church sex abuse scandal. Jessica Coblentz examines the history and contemporary relevance of the 1975 "Theology in the Americas" conference to identify and resist the "white Catholic theological racism" that was at work then and which persists in the academy today. In her paper, Dana Dillon discerns that Catholic higher education is in the midst of a kairos moment, challenged to build "cultures of inclusion" on our campuses in a way that embraces both Catholic identity and the pursuit of diversity and inclusivity. Mary Doyle Roche looks at how a particular version of the "American Dream" has been used to exclude a variety of groups, including the LGBTQ community. She suggests ways the church can move this "dream" to become inclusive of LGBTQ youth by attending to their particular experience. In his paper, Nicholas Mayrand raises a cautionary flag with regard to many of the generalizations made from polling data about the "nones" and argues that theologians must always attend to the "messy particulars" in their research and teaching. John Sheveland's essay sets the church's approach to the sex abuse crisis within the field of trauma studies and in so doing appeals for "a new way of being church in which the total body of the church understands itself as a dynamically interdependent community vulnerable to and affiliated with the lives of those facing traumatic experience of any kind."

"Resources for Renewal within American Catholicism," the third and final part of this volume, consists of papers that explore the tradition(s) of American Catholicism for exactly that: sources and signs of renewal. Bishop Blaire opens this section with his plenary address. Blaire discusses "popular movements"—and Pope Francis's encouragement of them—and encourages theologians to see them as sources of creative energy and inspiration for American Catholicism. Michael Baxter turns to the Catholic radicalist tradition to understand the fears of fascism that have arisen since the 2016 election. He argues that for radical Catholics these fears are long-standing and signal the reality that the United States has never been a welcoming—let alone "providential"—place for Catholicism, as some have claimed it to be.

Alison Downie looks at the work of contemporary American Catholic authors Nancy Mairs and Mary Karr as pointing to a new way to think about the holiness of sainthood and draws attention to the "graced holiness within the ordinariness of messy life." Steven Harmon presents a brief history of the partnership between the CTS and the National Association of Baptist Professors of Religion Region-at-Large, and argues that this partnership has had an important influence on the Baptist-Catholic dialogue and might serve as a model for other ecumenical discussions. Daniel Horan turns to the writings of Thomas Merton as a source of "a spirituality of resistance" for Catholics in opposition to structural racism in the United States today.

Laura Taylor argues that the US–Mexico borderlands provide an important departure point for contemporary theological discourse in American Catholicism, and she holds up the story of Our Lady of Guadalupe as calling American Catholics "to a posture of seeking social justice for the most vulnerable and most marginalized in our midst." In the volume's last essay, Mathew Verghese presents statements on the environment issued by various US episcopal conferences in the twentieth century, the result of dialogue with local communities. He argues that these statements not only predate many of the theological themes in *Laudato Si'*, but also helped prepare for the reception in the United States of Francis's "integral ecology," with an emphasis on action and advocacy for environmental justice.

After all is said and done, this volume does not provide a definitive response to the meaning of "American Catholicism" at the start of the twenty-first century. It is used variously throughout these pages to denote in some places a hemispheric perspective on Catholicism and, in other places, to refer more specifically to Catholicism in the United States. A similar matter obtains with respect to the underlying questions. The contributors to this volume rightly address a plurality of crises, crossroads, and opportunities for renewal. Taken together, though, these scholars provide a reading of the signs of the times in American Catholicism today from their respective social locations as scholars and educators in the theological enterprise. Each of us is encouraged to do the same, to draw on the richness of their reflections, and to respond in kind—and in hope.

Acknowledgments

Many hands have been involved in putting together this volume—not to mention the CTS gathering from which it emerged. First, we acknowledge the CTS board of directors for their endorsement and support of this conference theme. Bill Portier and Sandra Yocum have been particularly supportive. Dave Gentry, who serves as Executive Director of National Conventions for the CTS, has been a steady supporter of our theme as well. We thank the many section conveners who translated this theme into their particular fields. Their work encouraged the preparation of remarkable papers that stimulated robust conversation at the conference and which, in turn, constitute the present volume. Thanks also go to the dozens of anonymous readers who reviewed the submissions. We extend a very special word of gratitude to Bill Collinge, who serves as the Chairperson and Editor of Research and Publications for the CTS, for his careful reading and editing of this volume. Thanks as well to Robert Ellsberg and Jill O'Brien at Orbis Books for their guidance. Finally, we acknowledge our families, Michelle Sherman, and Liza, Samuel, Ruth, Mary, and Thomas Peters for their patience and encouragement throughout the entire process, from conference theme proposal to annual volume publication.

PART I

REASSESSING

"AMERICAN CATHOLICISM"

Catholic History and College Theology in 21st-Century America

Timothy Matovina

The College Theology Society last took up American Catholic history as a conference theme in 1996. Sandra Yocum and Bill Portier edited the annual volume that year. Sandra's contribution to the effort sketched five sites of American Catholic intellectual traditions. The annual volume examined a variety of Catholic traditions in the United States under the general headings of praxis, aesthetics, and local theologies. Patrick Carey's essay, for example, provided an insightful history of the teaching of theology at Catholic colleges in the United States. Along with Sandra's more recent book on the history of our society's first fifty years, Carey's essay remains an important historical overview of how our craft and teaching vocation began and evolved. Bill Portier's summary introduction to that year's annual volume merits citation as a point of departure for our conversations this year:

> In the United States, the decades since the council [Vatican II] have seen a veritable *ressourcement* in American Catholic studies. It has happened in an interdisciplinary flurry on the back roads and the borders between history and theology and cultural studies. In a return to the sources comparable to the one that preceded Vatican II and energized subsequent theological renewal, new generations of scholars have begun to recover the American Catholic past and to reconstruct it along the lines of current historiography. . . . Teachers and scholars who want to situate their reflections in and address them to the lives of contemporary American Catholics have much to learn from the new historiography.[1]

The need to accentuate historical study and knowledge is even more urgent today in the moment some have called the age of Trump. More than half a century ago the distinguished British economist and writer Barbara Ward wrote:

> Nothing is more dangerous to the survival of a free Western society than the increasing neglect of history in our teaching and our interests. Dictators always attempt to distort or abolish history. . . . In our free society we are abolishing the past, not by rewriting it or forcefully suppressing it but simply by losing all interest in it. This is as fatal for a society as it is for a man to lose his memory.[2]

Ward's sentiments were echoed in a statement of the great church historian Owen Chadwick, who claimed that history "does more than any other discipline to free the mind from the tyranny of present opinion."[3]

Of course, history and theology do not always enjoy the most fortunate relationship, as is the case when the bias of church historians is excessively apologetic. The very first church historian, Eusebius of Caesarea, described the Roman Emperor Constantine as "an angel of God descended from heaven" whose "soul was visibly ornamented with the fear and adoration of God."[4] Subsequent analysts tempered significantly his laudatory assessment of a ruler who, while he legalized and supported Christianity, was by no means flawlessly angelic. The premier historian of Catholicism in the United States, Monsignor John Tracy Ellis, often railed against such sanitized views of church history. Monsignor Ellis liked to cite a mid-nineteenth-century letter of Dominican friar Jean-Baptiste Lacordaire to underscore his point. Lacordaire wrote to a colleague who held a professorship in church history at the Sorbonne:

> Ought history to hide the faults of men and Orders? . . . It was not after this fashion that the Saints laid open the scandals of their times. Truth, when discreetly told, is an inestimable boon to mankind, and to suppress it, especially in history, is an act of cowardice unworthy of a Christian. Timidity is the fault of our age, and truth is concealed under pretense

of respect for holy things. God indeed has conferred upon His Church the prerogative of infallibility, but to none of her members has He granted immunity from sin. Peter was a sinner and a renegade, and God has been at pains to have the fact recorded in the Gospels.[5]

In other instances historians make claims that, consciously or not, reduce theology to mere commentary on ancient texts. Anyone who has taught Scripture to undergraduates knows the pitfalls of leaving the impression, intended or not, that the historical critical method makes biblical study a narrow exercise of historical interpretation rather than an encounter with the living Word of God.

Nonetheless, examples of how knowing history can enrich theological studies abound. Think of the importance of knowing the political backdrop for the Council of Nicaea, the social and cultural dynamics that contributed to the differing theologies of the East and West, the influence of the black plague on Christian art and theology, the rising nationalism that shaped and was shaped by the Reformation, the questions the "discovery" of the New World posed for Christian anthropology as European theologians confronted the reality of a branch of humanity previously unknown to them, and the influence of the US experiment in democracy on the thought of John Courtney Murray and on *Dignitatis Humanae*.

Interdisciplinary collaboration holds great promise for mutual enrichment of our scholarly disciplines, as the work of Joseph Komonchak on the Second Vatican Council demonstrates. Komonchak examines what he calls three different meanings for the term Vatican II: texts, experience, and event. The first meaning, texts, includes the sixteen council documents, as well as their interpretation within the context and intentions of the bishops who produced them. Second, experience refers to all those—two popes, bishops, advisers, observers, and even journalists and others who watched the council unfold from afar—who were involved in the conciliar events from January 25, 1959, when John XXIII announced the convening of the council, to December 8, 1965, when Paul VI solemnly closed it. How did that experience shape their lives, the formulation of the council documents, and the subsequent efforts to live out the meaning of the council? Finally, event encompasses the effect, the impact, of Vatican II on the subsequent history of the Catholic Church and, indeed, of global history. Fifty years hence, we are only beginning to glimpse this impact with any depth. We need broader analyses of the council as an event in church history but also in global history. As Komonchak concluded,

> Of the Second Vatican Council is true what is true of all great historical events: They can only be understood, indeed only be identified, in the light of their consequences, intended or not. In that respect what the Second Vatican Council was as an event is still being determined. And it is being determined in and as the lived histories of the [local] churches.[6]

As members of those local churches, reassessing our current historical moment is critical for the renewal of our enterprise as scholar teachers of college theology.

The Historical Moment

Historical overviews of Catholicism in the United States tend to follow a paradigm of Americanization presumed to hold true for all Catholics. Charles Morris concluded his general history with the assertion that there is a "standoff between the tradition of Rome and the tradition of America [the United States]."[7] His claim is based on an understanding of US Catholicism as, in the words of Jay Dolan, a fledgling "republican" church after US independence that expanded into an "immigrant church" in the nineteenth and early twentieth centuries and after World War II had "come of age" as "American," a process often depicted as culminating in John F. Kennedy's election as president, which signaled for numerous Catholics the authentication of their full acceptance in US society.[8]

Some scholars question whether this tripartite periodization—Catholic minority in the early republic to immigrant church to Americanization—is the best lens through which to examine the US Catholic experience, even for the experience of European Catholic immigrants and their descendants. Others critique the language of "coming of age," noting that, whatever their level of formal education and status, European immigrants did not sojourn in a perpetual state of childhood immaturity, nor did adopting the English language and US social norms indicate that their descendants had advanced to the age of adulthood.[9] Nonetheless, the contention that US Catholics have become "Americanized" to a significant degree remains an important interpretive lens through which scholars, pastoral leaders, journalists, and other observers examine Catholicism in the United States.

Thus, a decisive challenge is to construct a history of US Catholicism that incorporates non-European groups but is not modeled exclusively on European Catholic immigrants' and their descendants' societal ascent and assimilation during the middle six decades of the twentieth century. Without discounting the interpretive contribution of the Americanization paradigm, particularly for understanding the experience of European-descent Catholics, this challenge necessitates a reanalysis of each epoch delineated in the standard historiography. Particularly important for our calling as college theology professors is understanding the period since World War II, as numbers of Asian, African, and especially Latino immigrants have constituted an increasingly significant portion of what was purportedly an established, Americanized, post-immigrant church.

Jay Dolan's introduction to the US history survey course exemplified a fundamental aspect of remapping our understanding of the colonial era. On the first day of class his custom was to ask his students the significance of three years in North American history: 1607, 1608, and 1610. At least one student was always able to recognize 1607 as the date for the founding of the first British colony, Jamestown. But rarely could anyone identify 1608 as the founding date for Québec, and 1610 for Santa Fe. Dolan attested that "the reasoning behind my pedagogical cunning is to impress upon the students the French and Spanish dimensions of American history as well as the more familiar English aspect."[10] Colonial US historians such as Alan Taylor have expanded on Dolan's treatment, noting even less-acknowledged developments within territories that later became part of the United States, such as Dutch colonies, Russian settlement in Alaska, and British incursions into Hawaii.[11] Implicitly, this approach answers an essential question for any overview of US history: Does the subject matter encompass solely the British colonists and other peoples and

territories *only when* they become part of the US nation, or does
it encompass the inhabitants of regions now part of the United
States both *before and after* their incorporation?

Rather than a story of thirteen original colonies and their
westward expansion, the latter perspective accentuates the encounter and conflict of peoples, primarily the southward-moving
French, the northward-moving Spanish, the westward-moving
British, the natives who already lived on the land, the enslaved,
and the immigrants who settled among them. Given that both
the French and Spanish colonists were from Catholic countries,
any comprehensive analysis of US Catholic history must examine
their foundational presence and the extent of their influence on
subsequent developments. Indeed, while Catholics were a small
minority in the British colonies, in lands from Florida to California
they constituted a more substantial population under Catholic
Spain. From the standpoints of original settlement, societal influence, and institutional presence, the origins of Catholicism in what
is now the United States were decidedly Hispanic. Furthermore,
African Americans and Native Americans were an integral part
of the US Catholic story from its inception. Historical studies of
the United States usually focus on the British and then US ascent
over French, native, and Spanish rivals in the formation of a new
nation. But the story of US Catholicism must treat the various
peoples who first lived the Catholic faith and established Catholic
institutional presence in places now part of the United States, and
then examine the contact and conflict between these groups as the
European powers, the natives, and the nascent US nation vied for
territorial control.[12]

Famine in Ireland and revolution in the German states accel-
erated Catholic immigration during the mid-nineteenth century,
making Catholicism the largest single denomination in the United
States by the 1850 census. Commenting on these and subsequent
waves of immigrants, Pulitzer Prize–winner Oscar Handlin would
later famously remark, "Once I thought to write a history of the
immigrants in America. Then I discovered that the immigrants *were*
American history."[13] But the growth and development of Catholicism in the United States during the great century of European
immigration (1820–1920) cannot be fully explicated without due
attention to non-immigrant Catholics. Native Americans struggled

to endure, some in communities that Spanish and French missioners had previously sought to evangelize, others within the new system of US laws, Indian reservations, and government-sanctioned Christianization efforts. The travails of African Americans were no less traumatic. Catholic laity, priests, and religious orders had slaves. Though there were some isolated outreach efforts to African Americans after Emancipation, and African Americans initiated some ministerial initiatives of their own, the Catholic hierarchy led no coordinated national attempt to support African Americans during Reconstruction and the Jim Crow era. The story of the first large group of Hispanic Catholics in the United States is primarily a tale of endurance in places where their Spanish and Mexican forebears had already created a homeland. As a common quip puts it, Mexican Catholics in the nineteenth-century Southwest were not immigrants who crossed a border, but had the border cross them during US territorial expansion. In one often-repeated phrase they were "foreigners in our native land" who survived the US takeover of northern Mexico.[14]

The history of Catholics such as these cannot be subsumed into a saga of immigrants. While historians, immigrant descendants, and national symbols like the Statue of Liberty enshrine immigrant ascendancy as a quintessential American story, the era of the "immigrant church" cannot be fully understood without knowledge of conquered Native Americans, enslaved African Americans, and Hispanics incorporated into the United States during territorial expansion. The endurance and uncommon faithfulness of Catholics from these backgrounds is an especially important element of the Catholic legacy from this era. Moreover, the conquered, the enslaved, and freed former slaves—along with the more numerous and influential immigrants—necessitate examining more deeply how the distinct experiences of entry into the United States shaped participation in church and society and thus to varying degrees the formation of US Catholicism.

By the 1920s new legislation severely curtailed the flow of European émigrés that had continued almost unabated over the previous century. The consequent waning numbers of first-generation Catholics from Europe hastened their transition to monolingual English and the acceptance of US cultural norms. John Tracy Ellis observed in his influential general history of American Catholics that the 1920s immigration laws "made a direct contribution to the maturity of the Church in the sense that during the [following] generation its faithful for the first time had an opportunity to become more or less stabilized."[15] Assessing Ellis's scholarly achievement, Daniel J. Boorstin, the editor of the Chicago History of American Civilization book series in which the Ellis volume appeared, wrote in his 1969 editor's preface to the second edition of the book that recent American Catholic history "is a peculiarly significant and inspiring chapter in the growth and fulfillment of American institutions."[16] More recently, Charles Morris has concluded that "except for the newest waves of Hispanic immigrants, American Catholics have long since made it in America. As much as any other religious body, they are middle-class, suburban, educated, affluent. They exercise control over their own lives in ways that their grandparents never did."[17]

Yet the Americanization of émigrés' descendants in the course of the twentieth century occurred simultaneously with another crucial historical trend: a significant new immigration of Catholics to the United States. Demographic growth in US Catholicism over the past half century is heavily rooted in immigration from Asia, the Pacific Islands, Africa, and particularly Mexico, the Caribbean, and Latin America. More than half the Catholics in the United States today are not of Euro-American ancestry. In the Archdiocese of Los Angeles, for example, the Eucharist is regularly celebrated in forty-two languages. The incorporation of these newcomers and their children and grandchildren into US church and society is occurring simultaneously with ongoing developments among the now largely Americanized descendants of European immigrants. Increasingly, both groups encounter and clash in the growing number of shared parishes, that is, parishes that regularly celebrate the Eucharist in two or more languages. Historical analyses must explore the implications of these striking phenomena.

Two parallel forces have been in motion within US Catholicism since World War II. New immigrants have arrived simultaneously with European-descent Catholics' rise to respectability as full-fledged Americans. In particular, Latino Catholics, previously a largely Mexican and Puerto Rican population concentrated in New York, the Southwest, and various Midwestern cities and towns, now encompass expanded contingents from every nation of Latin America and the Caribbean and extend from Seattle to Boston, from Miami to Alaska. Many Euro-American Catholics have only vague memories of their immigrant heritage. Today there are more Catholic millionaires and more Catholics in Congress than any other denomination. A majority of the justices on the Supreme Court are Catholic. As Allan Figueroa Deck, SJ, has noted, the Hispanic "second wave" of Catholic immigration to the United States has occurred just as "US Catholics have become comfortable with their hard-earned [US American] identity" and "achieved acceptance in a predominantly Protestant and rather anti-Catholic country."[18]

The current demographic Hispanicization of Catholicism in the United States also draws sharper attention to the transnational intersections of US and Latin American history. Following the Spanish colonial presence in lands now part of the United States, US political and economic expansionism led to the conquest of nearly half of Mexico's national territory at the midpoint of the nineteenth century, consolidated US occupation of Puerto Rico five decades later, fueled economic shifts that led to the origins of late nineteenth- and early twentieth-century immigration from Mexico, resulted in a US presence throughout the Caribbean and Central America that helped induce migrations from those regions, and has driven the globalization process that in recent decades fed immigration from throughout Latin America. This latter process blurred the border between Latin and North America, accelerating the development of previous links between Catholicism in the United States and Catholicism in the rest of the Americas.

A hemispheric perspective on Catholicism requires attention to migratory flows in all directions, which in the last half century have encompassed a relatively small but influential group of US Catholics who have visited Latin America or served in church ministries there. Often their experiences transform their understanding of Catholicism, as well as their attitudes toward the foreign policy of the United States. Women religious, priests, and lay missioners have established significant and vital links between the United States and the rest of the Americas through missionary institutes, most notably Maryknoll. Other Latin American links include US Catholics' awareness and involvement with liberation theology, the civil wars in Central America during the 1970s and 1980s, well-known incidents like the 1980 assassinations of Archbishop Oscar Romero and four US church women serving in El Salvador, and the numerous delegations of students, scholars, and church leaders who have visited and established contacts in Central and South America and the Caribbean.

Contemporary church officials have promoted vital links they deem conducive to stronger Catholic faith and evangelization in the hemisphere. The Latin American episcopal conferences at Medellín, Puebla, Santo Domingo, and Aparecida, as well as the 1997 Synod on America, have increasingly taken a more hemispheric focus. In a homily at Yankee Stadium on his first visit to the United States, Pope John Paul II boldly likened the split between the richer and more powerful nations and the more economically impoverished nations of the world to the rich man and Lazarus of Luke 16. He avowed that one of the great challenges in the American hemisphere and in our world today is to see that the destinies of the richer northern and poorer southern halves of the planet are intimately conjoined.[19] Significantly, in subsequent teachings John Paul II did not speak of "America" in the plural, but in the singular. In his apostolic exhortation *Ecclesia in America*, the title of which itself denotes the interconnectedness of the hemisphere, he noted explicitly that his "decision to speak of *America* in the singular was an attempt to express not only the unity which in some way already exists, but also to point to that closer bond that the peoples of the continent seek and that the church wishes to foster as part of her own mission."[20] Pope Francis, the first American pope, has promoted a similar hemispheric focus, as was evident in his leadership at the 2007 episcopal conference at Aparecida.

Interpreters of the past do well to adopt such a vision of the hemisphere, reimagining national histories within the context of an international American Catholicism and social reality. In this approach the term "American" itself, usually employed in the United States to designate the national ethos, connotes historical links and the need for solidarity across international borders. In sum, the US Catholic Church was never exclusively an immigrant church, nor is it solely an "Americanized" church today. Rather, it is a church built on the founding faith of migratory, conquered, and enslaved peoples that currently is largely run by middle-class, European-descent Catholics with growing numbers of Latino,

Asian, and African immigrants, along with sizable contingents of US-born Latinos, African Americans, Asian Americans, and some Native Americans. Moreover, Catholics in the United States share a common background and a common destiny with sisters and brothers throughout the hemisphere, and indeed throughout the globe. This is the past and present reality of the church we must bear in mind and heart as we seek to educate our students.

Renewing Our Theological Enterprise

The ambitious project of a hemispheric approach to Catholicism in the United States places our work as instructors and researchers within the broad context of the encounter and clash of the Old and the New Worlds. Conquest, settlement, enslavement, immigration, and exile were the human—and too often inhuman—experiences that constituted this massive intermingling of diverse peoples. Wars to establish nation-states independent of European rule and struggles to this day for life, dignity, and self-determination are part of the painful legacy of violence and conquest that gave birth to the hemisphere Europeans named America. Despite rampant injustices, Native Americans, Africans, Europeans, their mixed-race offspring, and later Asians have all contributed to the formation of new societies, cultures, and traditions. As instructors of theology we need to address all these peoples and experiences within the current borders of the United States, but against the backdrop and comparative framework of the American continents.

Understanding the current historical moment has at least three implications for our work. Perhaps the most obvious is the need to encompass in our reflections the diverse experiences of our forebears, as well as the diverse experiences of our contemporaries, including the students we meet in our classrooms. This entails a deeper understanding of the nature of pluralism, particularly in the scholarly enterprise. Various contemporary issues illustrate ongoing debates about authentic pluralism, such as the possibilities and limits of interreligious dialogue, continuing immigration controversies, and the role of Spanish and other non-English languages in church ministries. Consciously or not, frequently those who discuss such issues presuppose that the primary question is the degree of diversity that a dominant group can or should tolerate. But for some time now the presumption of a consensus dominant group or perspective has not been universally accepted. Assessing the challenge US Latino/a theologies pose for theological pluralism, for example, Roberto Goizueta reminds us that "pluralism can . . . become an instrument for exercising greater control over the parameters of theological discourse, while at the same time creating the appearance of genuine dialogue." He notes that, ironically, courses on liberation theology, Latino/a theology, black theology, and feminist theology can unintentionally exacerbate the problem, since such offerings are usually elective options that marginalize their discourse away from the required core curriculum.[21] Theological pluralism requires that such theologies be addressed not merely as the voices of marginal persons and discourses, but as contributors to the fundamental theological enterprise. Indeed, any authentic pluralism entails the recognition that various groups and perspectives can coexist without one occupying a presumed privilege of authority or dominance. As David Tracy put it, "There is a price to be paid for any genuine pluralism—that price many pluralists seem finally either unwilling to pay or unable to see. . . . The others are not marginal to our centres but centres of their own."[22]

Related are the researching and teaching works that have emerged from the five centuries of faith and struggle in the American hemisphere. In my own area of specialization, the growing effort to retrieve the theological treatises of Latinas and Latinos in the Americas has advanced this worthy endeavor. Contemporary works that recover such theologies include Luis Rivera-Pagán on the sixteenth-century theological debates about the evangelization of the New World, Gustavo Gutiérrez on Bartolomé de Las Casas, Alejandro García-Rivera on Martín de Porres, Claudio Burgaleta on the sixteenth-century Peruvian Jesuit José de Acosta, and Michelle Gonzalez and Theresa A. Yugar on Sor Juana Inés de la Cruz.[23] Other scholars have begun to critically examine hemispheric trends in theology and religious studies, such as Alex Nava's exploration of the sense of wonder and displacement that spans five centuries of exploration, conquest, intermingling of peoples, and literary output in the New World; Michelle Gonzalez's analysis of religious studies and liberation theology discourse on religion in the Americas; and Christopher Tirres's comparative study of pragmatists and Latino/a liberationist theologians.[24] As Gonzalez explains, "The *ressourcement* movement in twentieth-century Roman Catholic theology was an appeal for theologians to return to historical sources to inform contemporary understandings." This does not mean merely examining ancient sources in their historical context, but rather "a revival of historical sources" that enables a critical engagement between past formulations and present realities.[25] Thus, just as renewed study of the church fathers was a key intellectual precursor to the Second Vatican Council, the *ressourcement* of theological works such as those of Latinos/as in the American context is a crucial step in the project of developing theologies that are rooted both in the wider Christian tradition and in the life, faith, and struggles of contemporary communities in the hemisphere. Though not all of us will dedicate our research efforts to the recovery of such sources, we can all be aware of them and employ them appropriately in our teaching.

The mutual engagement of the Christian tradition and our American past has an even more significant implication for college theology teaching: such an engagement recalls and deepens our understanding of theology itself. Let me demonstrate this through the work of the late Virgilio Elizondo. As Roberto Goizueta and Timothy Matovina recently wrote in a journal article on Elizondo, Vatican II was foundational for his life work and witness.[26] Arguably the conciliar document that most shaped Elizondo's theological vision was *Dei Verbum*, and particularly a key passage from its opening paragraphs: "This plan of revelation is realized by deeds and words having an inner unity: the deeds wrought by God in the history of salvation manifest and confirm the teaching and realities signified by the words, while the words proclaim the deeds and clarify the mystery contained in them" (no. 2). In one of his first published articles, Elizondo presented an extended reflection on this text. He underscored that "evangelization is not just a word" but "a creative act." Words and acts are intimately united and mutually revelatory: "Jesus in his deeds and words *is* the Gospel." He is the gift of God's "selfless love unlimited" who invites humans to conversion and participation in the divine life.[27]

The title for Elizondo's article accentuates the understanding of revelation at the core of his theological project. "Biblical Pedagogy of Evangelization" emphasizes that the Scriptures and Christian tradition testify to the past words and deeds of God in order to instruct us in divine pedagogy. Citing the "dynamic process" of deeds and words in the vocation of Abraham, the Exodus, and the prophets, Elizondo concludes that the biblical history of Israel "is not just the history of a human group" but an illustration "of how God is working in humanity." Thus it is not surprising that early Christian communities were "not interested in simply canonizing the specific deeds and words of Jesus." Indeed, the evangelists "do not hesitate to bring out the meaning of the words and teachings of Jesus in the light of the problems, needs, customs and vocabulary of their particular people." This striking claim encapsulates Virgilio's perspective on divine pedagogy: the gospel writers were not merely recording what Jesus said and did, but already discerning how his words and deeds addressed concerns in each evangelist's community. Moreover, because God spoke and acted in certain ways in the past, and it's the same God speaking and acting in the present, then by knowing this past we can more faithfully discern God's message and calling today. This remains the fundamental theological task. In Virgilio's words, "Today the starting point, the locus, of God's revelation is the present-day tensions, crises and emotions which arise out of [our] struggle for a more human existence in our world."[28] Inspired by Medellín's challenge to become a church of the poor, he insisted that the poor and marginal are the privileged bearers of divine revelation, so the sources of faith must be engaged through their eyes. In this way he brought this epistemological privilege of the poor to bear on the interpretation of Vatican II, and specifically *Dei Verbum*.

Thus, for Elizondo the theological task centers on examining how God spoke and acted in the past to discern God's ongoing revelation in history, by which he means very particular times and places of history like the past, present, and future of locales within our American continents, and particularly the marginalized places of marginalized peoples. Nowhere was this element of his pastoral theological work more evident than in his creative reexamination of two foundational sources of faith in his borderlands Mexican-American community: the Galilean Jesus and Our Lady of Guadalupe, the latter, of course, regarded by many as the most influential religious phenomenon indigenous to America. In his various writings on Guadalupe,[29] Elizondo mined the theological content of the *Nican mopohua* (literally, "here is related"), the Nahua-language account of the Guadalupan apparitions to Juan Diego. He averred that in this holy text:

> Through the beauty of the image (flowers) and the melodious sounds (poetic words) the divine could be gradually experienced, and one could gradually come to share in the divine wisdom. Thus the Guadalupe event marks the opening of a divine-human encounter and of a divine communication. This harmony, this symmetry, was an essential element of the Nahuatl vision and hence of this revelatory poem.[30]

In his pastoral leadership Elizondo enacted this theological vision through organizing with his parish community the dramatic proclamations of the apparition narrative. I witnessed this ritual as a parishioner at San Antonio's San Fernando Cathedral during the early 1990s when Elizondo served as cathedral rector. The congregation observed with hushed reverence at the climactic moment when Juan Diego dropped roses that grew out of season and presented the image of Guadalupe that miraculously appeared on his *tilma* (cloak). As the previously unbelieving bishop and his assistants fell to their knees in veneration, applause erupted throughout the cathedral.

The San Fernando congregation was predominantly composed of ethnic Mexican, mostly working-class worshipers. What Elizondo articulates as the painful historical process of their *mestizaje*—the dynamic and often violent mixing of cultures, religious systems, and races—is echoed in many congregants' stinging memories of the polite disdain or outright hostility they meet in their dealings with sales clerks, coworkers, teachers, police officers, social workers, government employees, professional colleagues, and civic and church leaders. Thus, it is not surprising that they resonate with the liturgical drama of the lowly Juan Diego's rejection, his encounter with a loving mother, and his final vindication before the ecclesiastical leader of the Spanish conquistadores.

Celebrating the story of Guadalupe's maternal care and Juan Diego's struggle and triumph does not obliterate the painful daily realities of San Fernando congregants. But devotees at San Fernando and elsewhere find solace in Guadalupe's election of the unexpected hero Juan Diego, as well as hope in his unwavering faith and *aguante* (unyielding endurance). Though they recognize that their Guadalupan devotion does not eliminate all the *rechazos* (rejections) and social ills that beset them, most congregants do not consider themselves a dominated people, and they ardently attest that Guadalupe uplifts them as she did Juan Diego, strengthening them in the trials and difficulties of their daily lives. In a word, they confess that the Guadalupe narrative is true: it reveals the deep truth of their human dignity and exposes the lie of social inequalities and experiences that diminish their fundamental sense of worth.

As with the Galilean Jesus, in his analysis of devotees' relations with Guadalupe Elizondo presumes that discerning how God spoke in the past—specifically in this case to Juan Diego through the words and deeds of Guadalupe—enables us to grasp more deeply how revelation is operative in the lives of Guadalupe's faithful today. As Elizondo acknowledged on numerous occasions, "Today devotion to Our Lady of Guadalupe continues to grow, to be explored, and to be rediscovered. Our explanations do not make it powerful. It is powerful because it lives in the minds and hearts of the people."[31] For Elizondo the divine pedagogy enacted through Guadalupe is most evident in the faith of her loyal daughters and sons. Like the Galilean Jesus, the pastoral theological engagement of Guadalupe necessarily begins and ends with the engagement of people's relationship with her.

Elizondo's theology underscores the promise of interdisciplinary work that situates our teaching and research within the context of American Catholic history. Elizondo illuminates the Guadalupe tradition in multiple ways, including a theological analysis of the *Nican mopohua* as the foundational source of that tradition, a pastoral theological engagement of how that foundational story continues to affect the lives of Mexican Americans and other devotees today, and an exploration of Guadalupe's implications for contemporary ecclesial and social life. His is a corpus of theological work that clearly contributes to the authentic theological pluralism that our current historical moment requires.

More broadly, Elizondo presents a body of work that invites us to continue developing his rich *ressourcement* of this American faith tradition. His range of theological investigations examined the Guadalupe image, apparition account, and its historical context as a means to explore the collision of civilizations between the Old and New Worlds and the ongoing implications of this clash for Christianity and the emergence of new societies in the American hemisphere. His contribution invites continued research of the major epochs and events of Mexican history and the history of America—conquest, society building, racial mixing, independence, revolution, and the demands for justice of marginalized groups—through the lens of the Guadalupan message. In this sense the *ressourcement* of the Guadalupe tradition is an ongoing effort to articulate a Christian response to one of the most momentous events of Christianity's second millennium: the conquest, evangelization, and struggles for life, dignity, and self-determination of the peoples of America.

Most important, Elizondo's approach to theology deepens our understanding of the theological task itself. For Elizondo, theology is more than just critical thinking about faith. It is a spiritual discernment that examines the history and life of people in light of the gospels and the wider faith tradition, and then seeks to transform whatever obscures our innate beauty as creatures made in God's image. In the case of Guadalupe, his theology is an attempt to present a graced instance in which the experience of Christian disciples and their faith communities meet and retell the gospel story. This is a theology of America, or in its Spanish original América, a reading of the past, present, and future of our continent grounded in the divine pedagogy whose contours Christian believers have glimpsed in creation, in the people of Israel's encounters with their liberator God, and in the words and deeds of the Galilean Jesus. It is a theological attempt to write the history of America into the history of salvation told in the premier sources of revelation. Above all, it is an endeavor to name sin and grace in our history and call us to a present and future of greater faith, hope, and love. This is a theological examination of American history that merits not only our admiration but also our emulation in our vocation as collegiate scholars of theology.

Notes

[1]Sandra Yocum Mize, "On the Back Roads: Searching for American Catholic Intellectual Traditions," in *American Catholic Traditions: Resources*

for Renewal, ed. Sandra Yocum Mize and William L Portier (Maryknoll, NY: Orbis Books, 1997), 3–23; Patrick W. Carey, "College Theology in Historical Perspective," ibid., 242–72; William L. Portier, "Introduction," ibid., xi; Yocum Mize, *Joining the Revolution in Theology: The College Theology Society, 1954–2004* (Lanham, MD: Rowman & Littlefield, 2007).

[2] Barbara Ward, "The Battleground Is Here," *New York Times Magazine*, January 27, 1952.

[3] Owen Chadwick, *Freedom and the Historian: An Inaugural Lecture* (London: Cambridge University Press, 1969), 39.

[4] From Eusebius's fourth-century work, *The Life of Constantine*. See *A Select Library of Nicene and Post-Nicene Fathers of the Church* (Grand Rapids, MI: Eerdmans, 1952), 522.

[5] John Tracy Ellis, "Why Study History?" *Journal of Texas Catholic History and Culture* 1 (March 1990): 4–6.

[6] Joseph Komonchak, "The Council and the Churches," in *Catholics in the Vatican II Era: Local Histories of a Global Event*, ed. Kathleen Sprows Cummings, Timothy Matovina, and Robert Orsi (Cambridge: Cambridge University Press, 2017).

[7] Charles R. Morris, *American Catholic: The Saints and Sinners Who Built America's Most Powerful Church* (New York: Times Books, 1997), 431.

[8] Jay P. Dolan, *The American Catholic Experience: A History from Colonial Times to the Present* (1985; reprint, Notre Dame, IN: University of Notre Dame Press, 1992), 125, 417. See also James Hennesey, *American Catholics: A History of the Roman Catholic Community in the United States* (New York: Oxford University Press, 1981); Joseph A. Varacalli, *The Catholic Experience in America* (Westport, CT: Greenwood, 2006); James M. O'Toole, *The Faithful: A History of Catholics in America* (Cambridge, MA: Belknap Press of Harvard University Press, 2008); James T. Fisher, *Communion of Immigrants: A History of Catholics in America* (2000; new ed., New York: Oxford University Press, 2008).

[9] See, e.g., Michael J. Baxter, "Writing History in a World without Ends: An Evangelical Catholic Critique of United States Catholic History," *Pro Ecclesia* 5 (Fall 1996): 440–69; William L. Portier, "Americanism and Inculturation, 1899–1999," *Communio* 27 (Spring 2000): 139–60; and Peter R. D'Agostino, *Rome in America: Transnational Catholic Ideology from the Risorgimento to Fascism* (Chapel Hill: University of North Carolina Press, 2004).

[10] Jay P. Dolan and Allan Figueroa Deck, eds., *Hispanic Catholic Culture in the US: Issues and Concerns* (Notre Dame, IN: University of Notre Dame Press, 1994), 440.

[11] Alan Taylor, *American Colonies* (New York: Viking, 2001).

[12] For survey histories of Native American, African American, and Latino Catholic histories, respectively, see Christopher Vecsey, *American Indian Catholics* (3 vols., Notre Dame, IN: University of Notre Dame Press, 1996–99); Marie Therese Archambault, Mark G. Thiel, and Vecsey, eds., *The Crossing of Two Roads: Being Catholic and Native in the United States* (Maryknoll, NY: Orbis Books, 2003); Cyprian Davis, *The History of Black Catholics in the United States* (New York: Crossroad, 1990); Cyprian Davis and Jamie

Phelps, eds., *"Stamped with the Image of God": African Americans as God's Image in Black* (Maryknoll, NY: Orbis Books, 2003); Moises Sandoval, *On the Move: A History of the Hispanic Church in the United States* (1990; 2nd ed., Maryknoll, NY: Orbis Books, 2006); Timothy Matovina and Gerald E. Poyo, eds., *¡Presente! US Latino Catholics from Colonial Origins to the Present* (Maryknoll, NY: Orbis Books, 2000).

[13] Oscar Handlin, *The Uprooted: The Epic Story of the Great Migration That Made the American People* (Boston: Little, Brown, 1951), 3.

[14] Juan N. Seguín, *Personal Memoirs of John N. Seguín from the Year 1834 to the Retreat of General Woll from the City of San Antonio in 1842* (San Antonio: Ledger Book and Job Office, 1858), iv; Pablo de la Guerra, Speech to the California legislature, April 26, 1856, reprinted in *El Grito: A Journal of Contemporary Mexican-American Thought* 5 (Fall 1971): 19. Seguín's memoirs are reprinted in *A Revolution Remembered: The Memoirs and Selected Correspondence of Juan N. Seguín,* ed. Jesús F. de la Teja (Austin: State House, 1991).

[15] John Tracy Ellis, *American Catholicism* (1956; 2nd ed., Chicago: University of Chicago Press, 1969), 129.

[16] Ibid., ix.

[17] Morris, *American Catholic,* 431.

[18] Allan Figueroa Deck, *The Second Wave: Hispanic Ministry and the Evangelization of Cultures* (Mahwah, NJ: Paulist Press, 1989), 1.

[19] John Paul II, "Do Not Leave to the Poor the Crumbs of Your Feast: Homily of Pope John Paul II at Yankee Stadium (October 2, 1979)," *The Pope Speaks* 24 (1979): 312–17.

[20] John Paul II, *Ecclesia in America,* 1999, no. 5, English translation in *Origins* 28 (February 4, 1999): 565–92.

[21] Roberto S. Goizueta, "United States Hispanic Theology and the Challenge of Pluralism," in *Frontiers of Hispanic Theology in the United States,* ed. Allan Figueroa Deck (Maryknoll, NY: Orbis Books, 1992), 16.

[22] David Tracy, "On Naming the Present," in *On the Threshold of the Third Millennium* (London: SCM Press, 1990), 67.

[23] Luis N. Rivera, *A Violent Evangelism: The Political and Religious Conquest of the Americas* (Louisville, KY: Westminster/John Knox, 1992); Gustavo Gutiérrez, *Las Casas: In Search of the Poor of Jesus Christ,* trans. Robert R. Barr (Maryknoll, NY: Orbis Books, 1993); Alejandro García-Rivera, *St. Martín de Porres: The "Little Stories" and the Semiotics of Culture* (Maryknoll, NY: Orbis Books, 1995); Claudio Burgaleta, *José de Acosta, S.J., 1540–1600: His Life and Thought* (Chicago: Jesuit Way, 1999); Michelle A. Gonzalez, *Sor Juana: Beauty and Justice in the Americas* (Maryknoll, NY: Orbis Books, 2003); Theresa A. Yugar, *Sor Juana Inés de la Cruz: Feminist Reconstruction of Biography and Text* (Eugene, OR: Wipf and Stock, 2014).

[24] Alex Nava, *Wonder and Exile in the New World* (University Park: Pennsylvania State University Press, 2013); Michelle A. Gonzalez, *A Critical Introduction to Religion in the Americas: Bridging the Liberation Theology and Religious Studies Divide* (New York: New York University Press, 2014); Christopher D. Tirres, *The Aesthetics and Ethics of Faith: A Dialogue be-*

tween Liberationist and Pragmatic Thought (New York: Oxford University Press, 2014).

[25]Gonzalez, *Sor Juana*, 8.

[26]Roberto Goizueta and Timothy Matovina, "Divine Pedagogy: *Dei Verbum* and the Theology of Virgilio Elizondo," *Theological Studies* 78, no. 1 (March 2017): 7–24.

[27]Virgilio Elizondo, "Biblical Pedagogy of Evangelization," *American Ecclesiastical Review* 168 (October 1974): 527.

[28]Ibid., 528, 529, 530, 537.

[29]See, e.g., Virgilio Elizondo, *La Morenita: Evangelizer of the Americas* (San Antonio: Mexican American Cultural Center Press, 1980); Elizondo, *Guadalupe: Mother of the New Creation* (Maryknoll, NY: Orbis Books, 1997).

[30]Elizondo, *Guadalupe*, 35.

[31]Virgilio Elizondo, "Mary and Evangelization in the Americas," in *Mary, Woman of Nazareth*, ed. Doris Donnelly (New York: Paulist Press, 1989), 160.

Redefining "America" for Millennials

From Freshmen in Flip-Flops
to Seminarians in Surplices

Paul G. Monson

In his 2015 address before Congress, Pope Francis deemed himself "a son of this great continent, from which we have all received so much and toward which we share a common responsibility."[1] This language of a single, shared "continent" unmistakably stems from John Paul II's 1999 post-synodal apostolic exhortation, *Ecclesia in America*, which also provocatively refers to "America" as one "great continent."[2] Commentaries on Francis's speech overlook this allusion, and almost all general histories of US Catholicism omit any reference to the apostolic exhortation.[3] Moreover, a broad spectrum of the US episcopacy found John Paul's definition of "America" to be a gross simplification of a complex and diverse hemisphere, with murmurs that the pope could benefit from better cartography.[4] Nevertheless, as the first pope to address Congress, Francis unmistakably employed his predecessor's definition of "America" to bruise the ego of exceptionalism among his Yankee audience. In adopting a distinctly "hemispheric" tradition in papal ecclesiology, Francis identified himself not only as the first Latin American pontiff in the church's history, but also as its first "American" pope—a point pregnant with profound symbolism and meaning for Catholics north of the Rio Grande.[5]

This essay explores the meaning of Francis's insight for the definition of "America" in classrooms inundated with so-called millennials. I contend that any course on American Catholicism must be taught with a hemispheric vision that informs the students' appropriation of the past, present, and future. To support this claim, I employ my own pedagogical experience of courses in "American Catholicism" in two starkly different environments: freshmen in flip-flops and seminarians in surplices. The first group consists of apathetic undergrads (mostly freshmen) looking for a core requirement at Loyola Marymount, a Jesuit university in Los Angeles drawing from diverse cultural and religious backgrounds; the second, and my current environment, includes zealous semi-narians looking to fulfill an upper-level graduate requirement at Sacred Heart, a seminary near Milwaukee drawing from dioceses in the region and throughout the United States. This study ad-vances a hemispheric ecclesiology of American Catholicism as a means to integrate dominant Euro-American narratives and pressing Latino ministry in an ever-growing post-Christian culture.

The Past: A Reassessment of Colonial Roots

In outlining this hemispheric approach, it is best to begin with America's colonial past. In 2014, on the eve of Francis's apostolic visit, I found myself taking cover in a hailstorm of controversy surrounding the legacy of Junípero Serra (1713–1784) in Califor-nia. The announcement of Serra's sudden canonization baffled my liberal colleagues and infuriated local Native American activists. Within a century, Serra had shifted from an icon of "civilizing" frontier California to a symbol of ethnocentrism, brutality, and injustice toward the state's indigenous populations. Many in Los Angeles clamored that the pope was aloof to history, while oth-ers, including the archbishop, sought to contextualize and defend Serra's labors.

As I prepared remarks on the topic for a university panel, this controversy profoundly altered my perspective of US Catholic history. I quickly realized that Pope Francis had an ecclesiologi-cal rather than a strictly theological or moral reading of Serra's life. For Francis, an imperfect missionary was no impediment to advancing a transcultural, hemispheric vision of the Catholic faith in the face of US chauvinism and Latino immigration. The canonization served as a subtle reminder that the year 1776 marks not only a colonial revolution on the Eastern Seaboard but also the establishment of a colonial mission named San Francisco on the opposite coast. For Francis, "America" is a land with artificial political borders, and Serra reminds one of the deep Catholic roots of the United States beyond its Atlantic shores.

Nevertheless, Serra's service to the classroom was all the more surprising. For many students steeped in Californian provincialism, the typical starting point of US Catholic narratives—Maryland and New England—were unintelligible distant lands. The figure of Serra, however, was familiar to both Catholic and non-Catholic students by virtue of crude elementary school projects on California history. At the same time, their knowledge of Serra was impoverished. Few realized that the San Gabriel Mountains towering over Los Angeles take their name from one of Serra's missions, and that this mission, which later gave birth to the city, emerged at the same time as the US Constitution. Suddenly, the city of Hollywood became a city of history. By beginning with Serra, Los Angeles transitioned in student consciousness from a superficial "City of the Angels" to a historic "City of Our Lady, Queen of the Angels" (the city's original name), to a city with an undeniably Catholic starting point. Instead of commencing the course's narrative with the arrival of English Catholics on the *Ark* and the *Dove*, the class began with the students' own California context. With this new starting point, non-Catholic millennials realized that the topic of the class, which they had reluctantly chosen, was worth learning at a cultural level; Euro-American Catholic students recognized themselves as guests in a Latino land; and Latino millennials, including young Latino seminarians from South America, have come to see their own cultural story as part of rather than peripheral to US history, to see themselves as heirs to this history rather than as foreign guests.[6]

In a similar manner, Francis's attempt to integrate US Catholic history is a lesson that extends beyond the classroom to the future of American Catholic scholarship. Our narratives must shift to the South and shirk a triumphalistic journey from John Carroll to John F. Kennedy. Beginning with the work of John Tracy Ellis and James Hennesey, scholars have gradually reincorporated the Spanish and French colonial roots of US Catholicism, yet earlier historiography continues to cloud American Catholic studies and its ecclesiology. For instance, James O'Toole's excellent work, *The Faithful*, recovers a genuine *sensus fidelium* and continues to be a valuable source for the millennial classroom. However, even O'Toole begins with the Catholic experience in New England and relegates the Spanish colonial experience to a paragraph.[7] One must nevertheless acknowledge that O'Toole avoids the tympanic triumphalism of other histories, and it is precisely here that Serra joins the chorus. Not a single California mission survived beyond the first decades of the nineteenth century, and Serra's immediate legacy bears all the marks of utter failure.[8] Overall, Serra helps both student and scholar appreciate how the story of US Catholicism lacks uniformity. American Catholics, in a truly hemispheric sense, were both a persecuted minority and a persecuting majority, both separate from the state and intimately wedded to the state, both witnesses to great growth and victims of utter collapse. At the same time, the church considers the fruits of failure to be paramount, as in the case of the seventeenth-century North American martyrs of present-day Ontario and New York.[9] Still US Catholics continue to forget that the first "martyr" of the United States was in fact the sixteenth-century Spanish Franciscan friar Juan de Padilla (1500–1542), who died in present-day Kansas. America's first martyr was indeed a Latino, a salient point for Euro-American seminarians who often need to be reminded that the seeds of the faith are not simply sown; they are often scattered and forgotten for centuries, as in the case of de Padilla and even Serra. In his selection of Serra, Pope Francis reminds us that American Catholicism begins with the South and West as much as the North and East. Pope Francis's Serra invites us to eschew the ecclesiological triumphalism and Pelagian chauvinism that continues to grip our common definition of "America."

The Present: A Reassessment of "Americanism"

For the present relevance of a hemispheric America, one shifts to a controversy of the 1890s. This decade witnessed a cohort of German American clergy locking horns with the indomitable Irish American archbishop of St. Paul, Minnesota, John Ireland (1838–1918). The Germans, many of whom retained memories of the Kulturkampf, accused Ireland of reckless accommodation to modern values and state education; Ireland, however, perceived the Germans as an obstinate impediment to the Catholic evangelization of America. The controversy primarily centered on three questions: (1) whether new immigrants (mostly German) should preserve their language and culture in order to preserve their faith or assimilate to American culture to better advance a universal, Catholic faith; (2) whether modern appeals to the conscience and the Holy Spirit amounted to shrewd apologetics or toxic subjectivism; and (3) whether the celebration of the United States as the harbinger of a new "age" and the crucible of the church's future announced new opportunities or baptized Manifest Destiny.[10] The end of this splenetic debate is often dated 1899, when Pope Leo XIII condemned what he termed "Americanism" in his encyclical *Testem Benevolentiae Nostrae.*

Although this complicated chapter of US Catholicism lies more than a century in the past, it continues to resurface as a polemical tool that misses the nail and flattens the thumb. Russell Shaw's recent books on US Catholicism serve as an example of this problem, with one book shrouded in the rhetoric of "Remarkable Rise" and "Meteoric Fall."[11] Some may jeer at such melodrama, but this particular title holds sway among some seminarians. Most problematic is Shaw's assessment of Americanism, which he reduces to the story of a prophetic Leo XIII anticipating late-twentieth-century American Catholic individualism and dissent.[12] One must praise Shaw in countering a pervasive historiography that lauds John Ireland as a forerunner of Vatican II and demonizes Leo as a grand inquisitor of a "phantom heresy," with Teutonic henchmen to boot. Shaw's assessment is sharper, yet he regrettably dabbles in historical tourism without wrestling with the details: he distills a complex controversy into a polemic against postconciliar liberalism. This distillation echoes in some American Catholic circles, most notably in a recent debate in the online Catholic magazine *Crux* between Charles Camosy and Richard Bulzacchelli. Camosy, who cites Shaw, compares staunch Catholic support for Trump during the 2016 presidential election with a heretical nation-before-God "Americanism," whereas Bulzacchelli identifies Americanism as little more than modernist metaphysics.[13] In overlooking the ecclesiological dimension of the controversy, Camosy, Bulzacchelli, and Shaw ultimately miss the point of "Americanism" for the present.

Questions of accommodation and subjectivism continue to

haunt US Catholicism, yet Leo's perennial critique in *Testem Benevolentiae* is his rebuke of US Catholic exceptionalism. Leo accused advocates of "Americanism" of harboring a desire to create "a church in America different from that which is in the rest of the world."[14] In overlooking this key line, contemporary discussions of "Americanism" continue to ignore a simple fact that eludes practically every history of US Catholicism: John Paul II promulgated *Ecclesia in America* in Mexico City on January 22, 1999, one hundred years *to the day* of Pope Leo XIII's *Testem Benevolentiae*. This gesture is beyond mere coincidence, and only William Portier notes it in print.[15] But even Portier overlooks the additional fact that the penning of Leo's encyclical coincided with his preparations for the first episcopal conference of Latin American bishops, hosted in Rome in 1899.[16] For Leo, these Latino bishops represented a more mature church in "America" that chastened younger sister sees in the United States (which, after all, remained under Propaganda Fide as canonical mission territory until 1908). Leo's milestone conference further laid the foundation for CELAM (Consejo Episcopal Latinoamericano) and its historic postconciliar gatherings in Medellín (1968), Puebla (1979), Santo Domingo (1992), and Aparecida (2007). In fact, the *Lineamenta* for John Paul's Special Assembly for America (1997), which led to *Ecclesia in America*, took its lead from CELAM's conference in Santo Domingo, which in turn inspired the post-synodal endorsement of Our Lady of Guadalupe as a patroness for all Catholics in the hemisphere, including the United States. Overall, *Testem Benevolentiae* and *Ecclesia in America* are inseparable and demonstrate a papal tradition wary of Yankee exceptionalism. The anti-Roman blinders of many historians and theologians in the United States could benefit from recognizing this tradition, especially in light of the precarious state of immigration from the South. Catholic scholars should reclaim the lessons of "Americanism" in the nineteenth century for a distinctly Catholic definition of "America" in the twenty-first century, advancing the conversation beyond polemics to a robust, hemispheric ecclesiology for the present.[17]

In addition to new lenses for scholarship, this convergence of dates is essential for the classroom. A survey of both papal documents and the epiphany of this 1899–1999 convergence jar unsuspecting undergrads out of a slumber that glibly dismisses the relevance of dates for learning. For non-Catholic students, John Paul emerges as a cunning advocate for the marginalized in American society. For Latino students, the papacy legitimizes their own experience, and for Chicano students *Ecclesia in America* assists them in their own tenuous relationship with the Guadalupe of their parents. As for seminarians, especially evangelical millennials steeped in deep Marian piety, the pope adds tremendous depth to what is often a shallow infatuation with Our Lady of Guadalupe, transitioning their focus from the miraculous to the ecclesiological. Guadalupe thus emerges as a symbol of not only evangelization but also a distinctly Catholic definition of "America" that is transnational and hemispheric. This lesson further provides common ground between Euro-American seminarians and ESL Latino seminarians. Suddenly both sets of seminarians see themselves as sons of the same America.

The Future: A Reassessment of the City of Angels

These papal critiques of American exceptionalism ultimately guide one from the present into the future of US Catholicism. Like other Americans, Catholics in the United States indulge in a regional sense of pride. In American Catholic historiography, such pride often extends to cities with a history of red hats: Baltimore, New York, Philadelphia, Boston, Washington, Detroit, St. Louis, and, perhaps more than any other city, Chicago. US Catholic narratives and ecclesiastical politics overwhelmingly focus on these cities while overlooking what is today the largest archdiocese in the country: Los Angeles. One of James O'Toole's greatest insights in the final chapter of *The Faithful* is a reflection on a hypothetical figure he names "Maria of Los Angeles," his symbol for the future of US Catholicism.[18] This symbol is a ready pedagogical tool for integrating colonialism, Americanism, and a hemispheric ecclesiology toward the end of a course on American Catholicism. As O'Toole aptly points out, the church in the United States continues to experience many of the challenges and opportunities of its past, but none is more obvious than the effect of immigration and the shift of American Catholic strongholds from the cities of the Northeast and Midwest to the "Sunbelt" of the South and

Southwest. In essence, the future of American Catholicism is playing itself out not so much in Chicago as it is in Los Angeles.

However, Los Angeles also reveals how the future of American Catholicism will take root in soil starkly different from its past. Naturally this future includes the tide of Latino and Asian Catholics who fill Los Angeles's largest (and often poorest) parishes. But the most striking difference, gleaned from the classroom, is how the largest concentration of Catholics in the United States finds its home in an aggressively post-Christian culture. Naturally, Los Angeles is not alone among US cities in its trend toward secularization.[19] Nevertheless, recent Pew Center Research highlights how the number of Catholics in Los Angeles is comparable to the number of residents who identify as "unaffiliated" with any religious tradition.[20] Such data reveal the startling juxtaposition of the nation's largest (and rapidly surging) Catholic population alongside an equally expanding population of so-called "nones." This phenomenon yields a palpable cultural dichotomy that more historic sister sees like New York and Chicago experience to a much lesser degree.

Among "Angeleno" students, moreover, this pervasive convergence of cultural difference manifests itself not so much in piety as in literacy. Unlike my experience of millennial students in the Midwest, most of my undergraduate students at Loyola Marymount were true religious "nones" with no firm religious background whatsoever. As a professor, I consequently found myself teaching a course on "American Catholicism" to students who had absolutely no religious literacy in the supernatural, let alone Christianity. In the "City of Angels," I discovered that secularization was beyond a pressing development; it was a simple, bald-face fact.

The future of American Catholicism rests in dealing with this reality and viewing it as an opportunity rather than as an impasse. In such a context, one must resist an "us-versus-them" mentality that conflates apathy with antipathy, for apathy is more malleable. Once again, Los Angeles unveils a future that hinges on literacy rather than piety. Catholic "evangelization" in this context is not so much catechesis as it is the instruction of millennials in an exotic foreign language with its distinct grammar, syntax, idioms, and dialects. At Loyola Marymount, this approach both intrigued and disarmed millennial students, for whom learning the foreign language of "Catholicism" was both fascinating and humbling (as one experiences with any foreign language). Pope Francis's call to "return to the basics" points precisely to this opportunity, to open the heart by opening the mind.[21]

The future of Catholic higher education depends on its ability to grapple creatively with these areligious millennials (and, for that matter, subsequent "post-millennials"). By instructing millennials in the language of Christianity, American Catholicism must show how the exceptionalism of a dawning post-Christian, "secular age" is mere myth. This post-Christian culture is not as original, bold, and free as it claims. Its opposition to dogma is itself dogmatic; its empirical rejection of the supernatural lacks empiricism; its histrionic history suffers from acute amnesia. And with respect to Catholicism, this post-Christian culture simply does not know what it is talking about. In the words of one scholar, the place of theology in the humanities today is to "sniff out small gods," the gods of a supposedly godless culture.[22] This is the task of American Catholicism in the twenty-first-century academy.

In a similar vein, the experience of the church in "godless" Los Angeles is the ecclesiological key for American Catholicism's future. Here a pedagogical experiment yielded remarkable success. In a project called "Catholics in LA," my millennial students had to study a Catholic "entity" (parish, school, organization, religious community, etc.) in the city, taking the bus, interviewing strangers, and sifting through local literature (and yes, often doing so in flip-flops). Students had to situate a local, tangible Catholic creation in the larger story of US Catholicism. The remarkable, underestimated result was a sudden sense of student ownership facilitated through the hemispheric "grammar" of Catholicism that the course provided. In learning about Serra, Leo, and John Paul II, students gradually gained an appreciation for the church's transcultural unity in intercultural diversity. In other words, students learned to view "Catholicism" beyond the obvious, to see faith in the streets as much as in steeples. In particular, non-Catholics found this most rewarding, with products that included a Hindu student's phone app for the cathedral, a dance major's discovery of an underground Catholic artist network, and several projects on the city's Chicano street murals. These millennial "nones" got American Catholicism through a hemispheric vision and its grammar of intercultural creativity. Once students learned that "America" is more than the United States, they quickly realized that the "Catholic Church" is more than the chapel on campus or the pope in Rome.

This lesson from Los Angeles further extends to the future of the American Catholic priesthood and my current students, seminarians in surplices. A clear trajectory for the future remains incomplete, but the transition from SoCal "nones" to Midwestern "clerics" has unveiled a stark contrast that ultimately reflects the paradox of Los Angeles and its lesson for the future of American Catholicism. If indeed the largest concentration of Catholics in "America" occupies one of the nation's most secularized cities, the future lies in bridging these two ostensibly opposed worlds. The seminary professor's task is now to teach "Evangelical Catholic" seminarians, who are almost exclusively millennials, how to engage post-Christian "America."[23] A flawless method eludes this study, but the same starting point of a hemispheric "America" is certain. Overall, Serra, Leo, and John Paul offer us an initial grammar for engaging both sets of millennials—those in the streets and those in the pews.

Conclusion: A New Starting Point

To conclude, this case for a new definition of "America" for Catholics on these shores, gleaned from pedagogical experience, proffers a foyer for the future. Our vision of the future is incomplete, but our new starting point is certain. Both a recovery of a hemispheric colonial past and a papal critique of Americanism in the present lie at the heart of a truly Catholic definition of "America." In this sense, the church in the United States continues to contribute its original insights to the church universal, yet does so in a manner that transcends not only national borders but also our narratives of the past. The church, in the words of G. K. Chesterton, is a "democracy of the dead," a democracy that begins with history. In a hemispheric "America," the church is also a democracy of the marginalized, of the immigrant, of the Body of Christ, a democracy that carries no eagle-emblazoned passport.

Notes

[1] Pope Francis, "Visit to the Joint Session of the United States Congress: Address of the Holy Father" (Washington, DC, September 24, 2015).

[2]Pope John Paul II, *Ecclesia in America*, no. 5. The first papal articulation of a single, hemispheric "America" appears in John Paul II's 1994 apostolic letter, *Tertio Millennio Adveniente*, no. 57.

[3]The only known reference to *Ecclesia in America* in recent works on US Catholicism is in Patrick Carey, *Catholics in America: A History*, updated ed. (New York: Sheed and Ward, 2004), 142.

[4]On Francis Cardinal George's discussion of a "Calvinist" US Catholicism distinct from that of the rest of the hemisphere, and Archbishop Rembert Weakland's favorable reaction, see Rembert G. Weakland, *A Pilgrim in a Pilgrim Church: Memoirs of a Catholic Archbishop* (Grand Rapids, MI: Eerdmans, 2009), 384–87.

[5]William Portier presents a similar insight in his inaugural lecture, "The First American Pope," for the "Francis Factor" series at Alvernia University. The author thanks Portier for sharing this work after the convention.

[6]Perhaps the best gesture of this reality is the choice to adorn the ambo for Serra's canonization in Washington with a simple iron cross supposedly brought by English Catholics to Maryland on the *Ark* and the *Dove*.

[7]James M. O'Toole, *The Faithful: A History of Catholics in America* (Cambridge, MA: Belknap Press of Harvard University Press, 2008), 100.

[8]Serra established only nine of the twenty-one Spanish Franciscan missions in Alta California. On the problem of conflating Serra's legacy with a monolithic "mission system," see Rose Marie Beebe and Robert M. Senkewicz, *Junípero Serra: California, Indians, and the Transformation of a Missionary* (Norman: University of Oklahoma Press, 2015).

[9]On the intentional transnational history of this canonization, see my article "Sacred Seeds: The French Jesuit Martyrs in American Catholic Historiography," *Logos: A Journal of Catholic Thought and Culture* 17, no. 4 (Fall 2014): 88–107.

[10]Carey, *Catholics in America*, 65.

[11]See Russell Shaw, *American Church: The Remarkable Rise, Meteoric Fall, and Uncertain Future of Catholicism in America* (San Francisco: Ignatius Press, 2013), and *Catholics in America: Religious Identity and Cultural Assimilation from John Carroll to Flannery O'Connor* (San Francisco: Ignatius Press, 2016).

[12]Shaw, *American Church*, 50. Shaw republished this exposé of Americanism in the *National Catholic Register*. See "'Americanism': Phantom Heresy or Fact?" ncregister.com, May 10, 2013.

[13]Charles C. Camosy, "Has the Time Come to Name 'Trumpism' a Heresy?" cruxnow.com, February 8, 2017; Richard Bulzacchelli, "No, Trump's 'America First' Is Not Actually a Heresy," cruxnow.com, February 22, 2017. In the second paragraph of his article, Camosy provides a link to Shaw's essay in the *National Catholic Register* (see note above). See also Camosy's response to Bulzacchelli in "What Kind of Heresy Is Trumpism?—A Response to Prof. Bulzacchelli," cruxnow.com, March 28, 2017.

[14]Pope Leo XIII, *Testem Benevolentiae*, in *American Catholic History: A Documentary Reader*, ed. Mark Massa with Catherine Osborne (New York: New York University Press, 2008), 67.

[15]William Portier, "Americanism and Inculturation, 1899–1999," *Communio* 27 (Spring 2000): 139–60.

[16]John Frederick Schwaller, *The History of the Catholic Church in Latin America: From Conquest to Revolution and Beyond* (New York: New York University Press, 2011), 187.

[17]The works of Allan Deck, Hosffman Ospino, and Timothy Matovina take seminal steps toward such an ecclesiology. See, for instance, Matovina, *Latino Catholicism: Transformation in America's Largest Church* (Princeton: Princeton University Press, 2012), 36.

[18]O'Toole, *The Faithful*, 266.

[19]By "secularization" I do not intend a monolithic, global phenomenon but rather the absence of broad religious literacy in a particular context compared to other contexts. On the difficulty of defining "secularization," see José Casanova, "The Secular, Secularizations, Secularisms," in *Rethinking Secularism*, ed. Craig Calhoun, Mark Juergensmeyer, and Jonathan VanAntwerpen (New York: Oxford University Press, 2011), 61.

[20]David Lauter and Hailey Branson-Potts, "US Has Become Notably Less Christian, Major Study Finds," *Los Angeles Times*, May 12, 2015.

[21]Pope Francis, *Misericordiae Vultus*, no. 10.

[22]Christopher Insole, "Theology and Politics: The Intellectual History of Liberalism," in *Theology, University, Humanities: Initium Sapientiae Timor Domini*, ed. Christopher Craig Brittain and Francesca Aran Murphy (Eugene, OR: Cascade, 2011), 191.

[23]These seminarians fit the description provided in William Portier, "Here Come the Evangelical Catholics," *Communio* 31, no. 1 (2004): 35–66.

Ressourcement and Inculturation

American Catholic Theology in the Key of Portier

Introduction
Derek C. Hatch and Timothy R. Gabrielli

William Portier has a spent a career taking seriously his location as an American Catholic theologian, convinced that all theology is woven within a cultural context. Thus Karl Rahner's theology is as much about post–World War II Germany and Edward Schillebeeckx's is as much about the Netherlands in the middle of the twentieth century, as John Courtney Murray's is about the United States in the Cold War era. By 1987, Portier was convinced that, in his words, "I am by training and deep conviction a historical theologian (can there really be any other kind?), I assume that one's religious thought is intimately related to one's religious life and is best interpreted faithfully when placed in its concrete historical setting."[1] Thus, for Portier, to do American Catholic theology is to work to understand our forebears and, for that matter, our contemporaries in the US Catholic Church who have lived, prayed, and thought through being Catholic in this cultural-national matrix, *mutatis mutandis*, and in so doing to understand something about God.

To take seriously one's location as an American Catholic theologian involves a kind of *ressourcement*, a return to the oft-overlooked theological contributions by American Catholics throughout the history of the United States. Before Murray there were Hecker and Brownson, McSorley and Slattery, Gigot and Driscoll, Rudd, Day, Michel, Falls, de Hueck, and Furfey, among many others. If these thinkers are not often seen as key resources for American Catholic theology, it is because our approach to

35

theology remains too narrow. Many American Catholic thinkers of the nineteenth century fit the mold of the patristic pastor-scholar, addressing questions ad hoc in a land where Catholic universities had yet to be established. Therefore, these important thinkers were not considered worthy contributors to theological discourse in the European university-centered model. Then, between 1910 and 1965, a rigid neo-scholasticism took hold in response to, among other intellectual and cultural developments, the fear of relativism incited by the advent of critical history. This is a legitimate and real fear. However, the exclusive reign of this school meant that creative theological thinkers often inhabited places and realms of discourse not strictly dubbed "theological." Given these marginalized, forgotten, or troublesome voices, Portier's historical-theological project faithfully bears "the burden of the dead." That is, in true *ressourcement* fashion, it gives voice to those who have suffered and whose lives bear witness to our inability to remain neutral (methodologically or otherwise). As Portier wrote in 1987, "The most rhetorically persuasive arguments against historical relativism as a theoretical position are ethical ones addressed to us in our neutrality by mice who have elephants standing on their tails."[2]

Beyond describing the contours of the elephant or the plight of the mouse, theology à la Portier seeks to find a religiously usable past for both sustenance and critique in the present. Therefore, whether American Catholicism finds itself at a point of crisis or renewal, if it stands at the crossroads as we commemorate the 500th anniversary of the Reformation, Portier's immense scholarly contribution gives us a method: First, to recognize that such observations about the state of the church in America are conditioned by our concrete historical setting; second, to see that such descriptors have been used before to describe a state of affairs in the church; third, to commune—in scholarly fashion—with those who have gone before in order to see more clearly what is happening in the present and what we might do about it.[3] A good measure of the embodied task of American Catholic theology involves sorting through mediation as inculturation. In other words, that "concrete historical setting" mediates God to us, in sometimes surprising ways. At the same time, imperial domination calls for rebuke wherever it rears its ugly head. The church works in and through its setting, undertaking the hard work of inculturation: seeking the logos, as did Paul in Athens, while discerning elements that must be rejected, as did the apostle in Corinth or Philippi.

We have lightly shaped this Festschrift for Portier, titled *Weaving the American Catholic Tapestry: Essays in Honor of William L. Portier* (2017), as a suitable introduction to the study of American Catholicism at the advanced undergraduate or graduate levels. As such, students of Catholic theology, American Catholic studies, and American religious history will find its essays of interest. It is only fitting that a volume in honor of Portier, who has spent the last thirteen years at the University of Dayton forming the next generation of theologians in American Catholic life and thought, is suited for the classroom. Collectively, the essays represent an introduction to major themes, figures, and methods in American Catholic historical theology. Each essay could be used as a launching pad for further research into the particular topic, and surrounding issues and questions, or as an entryway into the thematic questions of the relationship between theology and history.

Portier's dedication to the constructive retrieval of American Catholic sources has done a great service to the church. Readers will observe that the research in *Weaving the American Catholic Tapestry: Essays in Honor of William L. Portier*, edited by Derek C. Hatch and Timothy R. Gabrielli (Wipf & Stock, 2017) is deeply indebted to his gift.

Catholic Evangelicals and American Catholics
Curtis W. Freeman

Weaving the American Catholic Tapestry celebrates the scholarly contributions of William L. Portier. Anyone who takes time to read it will surely join in the festivity, and in doing so they will discover what those of us who are familiar with his work have understood for a long time—that he is one of the most insightful living interpreters of American Catholicism. Readers will not only know why this is so, but they will see how as a gifted teacher and colleague he has enabled others to share and extend his insight. What I find impressive is that eight of the fifteen essays are written by his former graduate students. The breadth of themes they address across the biblical, theological, and historical fields indicates the reach and scope of his understanding of Catholic modernity and his impact in shaping the next generation of scholars, who will serve as interpreters for a wider audience.

Yet surprisingly, his scholarship has not been as widely recognized as it deserves to be as an interpretive resource to aid confused Catholics or perplexed Protestants in understanding the intellectual and cultural currents that shape American Catholicism. What *Weaving the American Catholic Tapestry* confirms is that Catholics and Protestants alike would do well to look to Portier as a spiritual guide through the maze of US Catholicism.

But in suggesting that Portier's scholarship went under the radar for the wider public, it is important to note that his colleagues in the College Theology Society have long recognized his skill as an interpreter of Catholicism in American culture. One example is that his "Here Come the Evangelical Catholics," published in *Communio* in 2004, was awarded the best article that year—and for good reason.[4] As David O'Brien points out in his contribution to *Weaving*, Portier's article is a stunningly clear social, historical, and theological analysis of "Catholic Americanism." His critically sympathetic examination of a then emerging group of younger Catholics that had begun to catch the eye of people in the Catholic academy surprised some of his colleagues, who were not enthralled with the spiritual fervor and theological convictions of these young Catholics. But Portier's article made a persuasive case for how evangelical Catholics might be a source of renewal for all Catholics to reclaim an identity in being Catholic that is more determinative than being American.

Portier's influence goes well beyond helping US Catholics come to terms with the new cultural pluralism by renewing and retrieving a sense of catholicity. His participation in the doctoral program at the University of Dayton that focuses on Catholicism in America attracted evangelical Catholic doctoral students, but it also drew a steady stream of evangelical Protestants, who wanted to explore a sense of the wholeness of the church. They had grown weary with the fissiparous biblicism and schismatic sectarianism that divided their own theological institutions and denominations. They wanted to reclaim something more universal, more historic, more inclusive.

But it was not just these students that he guided in a recovery of a sense of catholicity in theology. I find it hard to imagine how I ever would have learned to give an account of evangelical Catholics "as a pilgrim community of contested convictions within the church catholic" apart from my conversations with Bill Portier.[5] I was so struck by William Collinge's chapter on Portier as a historical theologian that I immediately began reading the latter's book *Divided Friends*. My account of theological liberalism was thick with Protestants from Kant, Schleiermacher, Ritschl, and Harnack in Europe to Bushnell, Rauschenbusch, James, Tillich, and Niebuhr in the United States, but my sense of Catholic theology in modernity was limited to a caricature of Neo-Thomism with thumbnail sketches of Alfred Loisy, George Tyrrell, and John Henry Newman. Portier's book showed me how turn-of-the-twentieth-century Catholic Americanism transformed Catholic thought, creating a new scholarship that embraced modern historical and scientific investigation. What made this account so convincing is that it resisted the temptation to theorize or reduce to typologies. Instead it offered thick narratives of four lives to show how Catholic Americanism took shape.

When I began my theological journey, I was a proud Dixieland liberal, resisting the racial, political, social, and economic status quo of the evangelical Protestant established church culture. I was adapting to the New South with my progressive fellow pilgrims. Though my story was different from the stories of Catholic modernism, I could relate. We had our own little Protestant popes making pious pronouncements against the heresy of modernism from the safety of their ecclesiastical kingdoms. We had our own opportunists, who held up their fingers to the changing theological winds and pivoted from liberalism to fundamentalism. We had our share of disillusioned apostates, who lost the faith, and there were plenty of disenchanted moralists turned Unitarians among us, who continued to be disappointed with the church and its leadership. But there were some among us who trusted God to provide what is lacking despite our inability to resolve the conflict between intellect and will. To borrow a line from Portier, "I definitely wanted to be one of those men."[6] I hope I still do.

A Fuller US Catholic Story
Margaret McGuinness

When reading *Weaving the American Catholic Tapestry*, it is hard not to think of James Joyce's oft-quoted, rather pithy expression that Catholicism means "here comes everybody." Joseph McSorley, Felix Klein, John Courtney Murray, Teilhard de Chardin, Dorothy Day, Italian immigrants, and Catholic conscientious objectors are all subjects of essays contained in *Weaving the American Catholic Tapestry*. Here comes everybody indeed.

There has always been a tendency in US Catholic studies—and in all historical studies, perhaps—to separate people into good guys and bad guys. But we all know that it's not so easy to classify people in that way, and Andrew Black's essay on Orestes Brownson in the Portier Festschrift is a fine example of this. Black reminds us that many of Brownson's contemporaries believed that his conversion to Catholicism in 1844 was confirmation of his "mental and emotional instability." American Catholics of the mid-nineteenth century held a different opinion: they thought that his "spiritual and intellectual pilgrimage seemed to provide incarnate evidence that the Catholic faith and Catholic Church represented the only ultimate satisfaction for the hearts and minds of restless Americans." When you add to the mix the fact that Brownson just doesn't really fit into the traditional story of the nineteenth-century immigrant church, it's hard to know what to do with him. Even though Brownson doesn't fit any "good guy" or "bad guy" mold, Black offers us a way out of this dilemma.

Many scholars of American Catholicism have long bemoaned the fact that there is no good historical study of the priesthood in the United States. As I read the essays in *Weaving the American Catholic Tapestry*, though, I was struck by what we learn about the priesthood in the United States. Sandra Yocum's essay on Father Joseph McSorley reminds us that priests—and even bishops—were more than simply "God's Bricklayers." They were, in general and at least at the beginning of their careers, men with a strong faith and a desire to impart that faith to others. And the essays by Jeffrey Morrow and Patricia McDonald also shed some light on our knowledge of the pre–Vatican II priesthood from the perspective of the history of Catholic biblical studies. Lacking good studies of the priesthood, we have tended to focus on priests as kind of one-dimensional. According to most parish histories, for instance, all pastors were great and wonderful people. But the priests at the heart of these essays are viewed from another perspective—that of biblical scholarship.

Some essays in *Weaving the American Catholic Tapestry* will be especially helpful to scholars and teachers trying to examine Catholicism in the second half of the twentieth century and the early part of the twenty-first. Benjamin Peters, writing on World War II and what he calls "the flattening out of American Catholicism," demonstrates "something of the profound shift that occurred in American Catholicism as a result of the 'Good War,'" and suggests that "some of the silenced and ignored prewar Catholic voices, whose historical context of war and economic instability is not all that unlike our own context today, continue to be relevant to Catholics in the United States." Reading this essay reminded me of the profound impact World War II had on the demographics of US Catholicism. What would have been the story of American Catholics, and Catholic higher education, without the GI Bill?

Very much related to this is the following point: we need to pay a lot more attention to this notion of evangelical Catholicism. In the very first sentences of David O'Brien's essay, he asks: "American Catholics, who are they? Are they Catholics who happen to be American or Americans who happen to be Catholics?" According to O'Brien, Portier recognizes that the collapse of the Catholic subculture is the "single most important fact of US Catholic history." The subculture collapsed as a result of economic and educational changes after World War II, and American Catholics then had to "learn 'how to be truly Catholic in American pluralism without a subculture.'" I probably have a fair number of evangelicals in my classes, using that term a bit more loosely than David O'Brien does. I suggest that this idea of the Catholic evangelical is something that we ought to take more seriously than perhaps we have in the past—especially as we look at the decline of US Catholicism in general. And I also think we need to bring this discussion of evangelicals into our teaching of US Catholicism.

There are very few women even mentioned in *Weaving the American Catholic Tapestry*. Michael Baxter's essay focuses on

Dorothy Day and the Catholic Worker, and I note a couple of references to Frances Cabrini and Catherine de Hueck. Is there a way to bring other women into the conversation? Can we pray with Elizabeth Seton as well as with Father McSorley? Can we place some of these folks within the context of the work they did and the relationships they had with women religious, as Diane Batts Morrow does with John Slattery and the Oblate Sisters of Providence in Baltimore?[7] Is Madeleva Wolff, CSC, who called for the education of women religious in the 1950s—an education that included theology and scripture—eligible for a place in the annals of Catholic biblical scholarship in at least some way? And is Rose Hawthorne, daughter of Nathaniel Hawthorne and a convert, a worthy counterpart to Orestes Brownson?

As I write these names, I am struck by the fact that all of these women are women religious; and of course many of the men found in this collection of essays are priests. How are we going to get laywomen into this mix? Do we know anything about Father McSorley's interactions with the laywomen who read his books on prayer, for example?

This question about the place of women in this conversation is not meant to denigrate in any way the fine essays in *Weaving the American Catholic Tapestry* and the equally fine work that the editors have done in producing this book. But Dorothy Day is not the "typical" American Catholic woman—and we are in the process of moving her from one margin to another, bypassing the center completely. In *The World Will Be Saved by Beauty*, Kate Hennessy writes that Dorothy's daughter "grieved the loss of this vibrant woman to the annals of hagiography and the desire to see her as a saint."[8] Hennessy's observation gives US Catholic historians and theologians additional food for thought.

Theologizing America: A Tale of Two Prefaces
Frederick Christian Bauerschmidt

In responding to *Weaving the American Catholic Tapestry*, the collection of essays by the friends and students of Bill Portier, I want to take up a particular theological issue that is itself woven through those essays, and is also present in Bill's own most recent work, *Divided Friends*, which uncovers the history of Catholic modernism in America, a history that has been obscured by "phantom heresy" historiography that failed to see the theological kinship of Americanism and modernism. This is the issue of the relationship of nature and grace.

Let me say at this point that I think the standard story of the integrist victory over extrinsicism truthfully tells one part of the story of Catholicism in the twentieth century, and that I would, broadly speaking, identify with the tribe of Henri de Lubac and other "integrists." A division of theology into extrinsicist and integrist approaches, along with a valorization of the latter and a rejection of the former, is too simple. There are multiple ways to integrate nature and grace, some of which may be commendable and some of which may not. Likewise, there may be moments when a return to the clear delineation between nature and grace associated with neo-scholasticism might well serve our purposes.

To begin to map how all of the reflection that has taken place on nature and grace in the last hundred years might play a role in understanding our current situation, as well as to uncover some of the limitations of that thinking, I would like to look at two examples of liturgical inculturation: the proper prefaces for Thanksgiving Day in the United States found in the 1975 *Sacramentary* and the 2011 *Roman Missal*. If the adage that the rule of prayer founds the rule of belief is true, then we might look at these prayer texts to see how it is that we think theologically about America.

To begin with the preface from the 1975 *Sacramentary*, after an opening reference to creation, the preface continues, "Once you chose a people and, when you brought them out of bondage to freedom, they carried with them the promise that all men would be blessed and all men could be free." The prayer nowhere explicitly identifies who this chosen people is, but given the context of Thanksgiving, hearers might be forgiven for thinking that this is a reference to our pilgrim forebears. When the prayer goes on to say "What the prophets pledged was fulfilled in Jesus Christ," it becomes apparent that this chosen people is in fact the ancient Israelites, but by this point the typological connection between the Israelites and the founding fathers has been forged in the hearer's mind, a connection that seems confirmed later in the preface when it says that the fulfillment of the prophetic promise "happened to our fathers, who came to this land as if out of the desert into a place of promise and hope." America the New World is defined theologically over and against the Old World as the promised land of freedom. In other words, it may seem that we have here a thoroughgoing "Americanist" narrative. Yet the preface concludes by saying that "it happens to us still, in our time, as you lead all men through your Church to the blessed vision of your peace." This reference to the church suggests that what we have here is not simply an Americanized Catholicism, but something more like Hecker's vision of a Catholicized America.

This prayer is loathed by commentators on both the left and the right. When we look to why the prayer might be problematic, it is clearly not because it is "extrinsicist." Indeed, if anything, it is a thoroughgoing "integrist" text, suggesting that there is no secular history segregated from salvation history, no realm of pure nature, but one seamlessly single history in which the American experience can be integrated into the experience of Israel and the church. But the prayer is torn by countervailing tendencies in which now America, now the church, assumes primacy of place in the story of salvation that it seeks to tell.

If we turn to the preface from the 2011 *Roman Missal* we find a whole new composition, one that abandons any attempt to integrate the American story into the story of salvation. Instead of a compelling narrative, the prayer offers abstractions like "responsibility," "commitment," and "fundamental dignity." This seems to be what unaided reason might tell us about the human person, something quite different from (though not incompatible with) a full-blown Christian anthropology and more akin to the thin accounts that undergird liberal democracies. When the prayer then turns to the death and resurrection of Jesus and the "freedom from sin" that is our "ultimate redemption," this is not presented as something that emerges *from* our fundamental dignity, but is rather a purely gratuitous *addition* to the humanity that has previously been described. In other words, the two parts of the prayer, one describing our created nature and the other describing our redemption in Christ, might seem to be only extrinsically related, with the latter forming a second layer upon the first.

Comparing the two prefaces, we must say that while we have lost the vivid narrative of 1975, this might not be such a bad thing, given the confusing and problematic way in which that narrative theologizes America. The 2011 preface might be abstract and even boring, but it is clear in its refusal to theologize America by incorporating the emergence of America into a salvation-historical narrative. Nor does it seem to me that the thin account of human nature that it gives is necessarily being presented as a pure nature—indeed, the very thinness and abstractness of the account might suggest its own inadequacy and its need to be perfected by our redemption in Jesus Christ. If that is the case, then perhaps what some might call "extrinsicism" could be differently understood as a refusal of problematic integrations of secular events into salvation history, a refusal to sacralize the mundane in such a way that the Gospel loses its "over-and-againstness" vis-à-vis the world. And a recovery of a sense of over-and-againstness might allow for a different sort of theological narration of America—one that sees not only the flourishing of grace, but also the effects of sin, a narrative that might incorporate the Middle Passage and Wounded Knee.

All of which is to say that perhaps we need to rethink once again the theology of nature and grace. Perhaps the declaration of an integrist victory is premature and those bad old neo-scholastics still have something left to tell us. It might even lead us to go back and look again at their texts to actually see if there is in fact a unified neo-scholastic account of nature and grace, or a unified integrist opposition to it, and whether we might need to draw new maps with which to traverse the past, finding the old landmarks of extrinsicism and integrism to have outlived their usefulness.

Notes

[1] William L. Portier, "John R. Slattery (1851–1926), Missionary and Modernist: The State of My Current Research Project," *American Catholic Studies Newsletter* 14, no. 1 (Fall 1987): 9.

[2] Ibid., 10.

[3] William Portier's *Divided Friends: Portraits of the Roman Catholic Modernist Crisis in the United States* (Washington, DC: Catholic University of America, 2013) is an example of exactly this kind of work. It describes Joseph McSorley's path through the modernist crisis in the early twentieth century, while subtly offering McSorley's emphasis on history and holiness as a viable path for contemporary faithful scholars. On the burden of the dead, see especially 38–57.

[4]William L. Portier, "Here Come the Evangelical Catholics," *Communio* 31, no. 1 (2004): 35–66.

[5]Curtis W. Freeman, *Contesting Catholicity: Theology for Other Baptists* (Waco, TX: Baylor University Press, 2014), 257.

[6]Portier, *Divided Friends,* xix.

[7]See Diane Batts Morrow, "'Undoubtedly a Bad State of Affairs': The Oblate Sisters of Providence and the Josephite Fathers, 1877–1903," *Journal of African American History* 101, no. 3 (Summer 2016): 261–87.

[8]Kate Hennessy, *Dorothy Day: The World Will Be Saved by Beauty, An Intimate Portrait of My Grandmother* (New York: Scribner, 2017), xi.

The Pentecost Challenge

Proclaiming the Gospel in New Parish Cultures

Patricia Wittberg, SC

A Pentecost prayer service I once attended contained a meditation from the third volume of *Days of the Lord*, on the chapter in Acts (2:6) in which the Holy Spirit inspires the apostles to proclaim the Good News to people in their native languages:

> The event of Pentecost is a mystery of universal importance. The miracle of tongues unhesitatingly entrusts the proclamation of the Gospel to fragile human language, which is always changing. No longer is there a sacred language, determined once and for all or received from the past as the only one capable of authentically transmitting the good news. . . . The Spirit has been given to the Church so that it may assume every human language and all of the cultures expressed therein. In each one, the good seed of the Word must be sown with both hands, because in each, the fruits of the Spirit may be borne a hundredfold. In its calling, the Church is confronted with the challenge of constantly translating the Gospel into the native speech of "every nation under heaven."[1]

There is, the meditation said, no sacred language that enfleshes the Word of God perfectly, no cultural interpretation of the Gospel that is superior to all others.

I am not sure that everyone would agree with this—throughout the centuries, we Christians have canonized Latin, or Liturgical Greek, or Amharic, or Old Church Slavonic as *the* language for speaking to (and being spoken to by) God. And there are some good anthropological and sociological reasons for having a sacred, set-apart language and rituals for experiencing The Holy. But theologically and pastorally, there are also good reasons for *not* having one. Canonizing one single way of relating to God while cultures and languages change over time may dilute Christ's prophetic message, exclude outsiders, and/or hamper the church's missionary efforts. But translating the Gospel into fallible human languages and cultures also distorts it, in ways that each culture's members are blind to.

I wish to speak today about what it would mean to take the Pentecost challenge seriously: in our parishes, in our colleges and universities, and in our seminaries and houses of formation. Of all the Christian denominations in the United States, Catholic parishes are already the most ethnically diverse: a full third contain more than one ethnic group. At the same time, however, they are less diverse in other ways. Some parishes contain mostly senior citizens; a few primarily young adults. Some parishes attract traditionalists to their "high church" liturgies; others to their social justice focus.[2] Our schools, seminaries, and houses of formation also face challenges of diversity. What challenges does ethnic, generational, or theological diversity pose for US Catholicism today? What challenges does ethnic/generational/theological *homogeneity* pose?

We all necessarily relate to God through our own cultural worldviews and linguistic categories. So when we meet Catholics from another culture in our parishes or on our college campuses and are confronted with the different way(s) they live and worship, the different ways they image God, or their different assumptions about prayer, we may find them incomprehensible or threatening. Applying our own assumptions to other cultural groups may cause us to misinterpret their motives or dismiss their spirituality as undeveloped. With our "etic" (outsider) perspective, we have a keen vision of the flaws or defects in other cultural versions of Catholicism, while remaining blind to the ways they are challenging the flaws or defects in our own version. When is the presence of other Catholic cultures in our parishes and schools calling us to change or grow in our relationship with God? When, in contrast, are we called to challenge the other culture's blind spots and prophetically proclaim the Gospel message to them in *our* language?

Cultural Variations in Catholicism

Most Americans have some idea of the different aspects of "culture." We know that it includes material products such as cell phones or houses, behavioral practices such as how to greet a friend or celebrate a birthday, and value judgments about what is beautiful, desirable, or morally right. We are somewhat less aware of how these elements interact with and influence each other. Even less obvious to us are the deeper, subconscious "root paradigms" of cognitive culture that shape our very definition of reality.[3] These deep and subconscious cultural assumptions about who God is, what (if anything) God wants of us, and what purpose/meaning underlies our existence are the assumptions that we are the least aware of holding, and the least able to imagine how anyone could hold different ones than we do.

Even the seemingly superficial aspects of culture can cause disunity in a parish or university setting, because they often contain deeper messages that exclude others. Liturgical celebrations with chalice veils, drums, Gregorian chant, or speaking in tongues signal that "my kind of person" either is or is not welcome to participate. Practices that are expected in some cultures (e.g., bringing toddlers to an Easter Vigil celebration) may be considered out of place or distracting in others. More important sources of misunderstanding are the deepest "root paradigms" of our culture that we take for granted. Is it best to approach the divine directly or through a saint or a "holier" priest? In ecstatic experiences, formal liturgies, or centering prayer? Are men (or women) just naturally better at relating to God than the opposite gender is? Is going to church "unmanly," or "geeky," or something only "those people" do?

Dealing with Ethnic Cultures: A Historical View

The US church has had to deal with such questions before. During the nineteenth and early twentieth centuries, waves of immigrants from the Catholic countries of Europe raised the total number of Catholics in this country from thirty thousand at the end of the colonial period to over fifteen million in 1916.[4] Each newly arriving ethnic group experienced conflict with previously established Catholics, and sometimes with other immigrant groups as well. The Irish American clerics who dominated the US church's hierarchy after the mid-nineteenth century expected later immigrants to give up their "backward," old-country religious practices and conform to the accepted "American" way of worshipping. But the immigrants demanded their own ethnic parishes, headed by pastors of their own ethnic group, and the bishops were eventually constrained to provide them. By 1912, there were more than 1,600 ethnic parishes in the United States.[5] Most were located in the neighborhoods where the particular immigrant group they served had settled.

Homogeneous ethnic parishes served several valuable functions for the immigrants. They were "institutionally complete," meaning that they provided not only worship in the familiar language and symbols of the home country, but also parochial schools in the native language, social and athletic clubs, credit unions, and social welfare services—at a time when alternate sources of these benefits were scarce. In ethnically homogeneous parishes, the need to adjust one's way of worshipping to the preferences of other groups did not arise. One could live one's entire life cocooned by the "Sacred Canopy" of the ethnic parish, rarely exposed to other versions of Catholicism.[6]

There were pros and cons to this arrangement. On the one hand, it was easier to pass on the faith. Catholicism was in the very air the children breathed: they may never have met a non-Catholic, or even a Catholic of another ethnicity. The entire cultural atmosphere imparted by ethnoreligious festivals, language instruction in the parish school, and daily or seasonal home rituals or shrines, all made being Polish, French Canadian, or Italian synonymous with being Catholic. On the other hand, critics have charged that encapsulated ethnic parishes were less able to influence and enrich the rest of the US church or the larger society.[7] Outside observers were often scandalized by ethnic religious practices borrowed from a pre-Christian past.[8] Perhaps most serious, however, was the inability of homogeneous ethnic parishes to adapt to generational changes in the larger society and in their own ethnic group, or to make other, newly arriving, ethnic groups feel welcome.[9]

The second half of the twentieth century saw the dissolution of the ethnic parish model, which had been successful for almost 100 years. The restriction of immigration after the 1920s meant that ethnic neighborhoods had not been replenished by new arrivals for several decades. By the 1950s, the children and grandchildren of the immigrants had largely Americanized and, aided by postwar government policies, were moving into suburban areas. The Supreme Court's 1954 decision that "Separate but Equal" facilities were inherently unjust affected church decision-makers' willingness to establish separate ethnic parishes and schools for new Catholic migrants from Latin America or Asia. The call of the Second Vatican Council to participate in "the joys and the hopes, the griefs and the anxieties" of the modern world was enthusiastically embraced by US Catholics, who were perhaps naïve about the strength of secular American culture. It soon became clear that the larger American culture was influencing US Catholics far more than they were influencing it. As some critics have noted, while nineteenth-century immigrant Catholics had to figure out what it meant to be an *American* Catholic, their grandchildren and great-grandchildren had to determine what—if anything—it meant to be an American *Catholic*.[10]

Generational Cultures

If growing up in a particular ethnic Catholic environment means that one will be exposed to the sacred objects, ritual behaviors, religious values, and basic cognitive assumptions about God that are unique to that particular culture, growing up at a particular *time* has similar effects. According to sociologist Karl Mannheim, we all unreflectively absorb the values, behaviors, and cognitive root paradigms current during our childhood.[11] A 1940s child whose early experience of Catholicism included being drilled in the Baltimore Catechism by sisters in full habits, and whose seasons were marked by May crownings, Corpus Christi processions, and giving up candy for Lent, imbibed a Catholic culture that was very different from a 1970s child whose Catholicism was confined to a weekly hour of CCD and attendance at the Sunday youth guitar Mass—as different as if one had been raised Catholic in Ohio and the other in Burundi.

When persons reach adulthood, they become able to judge how well the culture they had absorbed as children corresponds to what they now experience. At that key time, they react to the events of the larger society that may contradict their childhood beliefs and values. The changes brought about by Vatican II had different impacts on Catholics, depending on how old they were at the time. Sociologists studying American Catholicism have divided US Catholics into four generational cultures—with, admittedly, some blurring of boundaries at the edges—depending on the amount and timing of their exposure to pre– and post–Vatican II practices:[12]

- **The Pre–Vatican II Generation** (born before 1943): This generation of Catholics reached their maturity before the Second Vatican Council began. They are the last generation to have passed both their childhood and their early adulthood within an all-encompassing Catholic subculture. This pervasive Catholic environment fundamentally shaped the cognitive and value aspects of their Catholic identity in a way that has resisted change ever since. To this day, surveys show they have a stronger religious affiliation than Mainline Protestants the same age, and much stronger ties than subsequent Catholic generations. There is a steep decline between this generation and younger Catholics in the percentages who attend Mass weekly, read Catholic periodicals, participate actively in their parishes, and consider themselves to be "strong" Catholics.

- **The Vatican II Generation** (born 1943–60): This generation experienced at least some of the same all-encompassing, traditional Catholic culture during their childhood, but came of age during the changes after Vatican II. Especially for the older half of this generation, the traditional socialization of their childhood Catholicism—however stultifying they may later have defined it as being—has made them more likely to remain in the church and push for change rather than simply to leave. As a result, they are disproportionately represented in the membership of organizations such as Pax Christi, Voice of the Faithful, and Call to Action.

- **The Post–Vatican II Generation** (born 1961–80): Catholics in this generation received their entire religious formation in the post–Vatican II era. Unlike earlier generations, they have had no experience of an all-encompassing Catholic environment to form their religious identity. Growing up in the post-Watergate era, and seeing many of their pastors and sister-teachers leave church service, they became more cynical and suspicious of institutions in general. If they did not agree with something the church or their pastors taught or said, they were more likely to leave rather than stay and press for changes. Contrary to the pattern of previous generations, most of them did not return to regular religious practice and parish participation after they married and began having children.[13]

- **The millennials** (born 1981–98): millennials are two generations removed from pre–Vatican II church. Neither they nor their parents remember the kind of all-encompassing religious environment that had shaped pre–Vatican II Catholics. Close to four in ten (39 percent) have become "religious nones," unaffiliated with any religion.[14] The same proportion say they have a "bad impression" of Christianity in general and would be embarrassed to be thought "too religious." The Catholic millennials who remain attached to the church tend to be only marginally so: less likely than Protestants their age to pray daily, to attend religious services, or to say that religious teachings have a strong influence on their lives.

- **The coming generation** (born after 1998): As those of you who teach college are well aware, the current batch of college students is different from those of ten or fifteen years ago. Having grown up after September 11, 2001, they have a more pessimistic outlook on the world than their older brothers and sisters, who had passed their childhoods in a more peaceful and prosperous time. Their modes of interpersonal interaction and community connection were shaped by smart phones and social media apps in their childhood, with results that are yet to be fully analyzed. Since this generation is only now reaching adulthood, it is too soon to say what their affiliation with Catholicism will be like.

Undoubtedly some of you are thinking that these overviews are too stereotypical, that you can name members of your own generation who do not correspond to the description given here, or that the millennial and postmillennial Catholics who populate your theology classes are actually more, not less, "Catholic" than older generations. No generation is perfectly homogeneous; there are regional, class, and ethnic variations. In addition, every generation contains what Mannheim called a "cognitive minority," persons who react to the overall tenor of their generational culture by saying, doing, and believing the exact opposite.[15] Among Catholic millennials, the "cognitive minority" may attend Mass daily, militantly proclaim their loyalty to the Magisterium, and adopt various "old-fashioned" devotional practices. Although almost all surveys estimate that this group constitutes fewer than 10 percent of all millennial Catholics, they are the ones who are the most likely to populate our seminaries and houses of formation. This has implications I will discuss presently.

The Present Situation

As is always the case, one generation is succeeding another in US Catholicism. In 1987, pre–Vatican II Catholics constituted 31 percent of Catholics in this country, Vatican II Catholics 47 percent, and post–Vatican II Catholics 22 percent. The relative proportions are very different today. Fewer than 10 percent of Catholics are members of the pre–Vatican II generation now; 33 percent are members of the Vatican II generation, 34 percent are of the post–Vatican II generation, and 23 percent are millennials. The median age of Catholics in the United States is younger than the median age of Mainline Protestants.

Figure 1. The Generational Composition of American Catholicism: 1987 and 2011

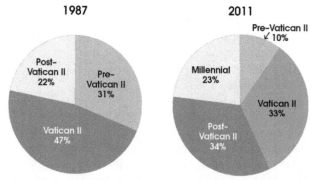

Source: D'Antonio, Dillon, and Gautier, *American Catholics in Transition*, 30.

But these generational changes are complicated by simultaneously occurring ethnic changes. Over three-fourths of the pre–Vatican II generation were non-Hispanic whites, whereas only slightly more than one-third of millennial Catholics are. Over half of millennial Catholics in the United States identify as Hispanic or Latino. In part, this is because migrating to a foreign country is usually done by young adults. In part, however, it is also due to the increasing alienation of younger, non-Hispanic Catholics from the faith of their childhood. In comparison to the oldest generation of US Catholics, non-Hispanic millennial Catholics are much less likely to say they attend Mass regularly or to say that the church was an important part of their lives, and much more likely to say they might leave Catholicism altogether in the future.[16] This alienation is especially strong among Catholic millennial women. Among the pre–Vatican II generation Catholics, women are more likely than men to attend Mass and say that the church is important in their lives, but this gap has been erased, or even reversed, among the youngest generation of Catholics.[17]

This alienation puts most millennial Catholics at odds with the cognitive minority of their generation who have entered church service. As I have already mentioned, this cognitive minority has tended to be more conservative and doctrinally orthodox than their age peers. To the extent that a new, young pastor attempts to conform a parish to his liturgical and doctrinal model of Catholicism, the current parishioners may simply leave, and new ones will be less likely to join. Reports are beginning to surface of Catholics seeking elsewhere for the kind of worship community they prefer. This is true of Hispanic as well as non-Hispanic Catholics: 25 percent of the Hispanics in the United States are former Catholics, and the percentage rises with each successive generation.

Proclaiming the Good News to Many Parish Cultures

Most Catholic parishes, colleges, seminaries, and houses of formation are, therefore, confronted with the necessity of fostering several different cultural versions of Catholicism. They probably contain parishioners/students from several different countries. Parishes may contain—or hope to attract—young members as well as older ones. Seminaries and houses of formation, while composed predominantly of millennial-aged students, must nevertheless attempt to foster relations between them and an older generation of faculty. There may be a wide spectrum of theological orientations among the parishioners/students/faculty, based on their respective ethnic or generational cultures. Each of these different cultural versions of Catholicism will have different preferences for how, when, and how often to pray, for what kinds of music best foster prayer, for the proper balance between the authority of the pastor/ dean/professor in matters of faith and morals and the individual's autonomy, for how much family involvement there should be in sacraments or studies, and a host of other variations. And these cultures are not static. A parish that structures itself to meet the needs and desires of a particular immigrant group (or a seminary that trains its future priests to do so) may not be able to attract or retain the immigrants' children and grandchildren. Local alumni may no longer feel "at home" at the vibrant college student Mass they had so enjoyed in the past, now that they have jobs, spouses, and children. A pastor or college chaplain who could relate easily to one ethnic group or generation may be at sea when attempting to relate to another.

How to meet these challenges? Should we invite all the different cultural groups in our parishes, schools, and seminaries to a common set of liturgies, classes, and social groups, so that we can all learn from and be challenged by each other's unique cultural "language" for envisioning God? Or would this dilute the distinctiveness of some cultures by assimilating them to mainstream American Catholicism? Should we retain separate liturgies, separate classes in theology and spirituality, separate social groups and parish committees for each cultural subgroup we are called to serve? This latter pluralistic approach will preserve the unique insights and practices each ethnic group, social class, or generation may have about the Divine. But will it fossilize a version of Catholicism that subsequent generations can no longer relate to?

The church is called to attempt to strike a balance between assimilation and pluralism in how it attempts to serve the multitude of ethnic, generational, and ideological cultures that populate our parishes and institutions. We must neither force them to discard their own ways of praying and acting before they are ready to do so nor allow them to cling to how "we have always done" something while their own children and grandchildren chafe for change. In discerning when to pursue assimilation and when to celebrate pluralism, we will alternate strategies between the two poles, and often we will make mistakes. But this, I believe, is what we were called to do by the Holy Spirit in Acts.

Assimilation Strategies

True assimilation does not require newcomers to discard their own culture and adopt another. Instead, it assumes that *both* sides will be profoundly changed, learning from and adopting some of the practices, vocabularies, values, and cognitive structures that the other side uses to image and relate to God.

Before this can happen, however, newcomers from other ethnic and generational cultures have to be persuaded to show up. This involves actively inviting them to our liturgies, paraliturgies, prayer services, and celebrations. In order for these invitations to be successful, we must first meet and get to know them where they are: as our co-workers, our neighbors, fellow members of our softball team or social club. It means finding out their cultural values, their deep, unconscious assumptions about who God is, and the material and spiritual services they most need and long for. For newly arrived ethnic groups, it may involve providing practical services like language instruction, legal assistance, and family counseling as well as liturgical celebrations that are meaningful to them. For millennial and postmillennial generations, it may involve offering opportunities to engage in group discernment prayer, the quiet of Eucharistic Adoration, or mindfulness training.[18]

Inviting members of other cultures to parish liturgies and functions also means deliberately welcoming them when and if they come. A parish or campus ministry could deputize a dozen or more extroverted persons from the various ethnic or generational cultures it wants to attract and ask them to watch for new arrivals standing hesitantly at the door, approach them, and take them under their wing until they feel at home.

Pluralism Strategies

Parishes and campus ministries also need to consider what they are inviting new members *to*. What prayer styles help a particular ethnic or generational group relate to God? What types of social gatherings or service projects most appeal to them? It is possible, for example, that the second-generation youth of a particular ethnicity (those born in America to immigrant parents) will not be attracted either to a parish's ethnic ministries, which target adults, nor to its youth ministry, which target Anglo-American youth. Some authors have suggested having separate RCIA or CCD programs for the different subcultures in a parish, and some racial or ethnic groups have asked colleges and universities to create dorms, dances, and fraternities/sororities restricted to their group only. When do such strategies honor the cultural identity of the newcomers to our parishes, seminaries, and college campuses, and when are they simply divisive?

In the end, no strategy is perfect. Nor, given that the larger society and its component cultures are constantly changing, is any strategy a permanent solution. Eventually, flaws will surface in the way(s) any parish, college, seminary, or house of formation chooses to address the challenge of articulating the Good News in the language of those who come to them. Which brings us back to the Pentecost mystery: that the Spirit, for incomprehensible divine reasons, chooses—over and over again—to entrust the Good News to our fallible and culturally bound hands.

Notes

[1] *Days of the Lord*, vol. 3, translated by Gregory LaNave and Donald Molloy (Collegeville, MN: Liturgical Press, 1993), 273–74.

[2] See, for example, Jerome Baggett, *Sense of the Faithful: How American Catholics Live Their Faith* (New York: Oxford University Press, 2009).

[3] See William E. Biernatzki, *Roots of Acceptance: The Intercultural Communication of Religious Meanings* (Rome: Gregorian Pontifical Institute, 1991), for a discussion of root paradigms.

[4] Patricia Wittberg, SC, *Catholic Cultures: How Parishes Can Respond to the Changing Face of Catholicism* (Collegeville, MN: Liturgical Press, 2016), 11–13.

[5] Ibid., 12.

⁶Peter L. Berger, *The Sacred Canopy: Elements of a Sociological Theory of Religion* (Garden City, NY: Doubleday, 1967).

⁷See, for example, John Tracy Ellis, "American Catholics and the Intellectual Life," *Thought* 30 (1955): 351–88.

⁸See Robert Orsi, *The Madonna of 115th Street: Faith and Community in Italian Harlem, 1880–1950* (New Haven: Yale University Press, 2002).

⁹See Simon C. Kim, *Memory and Honor: Cultural and Generational Ministry with Korean American Communities* (Collegeville, MN: Liturgical Press, 2013), 47, 52, 81.

¹⁰Christian Smith, Kyle Longest, Jonathan Hill, and Kari Christoffersen, *Young Catholic America: Emerging Adults In, Out of, and Gone from the Church* (New York: Oxford University Press, 2014), 23.

¹¹See Karl Mannheim, "The Problem of Generations," in *Essays in the Sociology of Knowledge*, ed. Paul Kecskemeti (London: Routledge, 1952).

¹²This section is taken from Wittberg, *Catholic Cultures*, 70–75, and based on categories developed by William V. D'Antonio, Michele Dillon, and Mary L. Gautier, *American Catholics in Transition* (Lanham, MD: Rowman and Littlefield, 2013).

¹³Mark Silk, "Gen-X Catholic Debacle," Religion News Service (June 5, 2012).

¹⁴Robert P. Jones, Daniel Cox, Betsy Cooper, and Rachel Lienesch, "Exodus: Why Americans Are Leaving Religion—and Why They're Unlikely to Come Back," Public Religion Research Institute (www.prri.org), September 22, 2016.

¹⁵Mannheim, "Problem of Generations," 308, 316–18.

¹⁶D'Antonio, Dillon, and Gautier, *American Catholics in Transition*, 22–23.

¹⁷Ibid., 90–92.

¹⁸For further suggestions see Wittberg, *Catholic Cultures*, 46–54, 90–98.

Nearer the People?

Pope Francis and the Crisis of the American Parish

William A. Clark, SJ

A Theological Starting Point

The problems associated with Roman Catholic parishes in the twenty-first-century United States are usually dealt with as questions of pastoral organizational priorities. In what follows, I wish to keep the *theological* context of the parish particularly in view, beginning with some basic assumptions: Jesus Christ reveals the God he calls "Father" by sharing with his disciples his own *intimate communion* with him in the Spirit (which the church will ultimately recognize as Trinity). As Jesus draws us into that communion, the relationship displays other essential aspects: by virtue of his incarnation, it is a communion *embodied* and *sacramental*; by virtue of his shared life, not only with fellow human beings but with the heavenly Father, it is not an individual relationship but a *communal* and *inclusive* one; by virtue of his ministry of seeking the lost, it is a communion that is active in and engaged with the world, and thus *collaborative*.[1] These characteristics of communion, lived and shared within our local church communities, give those communities a proper practical *authority* within the universal church that is theologically warranted.[2]

It is hard to deny that leaders of local church communities need to listen, for practical reasons, to the People of God as represented by the parishioners of those communities. In an era of "parish shopping," this is how pastors ensure that parishioners will understand what is taught, support the staff's plans and projects, and even choose to remain in the community at all. Taking a theological view, however, it seems even more important to recognize the face-to-face church community as a primary locus for believers' direct encounter with Jesus's self-revelation. It occurs in Christ's embodied presence in the Eucharist and other sacraments, and in the actual gathering of believers who share this communion with Christ, and so with one another. The parish or other genuine local church community is where, far from looking past one another to some "individual experience" of Jesus, we must encounter one another in the depth of our encounter with him.

New Models of Parish: A Fundamental Shift?

Urgent e-mails in 2016 begged me (and anyone else who would respond) to help save Mt. Carmel Church in Worcester, Massachusetts, the city where I live and work. The rumbling traffic of a too-near downtown expressway has weakened the ninety-year-old sanctuary, now declared too dangerous for occupancy.[3] The parish had already been canonically merged with another; in civil law, all the temporary barriers to the church building's demolition were removed, and an appointment with the wrecking ball had been set.[4] A small group of parishioners distraught enough to appeal to the Vatican were attempting to delay the process, but they have not prevailed this time, as has occasionally happened elsewhere. Mt. Carmel will soon become another lost symbol of a vanishing form of US Catholic life.

In what has come to be thought of as the "traditional parish"—with its myriad social and spiritual functions, generations of dedicated parishioners, hard-earned financial resources, and physical plant—US Catholics have for nearly two centuries encountered the embodied Christ and his mission. That few typical parishioners have likely thought in such terms—while yet holding their faith implicitly and practicing it diligently—is simply further demonstration of how thoroughly incarnated that faith has been. The heartbroken parishioners of Mt. Carmel, in their frantic effort to save a condemned *building,* are holding on, until the very last, to a cherished *icon* (with all the sacramental significance of that word) of this incarnate Christ. They know that those walls were once anointed with holy oil, that parishioners have always blessed themselves upon entering and leaving, and that many of their most significant family events have taken place inside. A remnant within today's Catholic community thus witnesses to the value of the traditional American parish of the nineteenth and twentieth centuries. Yet times change, and the church must respond.

In the Apostolic Exhortation *Evangelii Gaudium*, Pope Francis notes that the parish "possesses great flexibility."[5] "If [it] proves capable of self-renewal and constant adaptivity, it continues to be 'the Church living in the midst of the homes of her sons and daughters,'" he declares, quoting John Paul II (*EG* 28). Both this adaptability and the need for even more of it have meant that the typical parish has not functioned in the way Mt. Carmel parishioners remember, for them or nearly anyone else, for some time now. Many of the Catholic communities of the nineteenth- and twentieth-century European immigrations have been assimilated and scattered. Many families who were their mainstays have lost their own solidarity of religious practice, and a thousand other activities compete for everyone's time. Those who persevere do so in a social situation that encourages personal choice of a convenient and attractive parish, more so than commitment to a stable community.[6] However, that very choice is increasingly limited in many regions as parishes merge, church buildings are closed, and parishioner relationships become more accidental than hereditary.[7] As such conditions prevail in much of the Northeast and Midwest, substantial areas of the country are nevertheless experiencing a steady influx of new Catholics. Non-European immigrant Catholics have become a significant presence in many places.[8] Concurrently, the general population shift toward the south and west has brought to these regions a broad representation of Catholics with roots in the more traditional strongholds.[9]

Neither type of growth, however, is being met by the steady creation of new parishes in the former mold. More frequently, existing parishes grow larger, just as do the remaining parishes in regions of population decrease. As the traditional model is left behind, what seems to be emerging is what some Catholics in Germany have taken to calling the "XXL parish." Comparable dynamics there have produced parishes with as many as 40,000 parishioners.[10] A May 2017 cover story in *America* magazine featured St. Matthew parish in Charlotte, North Carolina, with

10,000 families, the rough equivalent of its German counterpart for size.[11] "I think this is going to be the model parish in the future," one of the parishioners speculated in the *America* article. "You're not going to see a church on every block or in every town."[12] The recent CARA (Center for Applied Research in the Apostolate) study of parishes nationwide comes to a similar conclusion: "The neighborhood parish is being transformed into the regional community parish."[13]

While "megaparishes" like St. Matthew are still far from the norm, the shift toward fewer and larger parish communities, in a variety of distinct forms, is clear. The CARA study reports a 39 percent increase in the average number of parishioners since the last comprehensive data was collected twenty-five years ago[14] and suggests about a 10 percent decrease in the number of parishes over the same period.[15] Still, the shift away from neighborhood toward regional communities has come about almost accidentally, often without a great deal of prior reflection on the changing model. The canonical insistence on "some priest endowed with the powers and faculties of a pastor" (Canon 517.2) still seems to suggest to many diocesan bishops the sizing of parishes or clusters according to the number of priests available. Since the familiar shortage of clerical leadership is an operative factor everywhere, parishes continue to grow more in size than in number. This is true even in areas where burgeoning Catholic populations would in the past have signaled the recognition of many new local church communities. Faced with the prospect of huge congregations of anonymous worshipers, parishes such as St. Matthew (which grew from 237 to 10,000 families over a thirty-year period) have begun to seek ways to keep alive the neighborhood ideal of a unified and dedicated community. Quite consciously following a pattern set by Evangelical megachurches, they make use of the still largely unacknowledged principle of choice by inviting parishioners to find their own places amid myriad ministries, affinity groups, special programs, and small sharing communities.[16] St. Matthew even created a limited-service "satellite church" ten miles away that is nonetheless part of the one parish.[17]

In areas of decline, the regional parish is emerging from the practice of combining several "failing" smaller parishes. In what may be called the "administrative model" of parish merger—in which the failure of the communities to be merged may be more evident to diocesan officials than to parishioners (and, indeed, have more to do with diocesan priorities than with the strengths and weaknesses of any given parish)—churches are closed and parishes merged by rapid, decisive actions. The consultative process, such as it is, is often highly formalized, and the overall approach is apt to result in fractured communities and "one-size-fits-all" parish ministry. A more pastorally sensitive "community model" allows a slower evolution within a cluster of parishes, from autonomy to cooperation to a single pastorate, and perhaps then to a formal merger. This enables a more thoughtful response to the particular needs of a changing parish population, with the emergence of new administrative arrangements appropriate to the local situation.[18] A separate but often overlapping case involves the emergence of larger multicultural parishes in response to the arrival of a new ethnic or linguistic group in the neighborhood of a well-established parish. Unlike earlier arrivals, new Catholic immigrants are often greeted by parishes with elaborate physical plants, long traditions, and active members. Almost inevitably, at least two separate communities must then choose between a kind of institutionalized segregation, or a more demanding process of cross-cultural listening, growing cooperation, emerging friendships, and the hope of unity.

Amid these varied parish forms, a series of disturbing questions arises that begs for more careful thought about the transformation taking place. The larger scale of "XXL parishes" may be able to claim a greater efficiency in everything from purchasing supplies to training Eucharistic ministers; the offering of many groups and activities may meet ever more specialized needs and interests; but are these advantages able to compensate for the loss of the *immediate* sense, the here-and-now challenge, of catholicity? There is visible diversity in a large congregation, but might that visibility—kept at "arm's length"—begin to substitute, in the minds of some, for the inescapable presence of the annoying neighbor or the vaguely frightening "foreigner" who must be dealt with face-to-face and person-to-person, as a fellow parishioner? In a similar vein, what will change if parishioners no longer participate in the sacraments amid recognizable neighbors and day-to-day companions, but rather as part of an effectively faceless group? The tug of individual interior piety is strong under any circumstances; how, in the "mega-parish," are worshipers challenged by the transformative relational intimacy of Jesus and his disciples? Do added layers of infrastructure and bureaucracy (sometimes resembling more the reinvention of the *diocese* than of the parish) increase members' distance not only from leaders and one another, but also from the incarnate, communal Christ himself?

Partial responses to such questions are offered from many quarters, but the most valuable answers will only be found in ongoing dialogue between practical parish life and thoughtful spiritual reflection on the church's mission. What this approach highlights in the current crisis of parish models is the struggle to save a *community of faith-in-action*, as opposed to a gathering of religious consumers. To sustain an authentic response to Jesus's invitation to communion, the parish community cannot simply be created artificially and maintained by a bureaucracy. It will need to become a natural human community sustained by multiple deep and rich bonds that are served, not imposed, by the whole church.

Local Church Communities and Their Leaders

The traditional US parish, broadly speaking, has represented an implicit relationship between a bishop and "a certain community of the Christian faithful stably constituted" within his diocese (Canon 515.1). Originally, many of these parishes were established when a community appealed to the bishop for a resident pastor or when an itinerant priest appealed on their behalf or when one parish nurtured a growing subcommunity into its own parish status. Subsequently, a change of pastors has always been a highly anticipated moment—"Who will the bishop send us?" In extreme circumstances, appeals to the bishop for replacement of an unsuitable pastor have not been unknown, but the norm has been that pastors are accepted and welcomed: their arrival is an acknowledgment of the legitimate identity of the community itself within the larger church.

The crisis of the parish has seriously eroded this implied acknowledgment. The practice of individuals choosing their own parish suggests a weakening sense of the community's moral ownership, and speaks instead of a transactional image of the parish. The pastor seems increasingly like a proprietor, manager, or service provider. The previously described "administrative" style of parish consolidation has promoted a sort of "siege mentality" in many communities and given pastors—often unwillingly involved—the aspect of bureaucratic "hatchet-men," or perhaps that of beloved but ineffective "heroes of the resistance." It seems axiomatic that, as parishes grow, pastors cannot give the same sort of time to individual parishioners and families as they might have done with a smaller population. To succeed, they must efficiently and gracefully increase the distance between themselves and most parishioners, carrying on with inventing a new community and multiplying subcommunities for individuals and nuclear families to belong to.[19] As essential as this work may be under the circumstances, it seems inevitably to enhance the image of the pastor as a kind of entrepreneur rather than a servant leader linking a specific believing community to the universal church.

Such developments present important challenges to parish priests' traditional roles as community leaders and spiritual guides. With fewer ordained colleagues and ever-larger congregations, priests must face the potentially demoralizing role of "sacramental manager," with its dangers of exhaustion, frustration, and perceived irrelevance. While the prospect of building new models for the church to succeed could be invigorating for some, pastors are nonetheless always faced with the struggle of staying in active communication with a constantly changing Catholic people.[20] On the part of the laity, it is common to find parishioners (like those from the doomed Mt. Carmel) who are alienated by their loss of community identity.[21] Many do not feel empowered by administrative arrangements that emphasize, perhaps necessarily, trained professionals rather than community-wide volunteers.[22] It also remains to be seen whether the "small communities" that now often carry nearly the whole weight of parishioners' face-to-face experience of church will ever receive the kind of canonical affirmation that the traditional parish has had. In many other ways, of course, segments of the laity are energized, but anecdotal evidence suggests communities pulling in opposite directions, toward the excitement of a new endeavor or the individual appeal of a particularly dynamic pastor or, contrastingly, back toward the populist instinct to preserve an old community's distinctive ways.

Pope Francis: "Theology of the People"
and the Hope of a New Vision for Local Communities

In a well-known article published in *Theological Studies* in 2016, Argentine theologian Juan Carlos Scannone, SJ, lays out the basic characteristics of Pope Francis's version of *la teologia del pueblo*—an outgrowth of a distinctively Argentine movement—pointing out its manifestations particularly in *Evangelii Gaudium*.[23] The term "Faithful People of God" reveals a primary element of this thinking, encompassing the sense of the whole church as a pilgrim and evangelizing people, as well as the option for the poor, with a particular eye on popular religiosity and the ancient but often hidden wisdom that it transmits.[24] When this term is applied to the parish situation in the United States, an important and potentially instructive tension appears. In this context, at least, the Faithful People seems to tug the church in two quite different directions. On one hand, parishioners' initial reluctance regarding reorganization efforts offers strong reminders of essential values that could be lost along with the traditional parish. Could this be a call to *ressourcement* amid the reinvention of local church communities? On the other hand, the Faithful People also tends to push forward culturally, insisting that the church acknowledge changed conditions in ordinary life. "The church needs to be more up-to-date," is heard often—even from some of the faithful not well known for radical attitudes. Critically understood fifty years after Vatican II, this should be a call to *aggiornamento*. In our polarized situation, these two tugs will perhaps inevitably seem to oppose each other, but just as they were in the conciliar era (although not for long), they can be transformed by being held *together*. Is such cooperation an unrealistic hope?

Summarizing the context in which he wishes to reflect on the Faithful People, in *Evangelii Gaudium* 222–37, Pope Francis lays out his now well-known "Four Principles."[25] A look at these may offer both a sharper image of the challenges and a stronger sense of vision in the ongoing work of meeting those challenges:

"Time Is Greater Than Space." The first principle indeed loses something in translation, but means fundamentally that historical processes are more important than particular positions of power at given moments. This suggests that the people—the laity and clergy together—are more important than any particular institutional model or leadership structure. The central question thus becomes, "Where are the structures going as time unfolds?" rather than, "What place do they occupy in today's snapshot of society?" In pastoral situations, the first principle seems to recommend more flexible *listening* and thoughtful consideration, with fewer imposed solutions and less "empire building."

"Unity Prevails Over Conflict." Francis's discussion of this second principle is far deeper than the "Let's All Just Get Along" mantra that it may evoke. He means, rather, that *facing* conflict, not suppressing, ignoring, or hiding it, is essential to the strong and lasting unity that the church has always sought to maintain as one of the marks of its divine mission. The principle recommends attention to lowering walls of separation and to building communities of solidarity amid diversity. Rather than self-selected affinity groups or isolated individuals, these would have to be natural communities of people who live and work with, and depend on, one another, even without being quite aware of this interdependence initially, or even willing to admit it. Thinking this way would take us beyond faith-sharing groups, whose members may or may not see each other at the supermarket or walking their dogs, toward attempts to bring together as church the suburban homeowner and the immigrant worker who mows the lawn or packs the groceries.

"Realities Are More Important than Ideas." Ideas, says the pope in the third principle, ought to be understood as concepts that are *at the service* of "communication, understanding, and praxis" (*EG* 232). This approach again recommends attention to observation and listening, building toward a style of leadership that takes the people seriously, and does not simply replace the lives it encompasses with detached analysis. Such leadership can keep both flexible and generous the community's ongoing response to needs of all sorts, and to its own continual call to Christ's mission.

"The Whole Is Greater Than the Part." This final principle is not a dismissal of "the part," but rather a call to pay close attention to the roots and branches of a single tree or, to repeat Francis's better-known metaphor, to the varied surfaces of a "polyhedron" as opposed to a "sphere" (*EG* 236). The significance of either figure is that the parts, while they *must* form a whole with aspirations greater than each has individually, must also retain their own character, history, and hopes within the whole context. This principle recommends attention to and reverence for community distinctiveness, values, and ongoing growth—for their own sake but also for the flourishing of the whole church. Once again, both *ressourcement* and *aggiornamento*—drawing on tradition while reaching toward the future—find their way into the necessary balance.

The traditional parish has come to seem, for many who remain interested in the church, rather quaint and comforting. This "old shoe" feel may be one source of the nostalgia often found behind such causes as saving Mt. Carmel Church. Yet a comfortable, nostalgic vision of these old communities generally misses the realities of poverty, exclusion, uncertainty, and yet dogged determination amid which they were built. Francis's vision of parish, written into *Evangelii Gaudium*, may at first glance seem to echo traditional models, but it explicitly does not lose sight of actual circumstances and real communities gathered by parish institutions. The dynamism, openness, and strength of community in the pope's description, along with the caution at its end, form a useful pointer into the future of the face-to-face local church community:

> The parish is the presence of the Church in a given territory, an environment for hearing God's word, for growth in the Christian life, for dialogue, proclamation, charitable outreach, worship and celebration. In all its activities the parish encourages and trains its members to be evangelizers. It is a community of communities, a sanctuary where the thirsty come to drink in the midst of their journey, and a centre of constant missionary outreach. We must admit, though, that the call to review and renew our parishes has not yet sufficed to bring them nearer to people, to make them environments of living communion and participation, and to make them completely mission-oriented. (*EG* 28)

Notes

[1] This argument is briefly extended in William A. Clark, "Afterword: Further Notes on a Theology of Collaborative Leadership," in *Collaborative Parish*

Leadership: Contexts, Models, Theology, ed. William A. Clark and Daniel Gast (Lanham, MD: Lexington, 2016), 211–20.

[2]For a full discussion of the theological warrant for the authority of local church communities, see William A. Clark, *A Voice of Their Own: The Authority of the Local Parish* (Collegeville, MN: Liturgical Press, 2005).

[3]Brad Petrishen, "Worcester's Mount Carmel Church Holding Its Last Mass Today," *Worcester Telegram & Gazette*, April 30, 2016, www.telegram.com.

[4]Bob Kievra, "Controversial Worcester Church Merger Made Official," *Worcester Telegram & Gazette*, January 20, 2017, www.telegram.com. See also Diocese of Worcester, "Mt. Carmel-St. Ann and Loreto Parishes to Merge," *Roman Catholic Diocese of Worcester*, January 21, 2017, https://worcesterdiocese.org.

[5]Pope Francis, Apostolic Exhortation *Evangelii Gaudium* 28 (November 24, 2013), www.vatican.va. Further in-text citations use the abbreviation *EG* and relevant section numbers.

[6]Charles E. Zech et al., *Catholic Parishes of the 21ˢᵗ Century* (New York: Oxford University Press, 2017), 18, 102–3, 119.

[7]On declining number of parishes and increasing size of church buildings, see ibid., 15, 17.

[8]Ibid., 94–97, 107–18.

[9]Ibid., 9.

[10]Andreas Henkelmann and Graciela Sonntag, "A Crisis of Trust, a Crisis of Credibility, a Crisis of Leadership: The Catholic Church in Germany in Quest of New Models," in Clark and Gast, *Collaborative Parish Leadership*, 142, 150–51.

[11]Leah Libresco, "The Largest Parish in America: Lesson on Evangelization from a Catholic Megachurch," *America: The Jesuit Review of Faith and Culture*, May 1, 2017, 20–25.

[12]Ibid., 22.

[13]Zech et al., *Catholic Parishes*, 57.

[14]Ibid., 17.

[15]Ibid., 15.

[16]Libresco, "Largest Parish in America," 21–22; cf. Michael White and Tom Corcoran, *Rebuilt: Awakening the Faithful, Reaching the Lost, and Making Church Matter* (Note Dame, IN: Ave Maria, 2013), 156–69.

[17]Libresco, "Largest Parish in America," 22.

[18]A fuller description of these two categories in a study of two parish clusters is found in William A. Clark, "Toward a Culture of Dynamic Community: Parish Consolidation and Collaborative Leadership," in Clark and Gast, *Collaborative Parish Leadership*, 77–78.

[19]For examples, see White and Corcoran, *Rebuilt*, 151–70, 189–203; also James Mallon, *Divine Renovation: Bringing Your Parish from Maintenance to Mission* (New London, CT: Twenty-Third Publications, 2014), 136–76.

[20]Substantially less than 50 percent of parishioners and pastoral leaders rate their parishes' communication strategies as "very successful." See Zech et al., *Catholic Parishes*, 64–65.

[21]Ibid., 143.

[22]CARA found fewer than 50 percent of regular church-goers report feeling strongly encouraged to participate in parish ministry; only 17 percent strongly agreed that they had a role in parish decisions. Zech et al., *Catholic Parishes*, 65.

[23]Juan Carlos Scannone, SJ, "Pope Francis and the Theology of the People," *Theological Studies* 77, no. 1 (2016): 118–35.

[24]Ibid., 126–27.

[25]Ibid., 127–30.

Part **II**

OPPORTUNITIES AND CHALLENGES FOR AMERICAN CATHOLICISM

Pressing Theological Issues and Questions in American Catholicism Today

This plenary panel offers a theological discussion of American Catholicism in the twenty-first century from a variety of historical and social viewpoints. The panel consisted of four CTS members—three of whom chose to include their thoughts in this volume—all scholars who have been trained in Catholic theology and who have worked across different times, places, and social locations. Panelists discuss what each sees as the pressing theological issues or questions in American Catholicism today. Our hope is that this kind of intergenerational and social diversity will highlight the fact that a theologian's historical and social location is as important in shaping how they do theology as any other factor.

Issues Facing the American Church Today: A Crisis of Ritual Formation
Katharine Mahon

It is popular for Catholic cultural commentators and theologians to lament the ritual and spiritual malaise that they see in American parishes and among young Catholics today. Faced with recent statistics about declining Mass attendance and Catholic membership, we cannot but wonder if they are correct. I believe that much of this decline is due to an anemic sense of liturgical participation and a shallow understanding of ritual that pervades much of American Catholic religiosity, a sense especially prevalent in white, middle-class, suburban environments, and affecting those formed following the Second Vatican Council most acutely. There is a crisis of ritual formation in the United States, stemming from the implementation of the liturgical and catechetical reforms of the Second Vatican Council. What follows is not a critique of those liturgical reforms, but rather an exploration into how their implementation in the United States may have contributed to the current crisis of ritual formation and a consideration of the effects of the crisis.

Most liturgical scholars would agree that the liturgical reforms following the Second Vatican Council, and the ways in which those reforms were applied and taught to priests and laity alike, have tended to overemphasize an intellectual manner of congregational participation. As a result, much liturgical catechesis has demonstrated a heavy rationalistic or didactic approach to ritual participation. It is not necessarily that the reforms of the rites themselves are poorly done or infused with faulty ritual theory, though critics of the reform have made those claims;[1] rather, the issue is how scholars and teachers have thought, written, and taught about participation.

The Liturgical Movement of the twentieth century was the driving force behind much of the theology of the liturgical reforms of the Second Vatican Council. As Timothy O'Malley has laid out in a recent essay, many of the leaders of the Liturgical Movement saw renewed liturgy and reformed rites as essential to combating secularism among Catholic populations in the West.[2] In summary, they believed that the laity's intelligent participation in the liturgy would form them into committed, informed Christians and inoculate them against the effects of secularization. To this end, they felt that rites should be reformed and catechesis should be renewed in order to enable the laity to participate more fully. The problem with their approach is that it exaggerates the role of the intellect in ritual participation to the detriment of other forms of participation. This serves to hasten, rather than hold off, the damage that secularization wreaks upon Catholics' spiritual lives. The liturgical theology of the leaders of the Liturgical Movement was not inherently flawed. Their endorsement of intelligent participation—intellectual comprehension of the words and symbols of the liturgy—as the highest means of ritual participation, however, does not seem to take into account the fact that ritual, by its symbolic nature, works beyond the cognitive level. As a result of this intellectual exaggeration, two approaches to liturgical participation have come to dominate people's understanding of how ritual works and how they participate in the church's liturgical prayer.

On the one hand is a rationalistic approach to ritual: the words and actions are mere symbols of deeper truths that can be comprehended. People come to see ritual as little more than a formality: a public enacting of a preexisting internal attitude, belief, or assent to the truths expressed in the ritual. On the other hand, an emphasis on the primacy of intellectual participation has combined with the Eucharistic liturgy being held up as the source and summit of the Christian life, so that Mass attendance becomes the pinnacle of Catholics' devotional lives, to the detriment of other extraliturgical forms of piety. Subsequently, liturgical participation is seen as an affective exercise: participation in the ritual means conforming one's affect to what is prescribed in the rite (i.e., sorrow for sins). In a perversion of this approach to ritual, participants come to view their participation as ineffective *unless* they achieve some sort of emotional response to the liturgy.

Both approaches demonstrate a pervasive individualism in liturgical theology that gives rise to a consumeristic approach to religious ritual. "Why should I go to Mass," the complaint goes, "if I don't get anything out of it?" There is expectation that participation is meant to lead to an intellectual insight or a confirmation of one's beliefs or some sort of emotional reaction. What we are to "get out of Mass," however, in the famous words of Robert Taft, SJ, is the "inestimable privilege of giving glory to Almighty God."[3] But this idea of setting aside sacred time, in sacred space, to simply be in God's presence and give God glory is a foreign concept to a population of laypeople who have been formed to see intellectual participation as the only way to participate in a full, conscious, and active manner. As our liturgies have grown more didactic and our faith more educated, Catholics have not only been influenced by secularization but have also internalized it: effectively splitting their bodies from their minds, their Sunday morning from the rest of their week, and their beliefs from their actions. Many Catholics have become convinced that faith is merely an intellectual exercise, so that religious identity is no more than acceptance of religious ideology. One then marks one's Catholic identity according to one popular Catholic political ideology or another, for if being Catholic is simply assent to a series of intellectual claims, then one's Catholic identity relies on how much one agrees with those claims. In essence, the exaggeration of intellectual participation in ritual has inevitably led people to understand membership in the church as little more than an intellectual endeavor. We have formed a nation of Catholics who hold a disembodied faith.

A Reconciling Faith in Polarized Times
Mary Doak

Not yet two decades into the twenty-first century, we find our country and world deeply and violently divided. Instead of the peace and unity promised by the end of the Cold War and the globalization of our economic and communication systems, we have worldwide terrorist networks, massive migrations of desperate refugees, and powerful nativist and xenophobic political movements. Within the United States, Americans are attacking each other over differences of race, religion, education, ethnicity, and ideology with astonishing levels of physical as well as verbal violence.

International and intranational conflict is, of course, nothing new. But it is a real question whether we can work together to solve our pressing global and national problems amid current levels of acrimony and mutual suspicion. Many are wondering whether our national institutions will even survive, given the currently toxic levels of polarization.

The tribal antagonism sweeping our country and much of the world is not only a political problem, however. It is also a theological challenge. In the Christian tradition, division, disharmony, and alienation are held to be effects of the sin that God's salvific grace is at work in the world to overcome. Indeed, as the Second Vatican Council taught, the church is called to be a sign and instrument of the union of all in God. What a difference the public witness of this reconciling faith could make at this time—in our nation as well as in our world!

And yet instead of being a force for reconciliation, Christianity (or more accurately "white" Christianity) has become one of the more aggressively defended forms of tribal identity in the United States. The scandal here is not merely that Christians are failing to live up to their beliefs, but that few recognize this Christian tribalism as the distortion that it is. Attacking others is hailed as evidence of strength of faith instead of being repented as sinful refusal of the harmony God desires. Even Catholics, who celebrate as their central sacrament the practice of communion with each other in God, have been practicing this politics of division—as if one were more faithfully Catholic to the extent that one vilifies other Catholics, especially those whose politics is deemed insufficiently oppositional. (When communion ecclesiology is wielded as a weapon to divide the church, surely something is very wrong!)

The fact that so many fail to see the contradiction inherent in a tribal, polarizing Christian faith suggests that the common understanding of Christianity in the United States is at best partial and inadequate. The theological anthropology of persons-in-community is forgotten; the full breadth of social and personal reconciliation is lost. When it is widely assumed that Christian redemption concerns only one's individual afterlife (or at most extends to the salvation of one's faith or other community), it is not surprising that Catholic Social Thought continues to be treated as peripheral to the practice of Catholicism. If the purpose of the church is to get individuals into heaven after death, then the obligations of justice, however clearly taught, will inevitably be understood as additional rules that, if not arbitrary, are clearly of secondary importance. And, in any case, who needs more rules to follow?

Catholic theologians, especially those of us in the United States, have an obligation to correct this distorted view of Christianity. Of course, all theological work intends in some way to clarify and deepen the understanding and practice of Christian faith. But I suspect that the fully social and relational Christianity assumed in most theology is often not communicated to our audiences. While we may think we are teaching further nuances about the depth and breadth of Christian salvation, our students—and wider public—may continue to fit these theological distinctions into a fundamentally individualistic or otherworldly framework. If theology is to address the current crisis of polarization (in the church and in the nation), we must make sure that the forest, that is, faith in God's salvific reconciliation of all creation, doesn't get lost as we explore the trees, branches, and twigs of our particular theological concerns.

Ultimately, of course, we need a conversion not only in thought but in practice. The diversity of contemporary American Catholicism presents Catholics with a great opportunity to witness reconciliation in our polarized society. Imagine the difference it might make if, instead of dividing into parishes of similar race, ethnicity, class, and (often) politics, our churches were truly diverse communities that fostered real relationships across these lines of division. Consider how Catholics (and other Christians) might influence the broader culture if, in the face of disagreement and division, we were committed to seeking mutual understanding, respect, and reconciliation rather than the victory of our side.

Stanley Hauerwas and others have been insisting for some time now that society needs the witness of the church being the church, and this is as true now as it ever has been. Yet the reconciling faith of the church cannot remain within the church alone. It is with good reason that Catholic sacramentality refuses to separate sign and instrument, witness and work. A reconciling faith must be lived not only in the (always imperfect) witness of the church community, but also in efforts to seek reconciliation beyond the bounds of the church, in our deeply divided society and world.

Some churches and many Christians, including Catholics, are already living this reconciling faith. They need, and deserve, the support of a Christian community united in the recognition that its identity lies in its commitment to inclusivity, to cooperating with God's healing grace restoring communion not despite but in and through our differences and disagreements.

The Anti-Incarnational Affect and Its Overcoming
Anthony J. Godzieba

Over a decade ago I had a conversation with a priest friend who teaches at a Catholic seminary. After relating to me how his students resisted reading Edward Schillebeeckx's *Christ the Sacrament of Encounter with God* because they believed theology from the 1970s was bankrupt, he made the offhand comment that, in his view, the students "don't believe in the Incarnation. They think the sacraments are magic." I want to discuss here that *anti-incarnational* or *antisacramental affect,* specifically the vague governing assumption that "secular America" or "the world" (a term that covers a lot of ground) is fundamentally Godless and devoid of grace. Here is my thesis: this affect or attitude is pervasive in American Catholicism—going back to the early years of the John Paul II papacy and exacerbated by the current apocalyptic frenzy in politics—and it has become a central feature of current American Catholic mythology; it is how many Catholics explain themselves to themselves and to others. The root theological claims at stake have everything to do with Christology and theological anthropology: What do you believe about the range of the power of the Incarnation? What do you believe about Genesis's *imago Dei* (Gn 1:26–27)? What do you believe about the sacramentality of the world and the worldliness of the sacraments?

My reflections here are guided by two representations of the Emmaus pericope in the Gospel of Luke (Lk 24:13–35). I am always deeply moved by the concluding verse: "Then the two recounted what had taken place on the way and how [Jesus] was made known to them in the breaking of the bread" (Lk 24:35). And as a hermeneutic and fundamental theologian, of course I love the pivotal role that interpretation plays in the resulting epiphany— the Scriptures, as Jesus reminds us, are not as self-evident as we would like. So: theory and praxis, interpretive application and Eucharistic solidarity—both are part of the fundamental core of Christian theology and of Catholic life.

Georges Rouault's 1936 print *Les disciples* (fig. 1) is an unusual depiction of the disciples' encounter with Jesus. All detail is stripped away: the fields and lakes on either side of the road are mere blotches of green and blue, and the village of Emmaus is one formalized red house in the far distance at the end of a mottled red road under an ambivalent sky. (The structure reminds me of an abandoned gas station or diner.) The cruciform pattern is unmistakable.[4]

Cleopas and his unnamed companion trudge from Jerusalem to what is probably their home village.[5] They are not the only members of the Jesus-movement to give up and return to the supposed surety of their earlier lives. Luke depicts the disciples deep in conversation, weighed down with disappointment and gloom (24:17). They are returning to their old certainties, but as Rouault illustrates, those certainties are as empty as our abandoned "diner" off in the distance. The stranger whom they meet joins their journey and their animated discussion. Perhaps this is the moment just before Jesus's rebuke of their stark misinterpretation of events: "'Oh,

Figure 1. Georges Rouault, *Les disciples*, 1936 (Plate XVI from *Passion* [Paris: Ambroise Vollard, 1939]). © 2017 Artists Rights Society (ARS), New York / ADAGP, Paris.

how foolish you are!'" he says, "'how slow of heart to believe all that the prophets spoke! Was it not necessary that the Messiah should suffer these things and enter into his glory?' Then beginning with Moses and all the prophets, he interpreted to them what referred to him in all the scriptures" (Lk 24:25–27). This itself is a small epiphany: The Scriptures are *not* self-evidently clear; they need a contextual *interpretation,* especially the context of Jesus's preaching of the Kingdom of God and its ongoing application. Rouault's image in turn demands an interpretation that fills in how the disciples get from the disaster in Jerusalem and the gloomy longing for the old certainties to the grace in Emmaus by means of their personal sacramental encounter with Jesus.

The second image is also unusual: *Kitchen Scene with Supper at Emmaus* (1603) by Pieter Aertsen, as engraved by Jacob Matham (fig. 2).

Figure 2. Jacob Matham after Pieter Aertsen, *Kitchen Scene with Supper at Emmaus,* Copyright © 1603 by the Museum of Fine Arts, Boston. Used with permission.

Aertsen was known for his "inverted" scenes of still life, a paradoxical style where "low" or common life is depicted in a classical "high" style.[6] Here, in the midst of a bustling kitchen full of everyday activities and spectacular fish, the revelation of the risen Christ to the disciples occurs in its own distinct space far in the background, yet in the midst of the goings-on of ordinary life. This is the sacramental imagination in a different key: an intense concentration on the ordinary reveals it to be extraordinary, and the supernatural does occur within the natural—but so subtly that you might miss it unless you were looking for it. Aertsen gives a sophisticated portrayal of the sacramental imagination nonetheless by emphasizing the divine "discretion" that is also part of the fundamental structure of creation: God pulls back to let creation be.[7] While still *theonomous* and thereby graced, the nondivine is granted *autonomy* as well. We are coaxed by the kitchen scene to discern the divine presence hidden among what look like merely everyday concerns.

These images help me parse the nagging undercurrents in

American Catholicism, specifically an undertow that seeks to drag Catholics back to the old certainties and the juridical policing of grace prevalent in the first half of the twentieth century. There is a precedent for my approach: if Hans Urs von Balthasar felt free to identify an *"anti-römischen Affekt"* (an anti-Roman attitude) toward ecclesial authority by noticing certain tendencies among clergy and theologians,[8] then I feel it is fair to observe certain tendencies within the American church and suggest that an *anti-incarnational or antisacramental attitude* exists, and has persisted since the American reception of the papacy of John Paul II.

In that reception, John Paul II's critique of a "culture of death," formulated with regards to medical-moral issues, was projected in its American reception to include all those elements of society thought to exclude Catholic values from public discussion.[9] Joseph Ratzinger's critique of the West and especially Europe of losing its Christian roots gave this projection a boost, and his nuanced analysis of the post–Vatican II theological climate as involving a "hermeneutics of discontinuity and rupture" and a "hermeneutics of reform" was spun into a simple binomial opposition: a "hermeneutics of discontinuity" versus a "hermeneutics of continuity."[10] In short, in the name of cultural resistance, over the past forty years some American Catholic thinkers and church leaders have been willing to denude the world, to strip it of its incarnational and sacramental moorings, in order to create the mythology of a dystopian hellhole that can be resisted only by the policing of grace according to juridical restrictions or Neoplatonic-style abstractions with a hefty dose of citations from Augustine's *City of God*.

This all sounds amorphous and vague—after all, how can one prove an "attitude"? I want to be clear: I am not accusing these thinkers and leaders of disbelief in the Incarnation and in the power of the sacraments. What I am pointing out is the power of certain modern and postmodern assumptions to swamp and resituate our stated beliefs. Over the past forty years American Catholics have been whipsawed by a loss of cultural status, declining numbers of practicing Catholics, declining vocations to religious life and the priesthood, the unraveling of a once vibrant Catholic educational system, colossal ecclesial failures such as the clerical sex abuse crisis, and more subtle ecclesial failures like the brutal discrediting of Cardinal Joseph Bernardin's pro-life "seamless garment" argument. It's no surprise that apocalyptic narratives of loss and spiritual and political revenge have been developed as coping mechanisms. We have all heard intense diagnoses of a "Godless world" from family members, students, and fellow parishioners who feel disrespected by a secular society that seems normally hostile to Christian values. The situation feeds the anti-incarnational/antisacramental affect that assumes the "bare, ruined" character of contemporary Western culture.

We could come up with a long list of examples. I offer two, both episcopal. In 2012, Cardinal Francis George, the archbishop of Chicago, made reference to a comment he made in a conversation that he had with a group of priests, saying that he "expected to die in bed, my successor will die in prison and his successor will die a martyr in the public square. . . . His successor will pick up the shards of a ruined society and slowly help rebuild civilization, as the church has done so often in human history." He contextualized the comment by saying that "I was trying to express in overly dramatic fashion what the complete secularization of our society could bring."[11]

In his recent book *Strangers in a Strange Land,* Archbishop Charles J. Chaput, taking a cue from Alasdair MacIntyre, examines major factors in contemporary American culture and concludes that each of them contributes to the construction of "a long, dimming corridor" populated by those formed by "the peculiar despotism innate to democracy" (citing Alexis de Tocqueville).[12] The social sciences, for example, "tend to reflect agnostic or atheistic thought committed to a particular brand of social reform." Liberal education is powerless to offset "the fragmentation in American culture [that] runs too deep," and young adults lack a sense of "moral gravity and duty" and instead are driven by "fear, fused with the lack of a demanding, morally coherent vision for university life, [that] helps drive the confusion, anger, hyper-sensitivity, and spirit of entitlement that now too commonly mark student life."[13] It is true that later in the book, Archbishop Chaput insists that "Christianity is an *incarnational* religion" and that "our creativity as creatures is an echo of God's own creative glory." But the persistent problem, he says, is that "God has never been more cast out from the Western mind than he is today." "Our urgencies hide a deep unease about the future," he claims, "a kind of well-manicured and selfish despair."[14]

We all recognize some truth in these critiques of post-Enlightenment and late capitalist Western culture; we have probably made similar arguments in our own work and no doubt appreciate the call to conversion, love, and service that Chaput and others make. However, within the framework of the anti-incarnational affect, the tone is relentlessly downbeat, even evacuative: the world is graceless, Godless, hostile to goodness and truth. To recognize any value in the "city of man" (the commonly employed Augustinian image) is to leave oneself open to toxic relativism and to tempt the abyss. In Chaput's view, Christians are "resident aliens" called to exercise "courage and a refusal to be digested and bleached out by the world around us."[15] It is a zero-sum proposition: materiality and culture must be minimized for God to be recognized.

Since the American reception of John Paul II's 1993 encyclical *Veritatis Splendor,* this anti-incarnational affect has been joined by a resolute juridicism that polices the boundaries of grace. In a culture seemingly evacuated of value and awash in relativism, many desire clear paths to follow; hence there is a juridical approach to grace that defines "orthodoxy" narrowly. The anti-incarnational affect is one of the sources of the controversies surrounding same-sex relationships and the readmission of divorced and remarried Catholics to the Eucharist—in other words, how in God's name could grace ever be found *there?*

This is why Pope Francis's approach rattles so many people. He sees grace as overflowing the boundaries, as his famous quip about a "messy" church attests,[16] and considers God's mercy as the untamable thread that courses through all reality. He is not governed by the anti-incarnational affect. Grace is available everywhere; whether its salvific power is activated depends on our willingness to be transfigured by Jesus, just as the Emmaus disciples were, and journey with him. In order to warm hearts just as "Jesus warmed the hearts of the disciples of Emmaus," the church must accompany those "disillusioned by a Christianity now considered barren, fruitless soil, incapable of generating meaning."[17] However, the pope is not naive. In a sermon preached during his 2015 visit to New York City, he remarked that "the rapid pace of change" makes us ignore all those whom society judges to have "no right to be part of the city." Despite this attitude, he said, "Jesus still walks our streets," and "God is living in our cities," and so we continue to have "a hope which liberates us from the forces pushing us to isolation and lack of concern for the lives of others."[18] In these and other examples, the pope challenges the anti-incarnational and antisacramental affect by means of affective appeals to convert to an alternative construal of reality, a reawakening of desire for life lived under the sign of grace, and the salvific transformation of the social world through the unfolding possibilities of mercy that is performed.

In conclusion, let's recall our two images. The juridical policing of grace, the drawing of boundaries, the branding of Catholicism are the "old certainties," and one cannot return to that empty diner as it stands and pretend that it represents a strong creation theology, the intensification of our participation in divine life in the incarnate Christ, and the transfigurative power of the Resurrection. Jesus rescues the abandoned disciples by performing grace for them and with them, by demonstrating that the created world is more like Aertsen's depiction: despite the hard toil, it is a world where the ordinary is extraordinary, which overflows with delights, always supported by the subtle, *sotto voce* presence of God whose grace lets things be.

The contemporary issue that I see for American Catholics, then, is not "how do we bring Christ to a dystopian hellhole?" but rather "how much grace are we willing to put up with?"

Notes

[1] For an overview of prominent criticisms of post-Vatican II liturgical reform and implementation, see John Baldovin, SJ, *Reforming the Liturgy: A Response to Critics* (Collegeville, MN: Liturgical Press, 2008).

[2] Timothy O'Malley, "Editorial Musings: Can Liturgy Heal a Secular Age?" *Church Life Journal*, March 6, 2017, http://churchlife.nd.edu.

[3] Robert F. Taft, SJ, "Sunday in the Byzantine Tradition," in *Beyond East and West: Problems in Liturgical Understanding*, ed. Robert Taft, SJ (Washington, DC: Pastoral Press, 1984), 33.

[4] My thanks to Fr. Dan Mackle for pointing this out to me.

[5] Cf. Joseph A. Fitzmyer, *The Gospel According to Luke X-XXIV*, Anchor Bible 28A (Garden City: NY: Doubleday, 1985), 1559.

[6] Aertsen was influenced by the Italian Mannerists. See James Snyder, *Northern Renaissance Art: Painting, Sculpture, the Graphic Arts from 1350*

to 1575 (Englewood Cliffs, NJ; Prentice-Hall/New York: Harry N. Abrams, 1985), 445; Reindert L. Falkenburg, "Pieter Aertsen, Rhyparographer," http://www.academia.edu/5166659/Pieter_ Aertsen_Rhyparographer.

[7]Christian Duquoc, "'Who Is God?' Becomes 'Where Is God?': The Shift in a Question," trans. John Bowden, in *Where Is God? A Cry of Human Distress, Concilium* 1992/4, ed. Christian Duquoc and Casiano Floristán (London: SCM Press, 1992), 3.

[8]Hans Urs von Balthasar, "The Anti-Roman Attitude," trans. Andrée Emery, *Communio: International Catholic Review* 8 (1981): 307–21.

[9]Pope John Paul II, Encyclical *Evangelium Vitae* (1995), http://w2.vatican.va.

[10]Joseph Ratzinger and Marcello Pera, *Without Roots: The West, Relativism, Christianity, Islam,* trans. Michael F. Moore (New York: Basic Books, 2006); Pope Benedict XVI, "Address of His Holiness Benedict XVI to the Roman Curia Offering Them His Christmas Greetings" (December 22, 2005), http://w2.vatican.va/. In his address, Ratzinger never opposed "continuity" and "discontinuity."

[11]Francis Cardinal George, "The Wrong Side of History," *The Cardinal's Column,* October 21–November 3, 2012, http://www.chicagocatholic.com.

[12]Charles J. Chaput, *Strangers in a Strange Land: Living the Catholic Faith in a Post-Christian World* (New York: Henry Holt, 2017), 144, 145.

[13]Ibid., 133 (social sciences), 136 (fragmentation), 139 (moral gravity), 140–41 (student life).

[14]Ibid., 229 (incarnational), 235 (despair).

[15]Ibid., 245 (resident aliens), 243 (bleached out).

[16]See the pope's speech to young Argentinian pilgrims during the 2013 World Youth Day celebrations in Rio de Janiero, http://w2.vatican.va/. Where the Spanish has "Espero lío" (I hope for a mess), the English translation has "I hope there will be noise."

[17]Pope Francis, address to the Brazilian bishops on World Youth Day, July 28, 2013, http://w2.vatican.va/, no. 3.

[18]Pope Francis, Homily at Mass at Madison Square Garden, New York City (September 25, 2015), http://w2.vatican.va/content/.

Forgetting and Repeating
the Theological Racism
at "Theology in the Americas"

Jessica Coblentz

In his 2003 address to the Catholic Theological Society of America (CTSA), Jon Nilson introduced the phrase "white Catholic theological racism" to denote how white theologians ignore, marginalize, and dismiss "that body of theological insight and challenge born of the Black struggle for justice, Black Theology."[1] Later, Nilson extended the phrase to white theologians' neglect of racism as a fundamental contradiction of the gospel.[2] Nilson's address echoed Joseph Nearon's early insight about racism in Catholic theology. Nearon, reporting to that same professional society in 1974, suggested that the racism of Catholic theology was "more the result of omission and inattention than conscious commission."[3] He warned his colleagues that having recognized the racism of Catholic theology as a sin of omission, they could no longer absolve themselves of their complicity in it. Despite this warning thirty years prior, Nilson confessed his own scant engagement with black and womanist thinkers and supported his point about the racism of the broader field with reference to James Cone's observations about Catholic theology in the year 2000. Cone conjectured that, "If one read only White Catholic theologians, one would hardly know that Blacks exist in America or had the capacity for thought about God."[4]

The aim of this essay is to expose the workings of white Catholic theological racism, past and present, for the sake of resisting it in our time. I join Black and antiracist theologians in this undertaking, including Nilson, who has presented statistics and concrete examples of Catholic theology's participation in racial injustice to awaken white Catholic theologians to this sin.[5] I will offer another concrete account of white Catholic theological racism by retrieving a pivotal and often-forgotten event in the history of theology in the United States—the first international, ecumenical gathering of "Theology in the Americas" (TIA), held in Detroit in August 1975. My analysis of TIA will lay bare the workings of theological racism in the history of our discipline. In view of this history, I will show how preparations for the 2017 College Theology Society (CTS) convention on "American Catholicism in the 21st Century" repeated some of the instantiations of theological racism that unfolded in Detroit. Finally, I will reflect on my own complicity in this and point to the controversies of TIA for strategies to resist the theological racism that persists today.

Preparations for Detroit I

The story of "Theology in the Americas" begins in 1974, when Sergio Torres, an exiled Chilean priest, joined other Catholic and Protestant theologians from North and South America to plan a conference they would host the following year in the United States. Organizers initially intended the gathering—commonly known as "Detroit I"—to explore how Latin American theology could serve as a "creative font" from which those in the "parched desert" of North America could drink.[6] Their work began with a preparation period in which approximately sixty small groups across the United States gathered locally to discuss the contributions of Latin American liberation theology and analyze the reality of Christianity and society in North America.[7]

Two preparatory documents from the organizing committee guided these small group discussions. The first exposed the injustices that plagued Latin America as a result of US economic and political policies. It summarized Latin American liberation theology's indictment of the United States and suggested that North America could learn from this theology, especially its interdisciplinarity, framework of praxis, and inductive methodology.[8] The second document provided logistical instructions for the small groups.

A series of letters among Torres, Rosemary Radford Ruether,

Gregory Baum, Avery Dulles, and Monika Hellwig vividly conveys the controversy that arose almost immediately after the release of these documents.[9] Ruether's letter, penned in February 1975, is the first on record. So dire were the sweeping generalizations about North America in the preparatory documents that Ruether summarized them this way: "The Latin Americans are to provide the 'theology' and the Americans the 'Devil.'"[10] She noted that the abject characterization of Christianity in the United States overlooked a long history of Americans who drew on local political and religious resources to resist oppression.

Seeking advice on how to respond, Torres forwarded Ruether's complaints to other theologians. Gregory Baum agreed that the preparatory documents uncritically assumed Latin American theology was the answer to all American evils.[11] He then pointed out the troubling oversight on which this pivot to Latin America depended:

> You should turn to liberation theology produced in your own country. There is the critical reflection of the blacks, of Mexican-Americans, of the women's movement, etc. And then there are American liberation thinkers. What about Rosemary Ruether? The interrelation between *theoria* and *praxis*, which is central in Latin American theology, has been with us for a long time. There are American thinkers who have made this the core of their theological reflections.[12]

Baum proceeded to emphasize the import of listening to perspectives beyond North America, but he challenged the assumption that North American society and Christianity had no liberating resources of their own.

Eventually, Torres forwarded Ruether's letter to Avery Dulles, who replied with the observation that TIA needed to clarify its aims: Was the conference about the problems and insights of Latin American liberation theology, including its critiques of the United States, or was it concerned with injustice in the United States and the development of liberation theologies in and for the United States?[13] By April 1975, Torres had decided on the latter. As a result, organizers commissioned Joseph Holland, John Coleman, and Frederick Herzog to prepare new preparatory papers that focused on US social and religious experience.[14] Again, conference participants quickly decried the racism and sexism of these new documents. With few exceptions, matters of racism and references to Black theology were absent. There was scarce mention of women's experiences and feminist thinkers as well. Furthermore, women and racial minorities had been excluded again from the production of these documents.

As a result of this criticism, the committee commissioned representatives from various "minority groups"—Black theology, feminist theology, Native American theology, and Chicano theology—to provide "up-to-date presentation[s] of the history, culture, and theological reflection" of their respective communities. These would supplement the official documents by Holland, Coleman, and Herzog.[15] By the time these minority reports were requested, however, the organizers claimed not to "have the time, the money, or the contacts necessary to find the most representative and capable spokespersons of each minority."[16] Torres and John Eagleson later admitted that "once again, in spite of good intentions, minorities were given a second place in the planning of the conference."[17]

Three Expressions of Theological Racism

Indeed, despite good intentions, theological racism marred Detroit I's preparatory period. First, the conference's initial focus on the problems and perspectives of Latin America reflected a long-standing tendency among white theologians who avoid US racial injustice by exporting their ethical concerns. This was common enough in the 1960s and '70s that Black theology's earliest thinkers identified it as a major obstacle to addressing white supremacy. J. Deotis Roberts articulated this in his 1974 monograph with reference to Dr. King's prophecy that "all Africa will be free before black Americans are free."[18] Echoing this concern, one TIA discussion group responded to the preparatory documents by asking, "Is white theology still more willing to look beyond its borders to find out the truth about itself rather than listening to the voices from within?"[19]

A second expression of theological racism concerns the committee's eventual turn to US injustice. Its new preparatory papers focused overwhelmingly on class at the neglect of other oppressive structures. This is probably because of the view that class disparities affected *all* Americans, whereas "minority" issues—racism, sexism—did not. This opinion appears in an early exchange between Dulles and Torres, where Dulles speculated that he would not be opposed to "the possibility of getting black, Spanish-speaking, and native American Indian theologians to expound what is in their traditions," but the "brunt of the conference should deal with the confusions and tensions felt by all of us, and not simply with minority groups, important though their testimony is."[20] Torres replied in "complete" agreement and assured Dulles that representatives from Black and other theologies would be integrated into the "global perspective of liberation that we have chosen as the focus of the conference."[21] In other words, they would be included to the extent that they reinforced the class focus of Latin American theology. This view resurfaced repeatedly throughout the conference.

Third, we see theological racism in the marginalization of the voices and experiences of black and other underrepresented communities, which were cast aside as peripheral to American experience and theological discourse. By originally depicting the United States as a monolithic source of imperial power, organizers elided complex power relations *within* the nation.[22] By presenting the continent as a "parched desert" without resources for resisting oppression, it erased the rich history of Americans who combated oppressive power. What's more, when racial and gender minorities decried their exclusion in the revised documents, there was no revision of the white-authored, class-focused documents on North America—only the brief addition of hastily commissioned, supplementary reports by and about these communities.

Had US racial minorities been included in the organization of the conference and its documents in the first place, then racial injustice might have been represented as a significant and inherent dimension of the US landscape. Their exclusion evinces that the conference organizers had, at the outset, marginalized issues of race and the theologians who addressed them. This reflects the larger problem of the committee's unfamiliarity with the scholarship of US minority scholars, which became apparent in their inability to identify authors for the rushed "minority reports."

Torres admitted this in his opening remarks at Detroit I, saying, "Most of the persons who initiated this present process are white and most of them had particular experiences in Latin America. It was inevitable that some would find the process too inattentive to the role of race. It only follows that they would be too little aware of the theological advances of the black community."[23]

The Events of Detroit I

"Theology in the Americas" commenced at Sacred Heart Catholic Seminary in Detroit on August 17, 1975. Present were twenty-five professional theologians from Latin America—most of them Catholic priests—and around one-hundred seventy-five participants from North America, including ordained and lay ministers, activists, and theologians who worked with a variety of "minority" communities.[24] A document synthesizing the reflection-group feedback had been circulated, and it directly addressed concerns that surfaced during the preparatory period. It repeatedly affirmed the consensus that Latin American theology could not "simply be imported" to address US injustices.[25] Likewise, it acknowledged that the particularities of American "racial and sexual oppression" were "not simply reducible to the question of class."[26] It recognized among African American participants a "strong and urgent plea to look honestly at their oppression, to listen to their theology, and to reflect on their constant striving for liberation."[27]

Nevertheless, patterns of racism continued. The first day's programing consisted entirely of presentations from Latin American theologians. The second morning was dedicated to social-scientific analyses of the North American context, which included some discussion of race but focused disproportionately on class inequality. The conference's theological racism reached a breaking point on day three. It began with a panel on Black theology that included Herbert Edwards and James Cone.[28] Edwards presented the black "minority report" from which a "lively and controversial dialogue" with the audience ensued. The conference proceedings record only excerpts from this exchange, but Torres offers a summary of what unfolded. He recounts that Latin American attendees, in particular, felt that Black theology's "insistence on racial oppression detracted from the global struggle."[29] They aspired to a united opposition against a single system of oppression—presumably class oppression, which was the focus of their agenda. In turn, "The black theologians responded that racial oppression cannot be identified with any other kind of oppression and that the Latin Americans cannot comprehend the historical and sociological roots of black oppression."[30]

The afternoon session that day was designated for "Emerging Theologies." It included concurrent presentations from Native American, Asian American, and US "Spanish-speaking" participants. Torres explains that "time limitations had led the conference organizers to schedule simultaneous panels, with the conference participants having to choose among them."[31] This garnered a "strong negative reaction," and caucuses formed among conference participants in response.[32] Twenty-seven conference participants assembled as the "Coalition of US Nonwhite Racial and National Minorities" and asked to present a collective statement to the entire conference.[33] Their statement identified the inadequacies of the previous day's social-scientific analysis of North America, which had "not express[ed] the conditions, experience, and theological reflections of the nonwhite racial and national minorities living within the United States."[34] They asserted, "The way the conference was structured perpetuated a tone of divisiveness among us nonwhites. We feel that the section on 'Emerging Theology' was a token one. We were forced into a situation which objectively appeared that we were competing with each other."[35] They also indicated a "lack of understanding [that] results in insufficient will, sensitivity, and understanding to embrace the oppressed US racial and national minorities and their liberation struggles."[36] In conclusion, the coalition offered three "indispensable" correctives for future planning and gatherings, which centered on the greater inclusion of minority persons. In response to this statement, Torres officially apologized to conference participants "for the [organizing] committee's deficiencies in planning."[37] In the published conference documents, he adds, "This session again demonstrated the importance and difficulty of obtaining just representation of the nonwhite minorities."[38]

The coalition's protest further exposed TIA's theological racism. Organizers prioritized foreign injustice over and against national oppression: Latin American theology had the opening session, and when Black theologians spotlighted US racial injustice days later, Latin American theologians insisted on the priority of global issues over the black struggle for justice.[39] This also represented the recurrent subjugation of racial injustice to other structural sins: Even on the day dedicated to injustice in the United States, speakers focused primarily on class inequality, offering only peripheral references to other national structural sins. This would continue through the conference's final, heated panel discussion.[40] Meanwhile, the voices and experiences of racial minorities were repeatedly silenced or marginalized: After dedicating stand-alone sessions to Latin American theology and to class-focused, social-scientific analyses of North America, organizers clumped into a single day the sessions that highlighted the perspectives and experiences of racial minorities, leaving them unheard by most conference participants.

Repeating Theological Racism

Some good things emerged from Detroit I, however. Kenneth Aman reported that by the end of the conference, it was clear that there was no single "theology of liberation for the United States; that we must for the indefinite future struggle with a variety of particular theologies which reflect the particular struggles experienced by various groups in the United States."[41] TIA moved forward with this conviction, establishing a network of affinity groups that gathered and worked together for years. This included the Black Theology Project, which Dwight Hopkins identifies with a major turning point in the development of Black theology.[42] These affinity groups significantly shaped the next major gathering of TIA in 1980, Detroit II.[43] The controversies of Detroit I also influenced the emergence of another important organization in the late '70s and '80s, the Ecumenical Association of Third World Theologians (EATWOT).[44]

These long-term positive outcomes and the temporal distance between 1975 and 2017 might tempt us to shrug off the theological racism of Detroit I as a by-product of its time. That was then, and things improved. In many ways, they have not. In 1986, the CTSA's convention centered on the theme "Catholic Theology in the North American Context." Reading the texts of its plenary speakers—all white men—Jon Nilson notes, "Patience and strong eyes are needed to ferret out the few mentions of racism and black theology. In fact, striking out those few remarks would leave the speakers' main arguments intact. Racism and black theology thus appeared as essentially marginal to the telling of the putatively 'real' story of Catholic theology in North America."[45]

We can also consider our own 2017 CTS convention—another conference on North American Catholicism. The official document presenting our theme, "American Catholicism in the 21st Century," repeats some of the transgressions that theologians decried at the very first TIA conference. Its presentation of "American Catholicism" includes no mention of racism, past or present. To paraphrase James Cone, if one were to read our conference theme, one would never know African Americans or the black struggle for justice existed at all. This is jarring when we consider the theme's repeated mentions of political "issues" and "turmoil," and its general concern for American "crises." If racism isn't an American crisis today—when, for example, African American men, women, and children are regularly and publicly killed by police officers with little to no recourse—then what *is* a crisis? And if racism is not a crisis that concerns *Catholicism*, then we Catholics must interrogate the relationship between our church and the Gospel.

Meanwhile, the convention theme identifies specific economic challenges as factors in American Catholicism, such as the 2008 "Great Recession." More than once it names Dorothy Day, who famously advocated for economic justice.[46] The inclusion of class and the exclusion of racism mirrors the blinding preoccupation with economic injustice that played out at Detroit I. This should spur CTS to consider why the society is more inclined to recognize economic inequality than the racial injustice that is woven into the fabric of this nation and its Catholicism.

While a number of presenters in the convention's concurrent sessions engaged matters of racial injustice, just as many did at Detroit I, their contributions do not excuse the omission of racism from the conference's official documents. That the CTS convention had one plenary speaker with expertise in Black theology, Cyril Orji, also does not necessarily evince a departure from the marginalization of black experience and perspectives. Orji was not given his own plenary session, but rather shared his time on a panel of white colleagues. This mirrors the "Emerging Theologies" session that epitomized the marginalization of racial-minority communities at Detroit I.

Remembering and Resisting Theological Racism

The story of Detroit I should alert us to the persistent sin of theological racism that white Catholic theologians perpetuate today. It certainly did for me. When I read that Rosemary Radford Ruether immediately spoke out against the misrepresentation of American experience, and James Cone protested the marginalization of Black theology as well as feminist theology at Detroit I, it left me wondering: *Why hadn't I spoken up?* Last year when I first read the CTS convention theme, I noticed racism's absence from the depiction of American Catholicism. I did nothing about it. I did not use my privilege as a white woman with professional connections in the society to raise concerns about this erasure. Unlike many of the dissenting participants of Detroit I, I did not give the colleagues who organized this conference the benefit of the doubt by pointing out this problem and its context in the history of theological racism, which organizers might have received graciously and acted upon correctively.

I now suspect that prior, more detailed knowledge of Detroit I and a deliberate attention to theological racism could have informed a constructive effort of resistance on my part. What's more, greater familiarity with Detroit I would have equipped me with tangible steps to counteract theological racism that I could have suggested. The agenda of Detroit I's dissenting participants remains painfully relevant today: our organization has yet to interrogate the white-supremacist assumptions underlying our depictions of "America," "Catholicism," and "American Catholicism." Leadership of our society must include and consult underrepresented communities, and then *prioritize* their perspectives in the work of CTS. This, according to the Nonwhite Coalition, could radically transform our organization in support of the flourishing of all people.

Knowing that history can aid us in avoiding a repetition of past transgressions and ready us for resistance against sins that reappear, I hope this retrieval and analysis of Detroit I begins to expose the unwitting racial blindnesses of white Catholic theologians like me, so that when a national theological society holds another conference on North American Catholicism, we will be already attuned to the white-supremacist history of our discipline and take for granted the need for a conference that prioritizes historically marginalized communities and reflects all of what "American Catholicism" is and ought to be. This will require dramatic conversion, however. White Catholic theologians would do well to begin by acting on the demands laid out by the critics of Detroit I forty-two years ago.

Notes

[1]Jon Nilson, "Confessions of a White Racist Catholic Theologian," *Proceedings of the Catholic Theological Society of America* 58 (2003): 64.

[2]Jon Nilson, *Hearing Past the Pain: Why White Catholic Theologians Need Black Theology* (New York: Paulist Press, 2007), 9.

[3]Joseph R. Nearon, "Preliminary Report: Research Committee for Black Theology," *Proceedings of the Catholic Theological Society of America* 29 (1974): 413.

[4]James H. Cone, "Black Liberation Theology and Black Catholics: A Critical Conversation," *Theological Studies* 61, no. 4 (2000): 741.

[5]See Nilson, *Hearing Past the Pain*, 12–21 and passim.

[6]Sergio Torres and John Eagleson, eds., *Theology in the Americas* (Maryknoll, NY: Orbis Books, 1976), 11.

[7]Kenneth Aman, "Liberation and Theology: The View from Detroit," *Commonweal*, September 20, 1975, 422–23.

[8]Torres and Eagleson, *Theology in the Americas*, 11–12.

[9]Although "Theology in the Americas" was an ecumenical gathering, this list of theologians accurately reflects the disproportionate influence of Catholics on this planning of the conference.

[10]Torres and Eagleson, *Theology in the Americas*, 84.

[11]Ibid., 88.

[12]Ibid.

[13]Ibid., 90–99.

[14]Ibid., 113–38, 139–74, 317–28; John Coleman, "Vision and Praxis in American Theology: Orestes Brownson, John A. Ryan, and John Courtney Murray," *Theological Studies* 37, no. 1 (March 1976): 3–40.

[15]Torres and Eagleson, *Theology in the Americas*, 175.

[16]Ibid.

[17]Ibid., 176.

[18]J. Deotis Roberts, *A Black Political Theology* (Louisville, KY: Westminster, 1974), 15–16. James Cone echoed Roberts's observation: "Most American theologians are too closely tied to the American structure to respond creatively to the life situation of the Church in this society," he observed. "Instead of seeking to respond to the problems which are unique to this country, most

Americans look to Europe for the newest word worth theologizing about." See *Black Theology and Black Power* (Maryknoll, NY: Orbis Books, 1989), 85.

[19]Torres and Eagleson, *Theology in the Americas*, 249.

[20]Ibid., 94.

[21]Ibid., 98.

[22]This is not to say that oppressed groups within the United States did not participate in or benefit from US imperialism. Rather, the monolithic presentation of the United States overlooks the disparities among those who had authority to execute and benefit from it.

[23]Torres and Eagleson, *Theology in the Americas*, 267–68.

[24]Ibid., x.

[25]Ibid., 251.

[26]Ibid., 249.

[27]Ibid.

[28]The published papers and commentary on the conference do not include a full list of presenters for this panel.

[29]Torres and Eagleson, *Theology in the Americas*, 351.

[30]Ibid.

[31]Ibid., 357.

[32]Ibid.

[33]Ibid., 359.

[34]Ibid.

[35]Ibid.

[36]Ibid., 359–60.

[37]Ibid., 357.

[38]Ibid.

[39]Attention to economic inequality and racial injustice need not be at odds, of course. Throughout Detroit I, however, they were often presented as competing concerns.

[40]The final panel on "Theology and Society" was, according to Torres, "set aside for reflection on the response of the prevailing theology—that is, the theology of the 'Western' white male theologians." See *Theology in the Americas*, 377. Beverly Harrison recounted a conflict that arose during this panel when Frederick Herzog, a white theologian, rejected the Marxist analysis and theology of grace that shaped Latin American liberation theology, instead favoring the antiracist analysis of Black theology and the theology of grace that accompanied it in that field. See Beverly Harrison, "The 'Theology in the Americas' Conference," *Christianity and Crisis*, October 27, 1975, 253–54.

[41]"Liberation and Theology: The View from Detroit," *Commonweal*, September 20, 1975, 423.

[42]Dwight Hopkins, *Introducing Black Theology of Liberation* (Maryknoll, NY: Orbis Books, 2004), 10.

[43]See Cornel West, Caridad Guidote, and Margaret Coakley, eds., *Theology in the Americas: Detroit II Conference Papers* (Maryknoll, NY: Orbis Books, 1982).

[44]M. P. Joseph, *Theologies of the Non-Person: The Formative Years of EATWOT* (New York: Palgrave Macmillan, 2015), 26–29.

[45]Nilson, *Hearing Past the Pain*, 14–15.

[46]That Day is widely known for her commitment to economic justice is not intended to suggest that Day was disengaged from the struggle for racial justice. Her antiracist activism is less known and consequently not a feature of her general legacy, which is my point here.

In the Image of an Intrinsically Social God

Theological Foundations for a Culture of Inclusion in Catholic Higher Education

Dana L. Dillon

In *Stand Your Ground: Black Bodies and the Justice of God*, Kelly Brown Douglas calls the current moment in the life of our nation, where police and vigilantes kill black bodies often with little or no accountability, a kairos time. Such a moment of "chaos and crisis" is "a decisive moment in history that potentially has far-reaching impact," in which we find "that God is fully present, disrupting things as they are and providing an opening to a new future—to God's future."[1] In this kairos time, many Catholic colleges and universities (like others), have seen student protesters demanding that our campuses become more aware of our institutional racism and more attentive to inclusion. This kairos moment puts us at a crossroads, and our response will determine whether we move toward crisis or renewal. Although some believe that we must prioritize either preservation of Catholic identity or movement toward diversity and inclusion, this essay seeks to offer theological foundations for a Catholic commitment to building cultures of inclusion on our campuses. Because of the pervasive presence of institutionalized racism in US history, engaging and addressing this cultural history is an imperative part of the mission and identity of Catholic colleges in the United States. We must commit resources to reshaping social structures to bring them more in line with justice and the dignity of the human person. This paper explores the nature of a Catholic university and its responsibility to upset cultural values at odds with the Gospel.

After displaying the pervasive nature of the cultural mind-set of domination in the United States, it suggests three key theological concepts that can serve as the foundation of a Catholic culture of inclusion: intrinsically social anthropology, an ecclesiology of communion, and the virtue of solidarity. Together they offer tools for Catholic universities to make this kairos time a time of renewal.

The Role and Purpose of the Catholic University

In *Ex Corde Ecclesiae*, St. John Paul asserts that Catholic universities exist "to help the Church respond to the problems and needs of the age."[2] Therefore, universities serve both church and society by helping the church to better respond to the needs of the community in each time and place and by becoming "an ever more effective instrument of cultural progress for individuals as well as for society" (*ECE* 32). John Paul calls for concrete contributions to a society's progress (*ECE* 34), shaped by interdisciplinary research that will seek to ameliorate the issues and problems a society faces, "cooperation in common research projects among Catholic universities" (*ECE* 35), and attention to the culture and history of the region in which each university is located (*ECE* 37). Catholic universities must consider the history and culture of the region and nation in which they find themselves. Developing and transmitting culture constitutes much of the work of the university: "By its very nature, a University develops culture through its research, helps to transmit the local culture to each succeeding generation through its teaching, and assists cultural activities through its educational services" (*ECE* 43). Catholic universities must participate in this work with a critical eye shaped by the Gospel and the culture of the church. Catholic universities must be "open to all human experience and . . . ready to dialogue with and learn from any culture" and should become "primary and privileged place[s] for a fruitful dialogue between the Gospel and culture" (*ECE* 43). The Catholic university should facilitate a dialogue between the Gospel and society that aims to better understand both "cultures of the world" and the "various cultural traditions existing within the Church" (*ECE* 45). Catholic universities serve society by clarifying and developing the values of a culture, including especially "the meaning of the human person, his or her liberty, dignity, sense of responsibility, and openness to the transcendent" as well as the "preeminent value of the family, the primary unit of every human culture" (*ECE* 45). They accomplish this by bringing such cultural values into dialogue with the Gospel message and Catholic teaching on these and other issues.

As a locus for this dialogue between the Gospel and culture, "all the basic academic activities of a Catholic University are connected with and in harmony with the evangelizing mission of the Church" (*ECE* 49). According to *Evangelii Nuntiandi*, a crucial component of evangelization is not simply preaching the Gospel "but also . . . affecting and, as it were, upsetting, through the power of the Gospel, mankind's criteria of judgment, determining values, points of interest, lines of thought, sources of inspiration and models of life, which are in contrast with the Word of God and the plan of salvation."[3] Catholic universities of any nation must examine areas where cultural judgments and values contradict those of the Gospel and work to upset those judgments and values in light of the Gospel and God's saving plan. For Catholic universities in the United States, the nature of a Catholic university compels serious analysis of the history and culture of institutionalized racism.

American Cultural Mind-set

African American essayist bell hooks recalls learning about Christopher Columbus and the first encounters between Europeans and the indigenous peoples of the Americas. These history lessons implied that "the will to dominate and conquer folks who are different from ourselves is natural, not culturally specific."[4] She recalls teachers and textbooks suggesting that if the natives had been smarter or stronger, they would have conquered the Europeans. Though texts did not explicitly root the Europeans' supposed superiority in their whiteness, the word "civilization" implied this. Further, hooks recalls learning that "whatever cruelties were done to the indigenous peoples of this country [were] necessary to bring the great gift of civilization. Domination . . . was central to the project of civilization. And if civilization was good and necessary despite the costs, then that had to mean domination was equally good."[5] Finally, hooks uses the phrase "imperialist white supremacist capitalist patriarchy" to denote that these interlocking systems of domination reinforce one an-other and have come to seem both normal and natural, as simply the way the world works.[6] Especially in the United States, "The assumption that domination is not only natural but central to the civilizing process is deeply rooted in our cultural mind-set."[7]

The cultural mind-set that hooks names—the understanding that domination is natural, normal, and essential to the civilizing process—lies at the heart of many arguments made for slavery, including Catholic ones. In 1861, Auguste Martin, the first bishop of Natchitoches, Louisiana, wrote a pastoral letter offering support and consolation to his diocesan faithful as the Civil War began. He exhorted their support of the Confederate cause and offered them theological arguments in defense of slavery. He argued:

> The manifest will of God is that, in exchange for a freedom which they are unable to defend and which will kill them, and in return for a lifetime of work we must give these unfortunate people not only the bread and the clothes necessary to the material life but also . . . their just share of truth and of the goods of grace, which may console them for their present troubles with the hope of eternal rest in the bosom of their Father, who calls them as well as us. From this point of view . . . slavery, far from being an evil, would be an eminently Christian work . . . the redemption of millions of human beings who would pass in such a way from the darkest intel-lectual night to the sweet . . . light of the Gospel.[8]

This argument, shocking to modern ears, represents a once per-vasive perspective, perhaps given its most famous expression in Rudyard Kipling's poem "The White Man's Burden."

> Take up the White Man's burden,
> Send forth the best ye breed
> Go bind your sons to exile,
> To serve your captives' need;
> To wait in heavy harness,
> On fluttered folk and wild—
> Your new-caught, sullen peoples,
> Half-devil and half-child.[9]

The white man's burden is that, through imperial conquests, he has become servant to the colonized. Kipling suggests that the European empires have the responsibility to civilize and improve the colonized peoples. Despite their efforts, ordered to nothing but the improvement of these peoples, they will likely be undermined by "Sloth and heathen Folly."[10] Much like Kipling, Bishop Martin conceives of slavery as "an eminently Christian work" that improves the enslaved by bringing these "unfortunates" to salvation and to the Gospel. Martin directly states his terrible assumption: these people's freedom "will kill them." On his view, white Christians must enslave and control these people for their own good. Only under the control of benevolent white Christians will they be directed toward proper choices, like work and the Gospel, for their salvation. Of course, this mind-set originated long before slavery in the United States and extends after it. However, the idea that people of color must be controlled both for their own good and the good of society pervades and characterizes American history and culture, including American Catholicism.

Scholars from various fields have offered accounts of this cultural mind-set of domination and control and its impact on racialized practices throughout history. Michelle Alexander has traced it from slavery to sharecropping to Jim Crow laws to the contemporary practices of US prisons and police, noting that these systems not only forcibly control Black bodies but also exploit Black labor for white profit.[11] Willie James Jennings has attended to similar dynamics, tracing them all the way to the killing of Michael Brown in Ferguson, Missouri, and noting that they are marked by a "sick Christianity" that has come to be at ease with violence toward Black bodies in the name of controlling white spaces.[12] Kelly Brown Douglas has traced Anglo-Saxon exceptionalism from its roots in Tacitus's comments on Germania to an American exceptionalism that becomes interlaced with white supremacy. These finally become the "stand your ground" culture that defends the "cherished property" of whiteness and results in the violent death of Trayvon Martin, as well as so many others.[13]

In their 1979 pastoral letter "Brothers and Sisters to Us," the US Catholic bishops acknowledge this history, saying that "racism has been part of the social fabric of America since its European colonization."[14] They condemn racism unequivocally as "the sin that says some human beings are inherently superior and others essentially inferior because of race," as "the sin that makes racial characteristics the determining factor for the exercise of human rights."[15] They say that racism mocks the golden rule, disregards the teachings of Christ, and denies the dignity of the human person communicated in the Incarnation.[16] They describe racism not as merely personal attitudes and actions that reflect and enact racial biases, but also as structural or social sin, saying:

> The structures of our society are subtly racist, for these structures reflect the values which society upholds. They are geared to the success of the majority and the failure of the minority. Members of both groups give unwitting approval by accepting things as they are. Perhaps no single individual is to blame. The sinfulness is often anonymous but nonetheless real. The sin is social in nature in that each of us, in varying degrees, is responsible. All of us in some measure are accomplices.[17]

This approach to social sin acknowledges some individual responsibility for upholding racialized social structures, but does not point to any means by which either individuals or groups could work to dismantle these systems. Bryan Massingale has pointed out that the bishops' approach focuses largely on personal attitudes and actions:

> The bishops presume that if the incompatibility of racist behaviors with Christian faith is pointed out, this will lead to personal conversion, which will result in social transformation. But the inherent limitations and constraints imposed on an individual's freedom, knowledge, and moral agency by what one prelate admits is an "enormity" of "cultural entrenchment" are neither acknowledged nor addressed.[18]

Given the entrenched cultural mind-set that is subtly (or not) and pervasively racist and the historical institutionalization of that mind-set, the cultural context of the United States stands in need of serious critique. Considering *Ex Corde Ecclesiae*, a Catholic university in the United States that fails to address the issue of race fails to be what a Catholic university is called to be. By its nature, a Catholic university must work to upset those cultural values and practices that stand in contrast to the Gospel, the common good, and the dignity of the human person. A failure to upset the cultural mind-set of domination and racialized injustice in the light of the Gospel is a failure to live out the identity of the Catholic university.

Theological Foundations of a Culture of Inclusion

To live the mission envisioned in *Ex Corde Ecclesiae*, Catholic universities cannot merely participate in cultural initiatives around improving racialized social structures, but must bring the light of the Gospel to this entrenched cultural mind-set and the institutions, attitudes, and practices that flow from it and form future generations in it. Catholic theology offers three interrelated concepts that can serve as a trajectory for such an approach: a Christian anthropology rooted in a Trinitarian God, an ecclesiology of communion, and the moral virtue of solidarity.

Christians assert the dignity of every person, made in the image and likeness of God, but many fail to understand that this dignity is personal without being individual. We are made in the image of a Trinitarian God, which means that we are persons-in-communion and intrinsically social beings. Christ not only reveals God to human beings but also reveals what it means to be human.[19] *Gaudium et Spes* argues that Jesus's prayer for unity in John 17:21–22 ("that all may be one . . . as we are one") "implied a certain likeness between the union of the divine Persons, and the unity of God's sons in truth and charity" (*GS* 24). The interpersonal communion of the triune God in whose image we are made reveals our social nature and reveals interpersonal communion with one another to be both our vocation and our destiny. As the *Compendium of the Social Doctrine of the Church* puts it, "Being a person in the image and likeness of God . . . involves existing in a relationship, in relation to the other 'I,' because God himself, one and triune, is the communion of the Father, of the Son and of the Holy Spirit."[20] Of course, this cannot mean an abstract, theoretical love or communion. It is a deep ontological claim about human persons. We are made in communion with one another, and our failure to act like it not only betrays our brothers and sisters but also makes us less than who we are made and called to be. Imagine if the Trinity were "separate but equal" or "friendly at a distance," assenting to the other's full and equal personhood in theory but without genuine communion. God would not be God. So, too, we fail to be fully human when we allow racial divisions to distance us from one another.

Drawing from *Gaudium et Spes*, the *Compendium* insists on a "parallel between the union existing among the divine Persons and the union of the children of God in truth and love" (*GS* 34). Because the image and likeness of the Trinitarian God is the foundation of human nature and human society, "'To be human means to be called to interpersonal communion,' which reaches its apex in the commandment of love" (*GS* 34). To be human means to be in communion, to be interdependent, to be united with the entire human family. The basis of our unity is the Trinitarian God's having made us in the divine image in union with one another, and drawing us all together into God's own life as persons-in-communion. Attending deeply to the intrinsically social nature of Catholic anthropology contributes something essential to conversations on race and practices of inclusion.

The second theological theme, an ecclesiology of communion, proceeds from the first. Drawing from the Second Vatican Council, Sister Jamie Phelps, OP, notes two central, interrelated insights about the nature of the church: "The Church is essentially missionary and her primary mission is that of communion, that is, to be a sacrament of unity with God and the whole human race."[21] By its nature the church is both united in Christ and sent forth to draw others into this unity. Phelps describes the mission of the church as threefold:

> First, the church creates a *community of believers* who grow in union with the triune God through their participation in the sacraments and the life of the church. Second, the church is called to be a *transformative agent in a divided community of believers* both Christian and non-Christian. And third, the church is called to be a *transformative agent in a world divided by sin and injustice*. These three parts are integrally related, and one without the others renders the mission of the church incomplete.[22]

Catholic universities must take all three components of this ecclesial mission to heart, committing to creating community on campus, working to overcome divisions, and fighting injustice everywhere. Rooted in Jesus's own mission, the goal of "enabling all human beings to live in the fullness of their humanity as free and responsible human creatures made in the image and likeness of God" is at the heart of every Catholic institution.[23] This mission is only possible with a radical communion of genuine love, at the service of human flourishing, freedom, and responsibility on every level. The church must be both a communion and a sacrament of unity, and must work with all people of good will to transform the social order to be genuinely directed to the common good. Theologians must further develop this ecclesiology and its implications for overcoming institutionalized racism in the United States.

Finally, a Catholic vision capable of upsetting the cultural mind-set of racism requires a theological account of solidarity. Solidarity flows out of the intrinsically social nature of the person and communion ecclesiology. In *Sollicitudo Rei Socialis*, St. John Paul II elevated the concept of solidarity to a moral virtue, defining it as "a firm and persevering determination to commit oneself to the common good; that is to say to the good of all and of each individual, because we are all really responsible for all."[24] Since the common good is "the good of all and of each," the good of one and the good of all do not compete with each other but mutually constitute each other. Created in the image of an intrinsically social God, the good of each human being interconnects with the good of all others, so that we all flourish best when we each flourish, and vice versa.

A Christian commitment to the flourishing of all and of each cannot be merely abstract. St. John Paul II calls us to a solidarity based on Christ's own paschal sacrifice:

> Solidarity seeks to go beyond itself, to take on the specifically Christian dimension of total gratuity, forgiveness and reconciliation. One's neighbor is then not only a human being with his or her own rights and a fundamental equality with everyone else, but becomes the living image of God the Father, redeemed by the blood of Jesus Christ and placed under the permanent action of the Holy Spirit. One's neighbor must

therefore be loved, even if an enemy, with the same love with which the Lord loves him or her; and for that person's sake one must be ready for sacrifice, even the ultimate one: to lay down one's life for the brethren (cf. 1 Jn 3:16). (*SRS* 40)

Considering a history in which the equality of people of color has been consistently and institutionally denied, white American Christians are called to commit to the institutional change that would finally recognize and embody this fundamental equality, even to the point of sacrifice and death. This not only embodies our true nature as persons-in-communion but, through this action, we participate in the paschal sacrifice of Christ and therefore in the unity of the Trinity. Our faithfulness in making a true commitment to our neighbors and dismantling the institutional machinery of racism is an essential measure of our connection to Christ and to the life of the Trinity. This theological trajectory draws a line from the nature of God through human interconnectedness to the need for a solidarity that can replace institutionalized racism with Gospel values.

At this kairos moment, "God [is] calling us to a new relationship with our very history and sense of self, and thus to a new relationship with one another, and even with God."[25] We must see our history in a new way, including the ways Catholic institutions have been more deeply shaped by the cultural mind-set of domination and exploitation of persons of color than by the Gospel and our theological commitments. We must make the cultural mind-set of domination—past and present—visible so that we can combat it. We should take concrete steps in curriculum development, research agendas, hiring, admissions, scholarships, and more to shift our institutions from the mind-set of domination to the practice of inclusion. We should amplify the voices of persons of color on our campuses as well as other historically underrepresented groups, making certain that the "we" at the heart of our institutional self-understanding is a "we" that reflects all our institutional stakeholders. We are not a white "we" working to include others, but a diverse "we," working together to make sure all of us are included in keeping with our theological foundations. Doing this work together can "move [us] toward unity in diversity through the empowering grace of the Holy Spirit, whose transforming power can enable us to become more inclusive than we think desirable or possible."[26] Grounded in trinitarian anthropology, communion ecclesiology, the moral virtue of solidarity, and the inspiration of the Holy Spirit, our institutions can become models for inclusion in ways that will serve our students and our society. In so doing, we can become the places of cultural renewal that the nature of the Catholic university calls us to be.

Notes

[1]Kelly Brown Douglas, *Stand Your Ground: Black Bodies and the Justice of God* (Maryknoll, NY: Orbis Books, 2015), 206.

[2]Pope John Paul II, *Ex Corde Ecclesiae* (1990), no. 31, http://w2.vatican.va.

[3]Pope Paul VI, *Evangelii Nuntiandi* (1975), no. 19, http://w2.vatican.va.

[4]bell hooks, "Columbus: Gone but Not Forgotten," in *Outlaw Culture: Resisting Representations* (London: Routledge Classics, 2006), 233.

[5]Ibid., 233–34.

[6]George A. Yancy and bell hooks, "bell hooks: Buddhism, the Beats, and Loving Blackness," *New York Times* (December 10, 2015), https://www.nytimes.com.

[7]hooks, "Columbus," 234.

[8]Quoted in Cyprian Davis, OSB, "God of Our Weary Years," in *Taking Down Our Harps: Black Catholics in the United States*, ed. Diana L Hayes and Cyprian Davis, OSB (Maryknoll, NY: Orbis Books, 1998), 25.

[9]*Rudyard Kipling's Verse, Inclusive Edition, 1885–1918* (Garden City: Doubleday, Page, 1922; Bartleby.com, 2013), lines 1–8, http://www.bartleby.com/.

[10]Ibid., line 23.

[11]Michelle Alexander, *The New Jim Crow: Mass Incarceration in an Age of Colorblindness* (New York: New Press, 2012).

[12]Willie James Jennings, "After Ferguson: America Must Abandon 'Sick Christianity' at Ease with Violence," *Religion Dispatches* (December 9, 2014), http://religiondispatches.org.

[13]Douglas, *Stand Your Ground*.

[14]United States Conference of Catholic Bishops, *Brothers and Sisters to Us* (1979), http://www.usccb.org.

[15]Ibid.

[16]Ibid.

[17]Ibid.

[18]Bryan N. Massingale, *Racial Justice and the Catholic Church* (Maryknoll, NY: Orbis Books, 2010), 71.

[19]Second Vatican Council, *Gaudium et Spes* (1965), no. 22, http://www.vatican.va.

[20]Pontifical Council for Justice and Peace, *Compendium of the Social Doctrine of the Church* (2005), no. 34, http://www.vatican.va.

[21]Jamie Phelps, OP, "Communion Ecclesiology," in *Uncommon Faithfulness: The Black Catholic Experience*, ed. M. Shawn Copeland with LaReine-Marie Mosely, SND, and Albert J. Raboteau (Maryknoll, NY: Orbis Books, 2009), 116.

[22]Ibid., 118.

[23]Ibid., 121.

[24]Pope John Paul II, *Sollicitudo Rei Socialis* (1987), no. 38, http://w2.vatican.va.

[25]Douglas, *Stand Your Ground*, 206.

[26]Phelps, "Communion Ecclesiology," 123.

Inclusive Church for the 21st Century

Dreaming beyond the Binary with LGBTQ Youth

Mary M. Doyle Roche

In order for the church of the twenty-first century in the United States to be more inclusive and fully participatory, Christians must risk dreaming about the future with those who challenge long-held theological-anthropological assumptions about persons and communities. A temptation for the church in the United States is conflating a vision for the church with the "American Dream." The church has played a role in shaping, and has been shaped by, the values of the American Dream. Even so, Christian ethicists, particularly those adopting Catholic social teaching and liberationist perspectives, have long been challenging many of these values (wealth, status, individual achievement, patriarchal family forms, and competition over cooperation). They have unearthed and challenged the racism, classism, and sexism in our society and our churches. As this vital work continues, we must add the task of challenging heteronormative and binary assumptions that shape the church's vision of what is possible.

The heteronormative and binary dream of a life well lived becomes a nightmare for many LGBTQ youth as they face bullying; hostile home, educational, and religious environments; high rates of mental health issues; and homelessness. Their plight has received increased attention in response to the 2016 "Dear Colleague" letter issued by the US Department of Justice Civil Rights Division and the US Department of Education Office for Civil Rights. The letter sought to provide guidance for schools based on an interpretation of Title IX that would allow students to use facilities and participate in programs based on their gender identity and not necessarily on the gender assigned to them at birth. The policy was recently rescinded by the Trump administration, a move that garnered praise from the United States Conference of Catholic Bishops.[1]

The voices of LGBTQ youth need amplification in the church and society. Their counternarratives add complexity to evolving understandings of gender and sexuality and challenge binary thinking: male/female; masculine/feminine; gay/straight; out/closeted; dreams/reality. Ta-Nehisi Coates's *Between the World and Me*, the moving letter to his son, is incisive in its critique of the Dream of people who think they are white. The stories of LGBTQ young people might similarly challenge *the dream of people who think they are straight* (a "queering" of James Baldwin's denunciation).[2]

Attending to the experiences of LGBTQ youth is helpful in moving beyond the binary and getting clearer on related but distinct concepts of sex, sexual orientation, gender, gender identity, expression, and performance. This practice will pave the way for a critique of heteronormative assumptions of the church's vision for human persons, relationships, and communities. A common good approach to the ethical practices of dreaming will be grounded in habits of inclusion and participation that can be more readily shaped, pursued, and attained by LGBTQ young people.

Voices of LGBTQ Youth

Two photo essays, *Speaking OUT: Queer Youth in Focus* (2014) and *Beyond Magenta: Transgender Teens Speak Out* (2014), provide insight into experiences of LGBTQ youth.[3] Here is some of what they have to say:

MANDY: I don't fit into the shape of your box.[4]

AMY: Love is bigger than labels and categories. Love is bigger than everything.[5]

MIKEY: In today's world, people are too concerned with labels. Life is about having the courage to accept yourself for who you are. I don't see being gay as a choice, rather just a mere part of who I am.[6]

KEVIN: This is me. One word is not enough.[7]

CAMERON: But for me, even describing it as a spectrum is too limiting because gender is explained somewhere in between girl and boy. That identifies gender the way society indicates, and that's not what it's about.[8]

MEGHAN: I live by being myself, not by defining myself. I have characteristics not labels. I have passions, hopes, flaws, ideas, desires, and dreams. So really . . . What's all the fuss thinking I'm different?[9]

JON: I am an eternal work in progress.[10]

After coming out to friends at the end of high school, Jessy says, "It was a good way to start college, knowing that my friends in high school accepted me as I am. When I went back to see them spring break of my freshman year, it was so different because by then I was a hundred percent me. It was beautiful."[11] Jessy goes on to say, "When I first started my transition, I wanted it to be complete, from one side to the other. But now I'm embracing my in-between-ness. I'm embracing this whole mix that I have inside myself. And I'm happy so forget the category. Just talk to me. Get to know me."[12] Jessy is clear, "God created me transgender for a reason. . . . I enjoy life from a different perspective."[13]

In listening to LGBTQ youth, several important and overlapping themes emerge. First, even as they search for identity, they also desire to move beyond categorization. Labels can liberate when young people self-identify as gay, lesbian, trans, or queer. Young people are liberated *from* identities they find suffocating and are liberated *for* new relationships of trust and solidarity. Labels can also confine when they are used derogatorily or to capture the whole of one's identity. People live at the intersection of multiple identities, roles, and relationships.[14]

Second, experiences of gender and sexuality are fluid and dynamic. LGBTQ young people's sense of who they are and who they want to be changes over time, which is not to say they are merely "going through a phase." For LGBTQ young people, self-discovery and the embodiment and performance of identity are quite intentional. According to one young person, LGBTQ youth are more like swimmers who must actively "do" gender rather than "float" about in heteronormative waters.[15] This requires ongoing deliberation and decision and prepares young people to participate in the process of social transformation rather than learning to "cope" or adapt to a heteronormative context.[16]

Third, though young people tell their stories in a loosely chronological fashion, researchers point out that they resist a linear pattern, especially when it comes to the "coming out narrative." Disrupting the closeted/out binary, LGBTQ young people are engaged in a complex and ongoing process of discernment about when, where, and with whom to disclose important parts of their lives. They carefully weigh advantages (the freedom that comes with self-acceptance, the access to communities of support and other resources) and risks (family alienation and loss of support, harassment, and violence). In/out is rarely a simple either/or, before/after proposition. Young people question whether being out is necessarily the more moral, socially responsible or "politically valuable" stance. Participants in one study of LGBTQ youth challenge the notion that the opposite of out is closeted; those who were not out to anybody, or who were out only to some people in their lives, were not necessarily living in shame and secrecy but rather living with the understanding that many factors affect their psychological health.[17]

Finally, solidarity that is explicitly voiced and embodied is crucial. LGBTQ persons do not want to be where they are merely tolerated, but rather where their presence is a source of joy. According to researchers, "LGBTQ youth do not want to have to guess or figure out if their parents and family members are supportive; they would like support to be verbalized."[18] They note that many young people felt that coming out was necessary but that the initial response from parents is frequently not positive. Young people often see their parents' faith and religious identity as a barrier in the relationship and desire explicit support from their families.

Authentic solidarity with LGBTQ persons requires moving beyond a deficit-based approach that considers LGBTQ young people primarily, if not exclusively, as vulnerable to mental illness, substance abuse, and homelessness. While statistics can't be ignored, young people are more than statistics. An asset-based approach to solidarity honors the whole person and empowers young people.[19] Participation in a "queer community" is also important, as is the adoption of "signifiers and shared norms."[20] However, once there are "shared norms," there is also the danger that even "mainstream systems of oppression" like transphobia will be replicated within the queer community. The LGBTQ community is not immune to human sinfulness, and so solidarity and ethical critique are not mutually exclusive.

Challenging homophobic and heteronormative environments requires empowerment, and it would be a mistake to think that the ability to resist is purely a matter of personal will or personality. The ability to stand up for oneself takes practice and multiple networks of support that nurture agency and interdependence.[21] Families, educators, health care personnel, and pastoral care workers also need support and guidance in how to advocate for the young people in their lives.

Challenging a Heteronormative Dream in the Church

How might experiences of LGBTQ youth challenge the heteronormative and binary thinking that characterizes the American and Christian dreams? Ta-Nehisi Coates is an insightful companion in this exploration. It is not the intention here to conflate the struggles of persons under the weight of slavery, Jim Crow, segregation, and racism in America with the struggles of LGBTQ persons. Coates's work does, however, prompt the exploration of dreams in new directions. In *Between the World and Me*, his moving letter to his son, Coates writes of a "gorgeous dream": "I have seen that dream all my life. It is perfect houses with nice lawns. It is Memorial Day cookouts, block associations, and driveways. The Dream is treehouses and the Cub Scouts."[22]

The scene painted by Coates, at once enticing and sealed off from his experience, is insidious not only because the structures of racism keep African Americans from achieving it, but also because these idyllic circumstances *are made possible* by the suffering of black people.[23] He also claims that many people, *believing themselves white*, are descendants of "dead 'races' (Frankish, Italian, German, Irish) later abandoned because they no longer serve their purpose—the organization of people beneath, and beyond, the umbrella of rights."[24] Racial and ethnic identity is a complex reality, and in a certain sense, "whiteness" is a myth that betrays the history of many peoples and is used to perpetuate and rationalize injustice.

Coates's provocative reflection generates new questions for Christians committed to justice and well-being for LGBTQ persons. Is there also a dream of people who think they are straight, who think they are cisgender? Do straight people protect this dream in order to maintain systems of power and privilege founded on inadequate and inaccurate categories? And if there is such a dream, what sleeping pills prolong slumber? Rules about who uses which bathroom? About who plays for which athletic team? About who goes to prom and what they wear? Restrictions about who is worthy of marriage and parenthood? If sex, gender, and sexual orientation are indeed more fluid, might everyone benefit from deliberately thinking about what makes us feel good in our own skin? About what is queer about who we are and long to be? About *who* (a loving Creator), rather than *what* physical characteristic or gender performance, makes us beautiful and in God's image? This is not to deny differences and uniqueness, nor to claim "queerness" in ways that rob it of meaning for particular persons, no matter how fluid that meaning might be. It is rather to suggest Christians might stand in awe amid wondrous diversity and shed binary masculinities and femininities that no longer have a purpose in a community where, as Paul tells the Galatians, all are one in Christ Jesus. Christians might let imagination play with gospel narratives, liturgical rituals, and theological traditions to uncover what is wonderfully queer about the body of Christ.

Waking from the heteronormative dream may be scary, but it is worth it, most of all because LGBTQ young people living a nightmare are waiting. *Speaking OUT* and *Beyond Magenta* are full of young people "fashioned like diamonds" under the immense pressures of a heteronormative culture. They are coming together through new languages, presentations, and art forms. With eyes "dancing with all the possibilities," they are living into a new reality with different visions of beauty for all of us, with implications for individuals, intimate relationships, and wider communities.[25] The pressure of homophobia and heterosexism has forged powerful resilience in many young people, but it has tragically crushed others. Social support and solidarity can make the difference.

Dreaming, the Common Good, and LGBTQ Participation

Many young people use the language of rights and freedom to be and become whoever they want to be; they believe that these rights should not face undue interference from others—live and let live. But what is also evident in their narratives is a deep desire to be in right relationship with themselves, their families, friends, intimate others, and even with God. There is a deep desire to participate fully in social life without discrimination, harassment, or violence. Those of us who are floating in heterosexual and cisgender waters want nothing less for ourselves but benefit from social conditions that allow us to pursue our deepest desires, and even some of our shallower ones. The USCCB statement in response to the Trump administration's rescinding the Dear Colleague letter reads in part,

> The Catholic Church consistently affirms the inherent dignity of each and every human person and advocates for the well-being of all people, particularly the most vulnerable. Children, youth, and parents in these difficult situations deserve compassion, sensitivity, and respect. All of these can be expressed without infringing on legitimate concerns about privacy and security on the part of all young students and parents.[26]

If the common good is the sum of social conditions that allow all people, as individuals and as communities, to pursue flourishing more easily, then the threats to "legitimate" privacy and security that gender nonconformity poses would need to be substantiated. The suggestion that children are being harmed through policies like those recommended by the Dear Colleague letter reinforces stereotypes about LGBTQ persons. Homophobia and transphobia, like racism, sexism, poverty, and violence are contrary to the common good. The bishops' statement fails to acknowledge that "difficult situations" are frequently caused by homophobia and transphobia, and not dysphoria or some other pathology. It also fails to acknowledge that religious faith arguments are "increasingly cited as a legitimate rationale for institutionalized discrimination" and undermine the human dignity of LGBTQ persons.[27] LGBTQ persons are thereby excluded from the common good of the body of Christ not only because they are denied access to some of the fruits of life in community but also because their contributions to shaping that common life have been marginalized and silenced.

In the memoirs and narratives of LGBTQ youth, children, more than adults in many cases, are more intuitive, more welcoming, and more patient with ambiguity around issues of gender. I do not mean to idealize or romanticize children in any way. They can be cruel. But many narratives of LGBTQ persons suggest that their cruelty frequently comes at the instigation of adults. Many more children seem to know that the child called Jack in class is really Jane; that in spite of their parents' protestations, a sibling has always been a brother and not a sister; that a parent is a boy-girl; and that a parent who is a trans woman will remain Daddy, whom they love and trust.[28] This is not to minimize the real confusion and pain that individuals and families may experience, but rather to approach it as James and Evelyn Whitehead suggest when they write, "We do not search for a safe exit from our confusion but for a place to kneel."[29]

Should people be shown respect, compassion, and sensitivity? Yes. But the USCCB statement also continues to reinforce the idea that gender-nonconforming persons are passive recipients of compassion rather than active contributors to building the common good for all.[30] The Christian community should not mistake the comfort of those at ease in the dominant culture for the common good. What is needed now is not caution, but rather prudence on the part of a community that sustains inclusive practices of dreaming about the future church and is skilled in knowing how to do the right thing, for the right reason, at the right time, and in the right place. This is moral growth, and it is often uncomfortable.

What might this mean for our institutional and communal practices around sharing dreams for the future church? Researchers Marilyn J. Preston and Garrett Drew Hoffman demonstrate that colleges and universities are "built for and around the needs of the majority culture."[31] So first, communities of higher education, especially Catholic institutions, need to attend to the "hidden curriculum" on campus, the one that operates in spite of what our mission statements and campus community policies might say about inclusion of persons irrespective of their gender, gender identity, or sexual orientation.[32] Preston and Hoffman propose adopting the perspective of queer theory as it "requires we turn our analytical lens onto ourselves, the languages we use, and our own identities, to elucidate how we reinforce particular notions of differences and how we can move outside of these discourses to imagine new potentials."[33] In analyzing campus discourses (including written text and visual images) through a queer lens, they find that college campuses claim to desire an atmosphere of safety and community but frequently fail to promote activism for social change among LGBTQ students.[34] "Successful" LGBTQ students are considered those who emphasize similarity with their peers and educate around issues of tolerance and acceptance rather than engage in practices that disrupt social norms.

Similarly, churches must examine the hidden curriculum found in liturgical celebrations, ministry priorities, and religious education classes. Our communities should be intentional about visual signs and signifiers that expand and encourage imaginative engagement with the world and the Christian story rather than narrow the possibilities.

Second, churches and other institutions should create time and spaces for young people and adults to reflect, imagine, and share dreams and hopes around identity and relationship. Let these be ministries and communities of solidarity rather than support groups. Support and ally groups have an important place in our institutions, but they may be limited in terms of structural trans-formation, leaving the basic architecture intact. Communities of solidarity are asset-based and so might also be training grounds for broader social action around issues of gender justice.

In this way, the church of the future can ask with Luke Timo-thy Johnson, "What is God up to in the world of real bodies?" "What is God up to in the sexual experience of actual humans?" He advocates for a church that is "a 'safe space' for discernment by individuals and groups concerned about gender."[35] Again, close attention to LGBTQ narratives reveals young people who have wrestled with and celebrated the "mystery" of the body and who have suffered in body and spirit. They do not need the mystery of the body and suffering preached to them. They are proclaiming the gospel and visualizing a new and mysterious creation and so may be in a better position to instruct adults who have been shaped by binary thinking.

Third, our communities need time and space for dialogue about the Christian dream and how best to live that dream into reality. Charles Camosy offers sage advice for dialogue around challenging issues on college campuses that is applicable to our churches as well: "Avoid binary thinking; avoid thin and dismissive language; lead with what you are for."[36] Yet leading with what we are for, while it keeps a positive tone, is itself part of the binary for/against. As Johnson recommends, conversation could lead instead with a question. How are things with you? What is your story? What gives you joy and what causes you pain? What are your fears? What are your hopes and dreams? What relationships allow you to be whole and free? What can I do for you and with you? Finally, "What do you think God is up to in all of this?" Participants should be ready for answers that lead beyond the binaries: male/female, gay/straight, in/out, us/them, same/different, good/bad, right/wrong, individual/community, dream/reality.

As Johnson reminds us, using the words of Saint Paul, we are all being transformed in a physical world that is passing away. Our creation, our becoming, is ongoing in human history and in eternal life where the "new creation" might not be a static fixed point, but rather a dynamic bursting forth of new possibilities in the Spirit. This frees the Christian community to dream anew, to dream boldly, and dream along with persons in the community whose stories are different. The practice of dreaming requires patience with ambiguity and uncertainty and openness to God's surprises. Christians must not let the desire for greater clarity and nuance about sex and gender warp into a desire for uniformity masquerading as unity. The ethical practice of dreaming with LGBTQ young people gives us new eyes, not rose-colored glasses, but rather eyes to glimpse the precious beauty beyond our wildest dreams that is present in our LGBTQ siblings, even now.

Notes

[1] United States Conference of Catholic Bishops, www.usccb.org. US Departments of Justice and Education, "Dear Colleague," www2.ed.gov.

²Ta-Nehisi Coates, *Between the World and Me* (New York: Spiegel and Grau, 2015), citing James Baldwin.

³Susan Kulkin, *Beyond Magenta: Transgender Teens Speak Out* (Somerville, MA: Candlewick Press, 2014). Rachelle Lee Smith, *Speaking OUT: Queer Youth in Focus* (Oakland, CA: PM Press, 2014).

⁴Smith, *Speaking OUT*, 26.

⁵Ibid., 61.

⁶Ibid., 62.

⁷Ibid., 69.

⁸Kulkin, *Beyond Magenta*, 101.

⁹Smith, *Speaking OUT*, 81.

¹⁰Ibid., 59.

¹¹Kulkin, *Beyond Magenta*, 10.

¹²Ibid., 29.

¹³Ibid., 25.

¹⁴M. Alex Wagaman, "Self-Definition as Resistance: Understanding Identities among LGBTQ Emerging Adults," *Journal of LGBTQ Youth* 13, no. 3 (2016): 212.

¹⁵Kulkin, *Beyond Magenta*, 103.

¹⁶M. Alex Wagaman, "Promoting Empowerment Among LGBTQ Youth: A Social Justice Youth Development Approach," *Child Adolescent Social Work* 33 (2016): 396–97.

¹⁷Kate Klein, Alix Holtby, Katie Cook, and Robb Travers, "Complicating the Coming Out Narrative: Becoming Oneself in a Heterosexist and Cissexist World," *Journal of Homosexuality* 62 (2015): 316, 319.

¹⁸Stuart Roe, "Family Support Would Have Been Like Amazing: LGBTQ Youth Experiences with Parental and Family Support," *Family Journal: Counseling and Therapy for Couples and Families* 25, no. 1 (2017): 58.

¹⁹Marilyn J. Preston and Garrett Drew Hoffman, "Traditionally Heterogendered Institutions: Discourses Surrounding LGBTQ College Students," *Journal of LGBTQ Youth* 12 (2015): 64–86.

²⁰Klein et al., "Complicating the Coming Out Narrative," 310–13.

²¹Tonya D. Callaghan, "Young, Queer, and Catholic: Youth Resistance to Homophobia in Catholic Schools," *Journal of LGBTQ Youth* 13, no. 3 (2016): 281, 284.

²²Coates, *Between the World and Me*, 10–11.

²³Ibid.

²⁴Ibid., 115.

²⁵Ibid., 118.

²⁶See USCCB, http://www.usccb.org/news/2017/17-045.cfm. James Martin, SJ, has taken up the bishops' commitment to compassion, sensitivity, and respect and offers pastoral recommendations for what this commitment looks like in concrete practice. See his *Building a Bridge: How the Catholic Church and the LGBTQ Community Can Enter into a Relationship of Respect, Compassion, and Sensitivity* (New York: Harper One, 2017).

²⁷Callaghan, "Young, Queer, and Catholic," 271.

²⁸Amy Ellis Nutt, *Becoming Nicole: The Transformation of an American*

Family (New York: Random House, 2015); Jennifer Finney Boylan, *She's Not There: A Life in Two Genders* (New York: Crown, 2003); J. Jack Halberstam, *Gaga Feminism: Sex, Gender, and the End of Normal* (Boston: Beacon Press, 2012).

[29]James D. Whitehead and Evelyn Eaton Whitehead, "Transgender Lives: From Bewilderment to God's Extravagance," *Pastoral Psychology* 63 (2014): 184.

[30]Martin's *Building a Bridge* highlights the need for reciprocal respect, compassion, and sensitivity.

[31]Preston and Hoffman, "Traditionally Heterogendered Institutions," 66.

[32]Ibid., 67.

[33]Ibid.

[34]Ibid., 73.

[35]David Cloutier and Luke Timothy Johnson, "The Church and Transgender Identity: Some Cautions, Some Possibilities," *Commonweal*, March 10, 2017, 15.

[36]Charles Camosy, "Teaching Difficult Conversations: Navigating the Tension," *Conversations on Jesuit Higher Education* 51 (Spring 2017): 26–27.

21st-Century Temptations

Nones, Polls, and the Allure of the View from Above

Nicholas Mayrand

This essay exposes problems lurking around contemporary appeals to the so-called "rise of the nones" and assesses the relevance for theologians operating within the context of US Catholicism.[1] The first section of the paper briefly introduces the murky conversation that swirls around America's "nones." The second features a critique of the none category from two angles, beginning with some analysis of the limitations associated with modern polling practices before turning to some serious concerns about the detached view from above that polling data encourages. The final section pinpoints some implications for the contemporary practice of theology, affirming calls to proceed by attending to messy particulars rather than retreating into broad universals.

Blame Those Nones?

In 2017 *Time* magazine created a stir with an article that recounted a property mogul's advice to young people, provocatively titled "Millionaire to Millennials: Stop Buying Avocado Toast If You Want to Buy a Home."[2] American millennials were thrilled to learn that the reason they have yet to buy houses can be traced to their debilitating addiction to trendy fruits that taste suspiciously like vegetables. The problem with this diagnosis of young people's problems was not hard to pinpoint; a slew of angry responses from millennials predictably made the usual rounds (even as many acknowledged that paying $18 for avocado toast is indeed ridiculous).

This essay will argue that something similarly unhelpful has been happening with recent deployments of the so-called "rise of the nones." For example, a 2016 issue in the journal *Teaching Theology & Religion* begins with the author's disgruntled reflections on his courses' waning numbers and the growing presence of "religiously indifferent" students.[3] The author bemoans the fact that his course evaluations are becoming increasingly populated by "mundane assessments" like "boring." This phenomenon, the author confidently explains, "can be traced to the rise of the nones" and the decline of the "religiously invested student." He then proceeds through a litany of polling data to support his conviction that millennials are narcissistic, materialistic, politically disconnected, and guilty of prioritizing leisure over hard work; he concludes that "there is no doubt that religion is of decreasing importance to this generation."[4]

This scholar is far from alone in making these assessments; a pervasive decline narrative undergirds many analyses of data on young people, particularly the young people who have been classified as "nones" because of their responses to pollsters' questions about religious preference. These nones, we are informed again and again, make up more than one third of the millennial generation in the United States. Polling data, we are repeatedly told, shows that as the number of professed Christians in America dwindles, very few nones seek a spiritual home in a traditional religious institution.[5] Perhaps the fabled twentieth-century thesis connecting modernization to inevitable secularization is finally beginning to have its day in the United States after all?

Keen observers, however, have pushed back against this tendency to point to the nones as a symbol of doomsday decline. Kaya Oakes's *The Nones Are Alright* stands as a manifesto in this regard. Oakes's interviewees provide human faces for anomalies in the polling data that undermine the notion that nones are a marauding band of religiously indifferent, hedonist narcissists.[6] Sociologists have been pondering these anomalies for fifty years now, beginning back in 1968 with Glenn Vernon's recognition that most nones were not atheists, which led him to call for a terminology shift from "nones" to "independents" in order to affirm that "nones" were not necessarily a-religious creatures, just as political independents were not apolitical beings.[7] More recently, a team of researchers including Robert Putnam noted that the nones are an incredibly fluid, heterogeneous group that resists hasty generalizations (e.g., charges like "religiously indifferent").[8]

William Portier has gone even further, arguing that demographic research on millennials and nones has reached a saturation point, that generalizations abound, and that explaining the shifts involved is "more a matter of speculative culture critique than demographic precision."[9] Portier, borrowing a phrase from John Henry Newman, suggests that to call someone such a label is to make them a "logarithm of their [true] self."[10] An autobiographical essay in the *Christian Century* provides a fitting illustration of Portier's point. Teri McDowell Ott, chaplain at Monmouth College, relates a chastening experience with a student named Thomas. Well versed in the polling data on the nones, Ott went into a coffee meeting with Thomas under the impression that she surely was going to be chatting with a none. She knew Thomas was from rural Illinois, that he described himself as interested in men, and that he was not one to show up to any campus ministry programming. Ott was astonished to find that Thomas happily called himself a Catholic and was quite willing to describe the church as his home despite his many disagreements with its theology and an admittedly spotty Mass attendance record. Ott found herself repeatedly pressing Thomas, but Thomas's responses pushed back against her expectations again and again. Eventually, Ott concludes that her problem was rather simple: "I thought I knew more about Thomas than I did."[11]

It is difficult to fault Ott for expecting to find a none in her situation. The Pew Forum and the many commentators who rely on its data repeatedly tell us that one in three millennials are nones, making "none" the largest religious group for the millennial generation. Christian groups are beginning to craft outreach programs to the nones, sensing a new mission field in their own backyards.[12] It would seem that theologians would be wise to attend to what these pollsters are saying in order to develop a better sense of where their students are coming from. I will be arguing, however, that now is a time for great caution for two related reasons. The first has to do with the practices of modern polling institutions, while the second relates to the dangers that accompany the view from above that polling data encourages.

The Great Temptations of the Opinion Poll

Buried in the fine print of a public opinion poll report is an important number: the poll's response rate. In a recent book on the polling industry (published prior to polling's 2016 presidential election debacle), sociologist Robert Wuthnow recounts a telling exchange that occurred at a 1996 panel discussion at the Roper Center for Public Opinion Research among three of the nation's leading pollsters, George Gallup Jr., Burns Roper, and Helen Crossley. While they differed in reasons why it existed, all three acknowledged the problem:

> Roper was especially concerned about the practice of reporting that results from a sample of a certain size were accurate within a particular range, such as plus or minus 3.2 percent. "It's not true [that] you can tell within 3.2 percent what the American public thinks," he said. "Actually, you can tell within 3.2 percent what the *cooperating* American public says and that's different. Thirty percent of the public doesn't cooperate. You don't know much about them."[13]

Roper admits here that polls really only tell us about people who are willing to participate in polls, which he believed to be about 70 percent of the American public. Keeping this point in mind, let us turn to the Pew surveys that fueled the explosion of interest in the nones during the last decade. On the surface, Pew's results appear rather impressive with sample sizes in excess of 35,000 people in both 2007 and 2014. A closer look at their methodology, however, reveals dismally low response rates of 24 percent in 2007 and under 11 percent in 2014.[14] Roper was concerned that just 70 percent of the public was willing to participate in polls, which for him meant that little could be said about the other 30 percent. But by 2014, nearly 90 percent of the people that Pew approached declined to participate, meaning, in Roper's words, "You don't know much about them."

Things grow murkier when we consider the challenges associated with polling millennials in particular. The 2014 Pew study relied solely on telephone calls to landlines and cell phones. But as many have bemoaned, texting, Snapchat, FaceTime, etc. have largely replaced the regular telephone call for younger Americans. Ian Bogost's fascinating piece in the *Atlantic* argues that design decisions may have more to do with this cultural shift than we realize; cell phones today are primarily designed to be carried, tapped, and pocketed, but not spoken into. As Bogost puts it, "True, iMessage and Facebook Messenger might seem more aloof and impersonal than calling by voice, but today's smartphone user is right to identify those experiences as the sensual, tactical [*sic*] successors to the telephone handset with its duplex of truncated 3 kHz voices echoing inside."[15] The point for our purposes is this: telephone polls are not suited for getting responses from the millennial generation. Ask millennials whether they ever answer phone calls from unrecognized phone numbers, let alone from the people they know. Given that a Pew pollster's number would fall into that unknown phone number category, it is a wonder that Pew found even a single millennial to poll.

The desire to turn to polls for clarity is not an easy one to shake, no matter how questionable the methods involved with producing representative samples. A range of brilliant scholars from Ludwig Wittgenstein to Michel Foucault have written about the human craving for generalizations, the desire for objectivity, and the eagerness to take up positions that allow us to view the world around us from above, controlling and reforming while avoiding the messiness of that world and the people in it. Running deeper than issues of response rates are the dangers that accompany this detached view from above, dangers that have been intertwined with the use of polling ever since polling's early forms emerged more than a century ago.

The polling industry and its none category are in many ways the offspring of the Progressive Era's social survey movement.[16] Enjoying generous funding from wealthy industry magnates like John D. Rockefeller, organizations in the early 1900s set out to reform the increasingly crowded northern cities. Influential religious groups like the New York City Federation of Churches and Christian Workers led the charge; these groups began to design and carry out increasingly detailed social surveys so that they could craft programs of civic evangelism. Their survey data allowed them to construct a new strategic view from above as they "scientifically" measured the efficacy of their evangelism efforts. For the first time, the religiously unaffiliated members of America's cities were systematically counted and concretized as a social problem to be solved through civic evangelism. For example, the aforementioned New York City Federation of Churches and Christian Workers was able to brag that its programs had dramatically reduced the percentage of religiously unaffiliated in their city.[17]

Unfortunately, the Progressive Era's deployment of social surveys in pursuit of its reforms has an underbelly that cannot be ignored. In his acclaimed book, *Stamped from the Beginning*, Ibram X. Kendi argues that Sir Francis Galton, cousin of Charles Darwin, provided the tools necessary for the flourishing of the social survey movement: "Galton created the concepts of correlation and regression toward the mean and blazed the trail for the use of questionnaires and surveys to collect data."[18] This might seem like little more than a bit of trivia about the so-called "father of modern statistics," but Sir Francis Galton's other nickname provides reason for extreme caution. Also known as the "father of eugenics," Galton used his statistical methods to, as Kendi writes, "popularize the myth that parents passed on hereditary traits like intelligence that environment could not alter."[19] Galton proceeded to advise governments to either rid the world of naturally unselected peoples or at least stop them from reproducing.

The myth at the heart of Galton's eugenics idea carried devastating implications in a US context marked by pervasive racist ideas. According to Kendi, Darwin's *Descent of Man* stopped short of Galton's bold eugenics, but Darwin's chilling comments about how the "civilized races" had "extended, and are now everywhere extending, their range, so as to take the place of the lower races" were well received in the United States: "Both assimilationists and segregationalists hailed *Descent of Man*. Assimilationists read Darwin as saying Blacks could one day evolve into White civilization; segregationalists read him as saying Blacks were bound for extinction."[20] Of course, it is possible that the social surveyors who deployed Galton's tools to carry out their reforming work were able to do so without allowing dangerous racist ideas to influence their endeavors; in fact, Wuthnow's aforementioned book's silence regarding race can leave one with the impression that this was indeed the case.

A closer look at Wuthnow's social surveying protagonists, however, shows that their "objective" positions did not always protect them from racist ideas that affected their work. For example, Rev. Walter Laidlaw, a leading social surveyor for the New York Federation, included "colonization movements" (i.e., movements advocating for the removal of Black Americans to places like Liberia) in his list of appropriate social service endeavors that represented "new forms of altruism's applications" as he praised churches for their role, stating that "it is an encouraging sign of the times that the church is not holding herself aloof from this generous humanitarianism. Genetically, of course, she is the mother of it."[21] Even the social survey movement's stalwart, W. E. B. Du Bois, was unable to escape the tentacles of the pernicious racist ideas that helped fuel the era's drive for reform. Du Bois's survey of Philadelphia's Seventh Ward was published in 1899 as *The Philadelphia Negro*, now considered a foundational sociology text. Antiracist in many ways, the book nevertheless characterized Black Americans as a social problem, reflecting Du Bois's belief at the time that the most important step toward progress between the races "lies in the correction of immorality, crime, and laziness among the Negros themselves, which still remains as a heritage of slavery."[22]

The point of this account of the social survey movement is not to vilify its protagonists as racists whose work must be summarily dismissed. The key here is to see that these social surveyors were forging a new way of observing others from above the fray in efforts to identify and solve what they believed to be social problems. Imbued with an aura of objectivity, their enterprise was nevertheless entangled with the racist ideas of the day. From their new vantage point, armed with statistics, powerful people and organizations were able to craft new ways to categorize human beings as problem groups, whether it be the "Black criminal," as Kendi's work documents, or the "religiously unaffiliated." These abstractions may make it much easier to craft strategies from above but they also reduce complex human beings to percentages and can lead to disastrous errors if based on flawed methods, as Kendi shows was the case with the statistics on Black crime that fueled the spread of the image of the menacing Black criminal.

In sum, the "religiously unaffiliated" category, which would soon become the "none" category as national polling grew out of the social survey movement, is an abstraction born of an ambiguous (at best) desire for reforms that can be carried out from a safe distance from positions of power. This drive for quantifiable, detached reform chafes against what we might call the drive for encounter that Pope Francis has been stressing as a central component of Christian witness. The abstract none category and the accompanying representative sketches that scholars like to draw based on the data—male, young, democratic/independent, non-Southern, etc.—may have some limited uses, but they can easily function as an excuse for avoiding the messier task of engaging real people whose stories will inevitably fail to align with the expectations that those portraits of the nones lead us to expect. These abstractions may help one rationalize increasingly disappointing teacher evaluations, but at what cost?

Implications for Theologians in Today's US Catholic Context

Polling data possesses a strange allure when it comes to learning about generations that seem different from one's own. This essay has been building a case for a concerted turnaway from that temptation. If polling data is not the answer to understanding others, particularly younger generations, then how might theologians proceed in a way that better connects with the hopes, fears, and questions of the younger Americans they encounter in churches and classrooms?

I submit that this critique of the so-called none category serves as another affirmation of the theological turnaway from broad, abstract categories toward the messy particulars of the lives of the people that we encounter. This turn to the minutiae of concrete human lives draws its vitality from the paradigmatic embrace of the particular: God's incarnation in the human person of Jesus of Nazareth. The scandalous particularity at the heart of the mystery of the Incarnation stands as a constant reminder that the Gospel does not take root through the imposition of broad norms and reforms on faceless, sweeping categories of people. Instead, God's enfleshment introduces a novel way for humans to join together in a love that obliterates the boundaries that come along with the labels that humans tend to create. As Charles Taylor, following Ivan Illich's profound theological reflections on the Good Samaritan parable, puts it:

> The enfleshment of God extends outward, through such new links as the Samaritan makes with the Jew, into a network, which we call the Church. But this is a network, not a categorical grouping; that is, it is a skein of relations which link particular, unique, enfleshed people to each other, rather than a grouping of people together on the grounds of their sharing some important property.[23]

In other words, God's turn to fully embrace our human particularities stands as a clear warning against the temptation to settle for generalized categories that allow us to theorize from a distance. Instead, the reality of God's enfleshment calls us to foster a new willingness to attend more closely to the particular experiences of the people who are right in front of us, including those that pollsters would like us to dismiss as nones.

This renewed focus on messy particulars does not entail a total surrender of the notion of profound theological truth with universal resonances. For a long time, many theologians have been calling their colleagues to take seriously the daily lived realities of particular human beings as the starting point for theological reflection that may have broader implications. For example, Virgilio Elizondo writes in a famous text on liberation theology that "the more universal one tries to be, the less one has to offer to others. Conversely, the more particular a thought is, the more its universal implications become evident."[24] More recently, scholars such as M. Shawn Copeland and Willie James Jennings have argued convincingly that the US context still suffers from the wounds of its colonialist moment, wounds that hide behind abstract categories masquerading as human universals. The antidote to these distortions comes in the form of privileged attention to the lives of the people who witness to the inadequacy of general categories that do violence to those that they claim to describe. For example, Copeland's work argues that theologies in the US context that proceed with generalized notions of the human tend to reflect the experiences of only the small subset of affluent, white males; these theologies often have very little to say to those who do not count as "human" in that limited sense. Copeland's corrective response to this problem thus posits a preferential-option-inspired turn to the daily realities of poor women of color.[25]

The point here, of course, is not to equate the status of poor women of color with those who might be mistakenly dismissed as vapid, indifferent nones. While this essay is indeed a call for a new attentiveness to the particularities of the lives of today's younger Americans, this endeavor must unfold in an intersectional manner with proposals like Copeland's, complementing without diluting them. In other words, this essay is not suggesting that the misunderstood nones should replace poor women of color as the privileged subject of theological reflection; instead, the key argument here is that the move to embrace lived daily realities in theological reflection should also extend to the way that theologians approach America's younger generations. In sum, the ongoing, challenging legacy of the Incarnation serves as a reminder that theologians belong not in the rarefied air of abstract categories and polling data, but down in the beautiful mess of human particularities.

Notes

[1]Special thanks to those who offered feedback and financial support during the course of formulating this essay, particularly the University of Dayton's Graduate Student Summer Fellowship program for the latter and Dr. Brad Kallenberg for the former.

[2]Jennifer Calfas, "Millionaire to Millennials: Stop Buying Avocado Toast If You Want to Buy a Home," *Time.com*, May 15, 2017, time.com/money.

[3]Randall Reed, "A Book for None? Teaching Biblical Studies to Millennial Nones," *Teaching Theology & Religion* 19, no. 2 (April 2016): 154–74.

[4]Ibid., 158.

[5]These assessments of the nones often trace back to data from Pew Forum polls that have been carried out over the past decade and popularized in columns in national media sources like the *Washington Post* and *New York Times*. For example, David S. Gutterman and Andrew R. Murphy primarily rely on Pew data as they talk of the "not secular, not seeking" character of the religiously unaffiliated in *Political Religion and Religious Politics* (New York: Routledge, 2016), 113–15. Elizabeth Drescher also invokes the Pew survey data regarding the nones' lack of interest in returning to any one particular religious tradition in *Choosing Our Religion: The Spiritual Lives of America's Nones* (Oxford: Oxford University Press, 2016), 24–25. In the fall of 2016, the Public Religion Research Institute (PRRI) released a report summarizing data from their recent polling project, "Exodus: Why Americans Are Leaving Religion—And Why They're Unlikely to Come Back," that has in turn spawned another set of think pieces in popular media outlets about the rising nones' indifference toward organized religious groups.

[6]Kaya Oakes, *The Nones Are Alright* (Maryknoll, NY: Orbis Books, 2015).

[7]Glenn Vernon, "The Religious 'Nones': A Neglected Category," *Journal for the Scientific Study of Religion* 7, no. 2 (1968): 219–29. Vernon concluded here that "the 'none' label carries negative evaluative implications, unwarranted by the limited research, and unproductive of further research" (229).

[8]Chaeyoon Lim, Carol Ann MacGregor, and Robert D. Putnam, "Secular and Liminal: Discovering Heterogeneity among Religious Nones," *Journal for the Scientific Study of Religion* 49, no. 4 (2010): 596–618.

[9]William Portier, "Newman, Millennials, and Teaching Comparative Theology," in *Comparative Theology in the Millennial Classroom*, ed. Mara Brecht and Reid B. Locklin (New York: Routledge, 2016), 42.

[10]Ibid., 41.

[11]Teri McDowell Ott, "Reflections of a College Chaplain: In the Realm of the Nones," *Christian Century*, January 6, 2016, 29.

[12]For example, see James Emery White, *The Rise of the Nones: Understanding and Reaching the Religiously Unaffiliated* (Grand Rapids, MI: Baker Books, 2014).

[13]Robert Wuthnow, *Inventing American Religion: Polls, Surveys, and the Tenuous Quest for a Nation's Faith* (New York: Oxford University Press, 2015), 156.

[14]The response rates are recorded in the reports on the polls. See page 117 of the report on the 2007 study and page 97 of the report on the 2014 study.

[15]Ian Bogost, "Don't Hate the Phone Call, Hate the Phone," *TheAtlantic.com*, August 12, 2015, https://www.theatlantic.com/.

[16]See Wuthnow, *Inventing American Religion*, chap. 2.

[17]Ibid., 20.

[18]Ibram X. Kendi, *Stamped from the Beginning* (New York: Nation Books, 2016), 210.

[19]Ibid.

[20]Ibid., 211.

[21]Walter Laidlaw, "A Plea and Plan for a Cooperative Church Parish System in Cities," *American Journal of Sociology* 3 (May 1898): 796.

[22]W. E. B. Du Bois, "The Conservation of Races," as cited in Kendi, *Stamped from the Beginning*, 283.

[23]Charles Taylor, *A Secular Age* (Cambridge, MA: Belknap Press of Harvard University Press, 2007), 739.

[24]Virgilio Elizondo, "Toward an American-Hispanic Theology of Liberation in the U.S.A.," in *Irruption of the Third World*, ed. Virginia Fabella and Sergio Torres (Maryknoll, NY: Orbis Books, 1983), 54–55.

[25]M. Shawn Copeland, *Enfleshing Freedom: Body, Race, and Being* (Minneapolis: Fortress Press, 2010).

Redeeming Trauma

An Agenda for Theology Fifteen Years On

John N. Sheveland

The most recent Vatican statement on child sexual abuse was delivered on February 12, 2015, by Sean Cardinal O'Malley, head of the Pontifical Commission for the Protection of Minors, at a consistory gathering of cardinals. The statement considers "best practices" for the prevention of child sexual abuse and refers to "damage, both spiritual and psychological" caused by abuse.[1]

This essay tests the appropriateness and scope of what O'Malley means by "best practices" up against the recent theological scholarship grappling with trauma studies. While the cardinal and commission are to be affirmed and supported in their efforts, the commission would benefit both from this literature and a robust commitment to address sexual abuse not only through the lens of prevention but, more fundamentally, through communal pastoral care. Without a decisive turn toward communally shared pastoral care informed by trauma studies, the prospects for ecclesial right relationship and healing appear bleak. Best practices require a shift in the paradigm that describes harm done to survivors—from mere "damage" to *trauma*. More than word choice is at stake, for we learn from trauma studies about the ubiquitous "temptation to cover over—to elide—the suffering."[2] Once the features of trauma are located in the concrete lives of persons and understood as bearing upon the community and the future, appropriate redemptive practices can be brought to bear.[3] One redemptive practice would be to shift from a bilateral mode of relating, in which the pope, other officials, or parish priests apologize to survivors, seek forgiveness from survivors, or even meet and spend short clips of time with survivors, to a new way of being church in which the total body of the church understands itself as a dynamically interdependent community vulnerable to and affiliated with the lives of those facing traumatic experience of any kind.[4]

I came to this material as someone immersed in graduate studies in Boston when the abuse scandal broke there in 2002 but who, like many, may have been saddened and shaken but not enough to integrate the experience within my study or career path. My response over these years may mirror the church's: deeply felt if delayed, and inattentive to the precise form of violence revealed as trauma and to the demands this violence exerts on the community. This changed fundamentally when, as a tenured faculty member, I developed and taught a course on religion and violence for the first time in 2014. With ISIS seizing the news cycle I knew it would be one of several deep-dive case studies we would explore, but my experience with interreligious dialogue reminded me of Edmund Chia's criteria for good dialogue articulated after Benedict XVI's Regensburg Address, namely, that it is better to lift up irrational or violent examples of religious commitment from one's own tradition than to cherry pick conveniently from others'.[5] I chose sexual abuse precisely as a Roman Catholic case study of religious violence alongside ISIS and Hindu nationalist violence against Muslims, even as the developing literature on religious violence gives scant attention to predatory sexual abuse, much less clergy sexual abuse. That literature favors group-on-group violence, ethnoreligious nationalisms, and violent political extremism.[6] I did not know what I was getting myself or my students into.

We swiftly discovered that sexual abuse was anything but violence "lite." The trauma we studied, alongside the conditions of its possibility, functioned on the one hand to grow our capacity to recognize cynical manipulation of religious categories, symbols, and power differentials by predator priests to groom, isolate, and intimidate their victims. On the other hand, we glimpsed the trauma inflicted on the psychological landscape of survivors such that the violent acts continue to be experienced psychologically as intrusive, threatening, and unmanageable in the present and future tenses. Traumatic wounding functions as a present, progressive, and continuing experience. It is what Shelly Rambo calls "the suffering that remains."[7] When we began looking at the material, we did not know just how violent it would be, how overwhelming it would be for victims and indeed some students and at times myself, nor that the framework of death would be fundamentally appropriate. The professor did not anticipate the numbers of students who would find their own traumatic wounding triggered through our study. These chilling moments revealed our learning environment to be a posttraumatic university and posttraumatic church, converting the classroom into a sacred space, a *memoria passionis* of the victims studied and of the victims studying.

Nor did I anticipate in 2014 that the church's response would remain in its early stages, not markedly progressed beyond John Paul II's rather symptomatic 2002 address to the US cardinals gathered in Rome in the wake of the US scandal. Positive developments in O'Malley's 2015 address include improved commitments to protect minors and to communicate cross-culturally among the bishops' conferences, transparency, and zero-tolerance, and a clear refusal of the mythology that abuse was to be hidden because it caused scandal.

Important as they are, these developments do not communicate sustained realization of the church—as the body of Christ—existing as a posttraumatic community in which ministry and right relationship have become core ecclesial commitments. We do not see appropriate concern translated into ministry toward, with, and by persons suffering from traumatic experience. Even for this new Pontifical Commission and its most recent statement, survivor experience remains somewhat invisible on the periphery.[8]

The first guideline contained in O'Malley's address reiterates the 2011 CDF requirement that bishops' conferences provide the name of a local contact person in their country with whom Rome could liaise. O'Malley writes: "Unfortunately some countries have not yet responded, and others have presented norms that seem too vague or ineffective." While O'Malley's frankness is appreciated, it is of concern that some or many global bishops' conferences are unwilling to produce the name of a local contact, and that some continue to think the problem is solely an American one. This admission implies cultural and ecclesial challenges in the very recognition of sexual abuse as a problem. This is particularly disappointing given that Pope Francis's precise charge to the commission includes collaboration with episcopal conferences: "Our task is to advise the Holy Father, to recommend and promote best practices and procedures, to promote education and prevention in the Holy See and in the Episcopal conferences throughout the world." The much harder work of pastoral presence and care is not part of the commission's charge, nor a focal point in O'Malley's address. Moreover, O'Malley's curious clarification that clergy sexual abuse "is not a Catholic problem or even a clerical problem" but "a human problem" somewhat belies established facts, for instance that abuses in Roman Catholic parishes outnumbered other denominations, which raises questions. One must ask which understandings of church and community, parish, and priest help explain the disproportionate preponderance of predator priests and child victims. What are the mechanisms by which bishops' conferences are enabled or allowed to disregard the CDF's instruction from 2011 to appoint a person from within each country to liaise with Rome, which lacked compliance as late as February 2015?

As well, O'Malley's words are in tension with the historical record when he indicates that Pope Francis has committed "to address the errors of the past and to continue Pope Benedict's and St. Pope John Paul's initiatives to remove abusive priests from ministry." To recall but one example, the notorious case of Marcial Maciel demonstrates that the prior popes struggled to remove known abusers from ministry. Maciel was the Mexican priest who founded the Legionaries of Christ and was perhaps the greatest fund-raiser of the twentieth century. He was openly celebrated by John Paul II even after fellow Legionaries like Father Juan Vaca disclosed in a letter to the Vatican Maciel's decades of horrendous abuse of many children, which included his own biological children. John Paul's enthusiasm for Maciel, along with support from Cardinal Angelo Sodano, may have impeded Benedict from disciplining or defrocking Maciel even with damning evidence in hand. Maciel died without having to confess or apologize and without his victims having the chance to reconfigure their own traumatic experience within a listening community modeling witness and truth-telling. Pope Francis spoke more adequately in a Spanish-language interview with Univision in which he referred to Maciel as "una persona muy enferma"—a very sick person.[9]

Additional guidelines in the address include passing references to the following: that the abuse scandal is second to none in priority; that pastoral concern for the protection of children is a requirement for a bishop; that pastors "be available" to meet with victims; that the commission has been "in contact with best practices and well-credentialed professionals throughout the world." Neither the best practices nor the professionals are elaborated on or described.

Section 2 of O'Malley's address, "Education Programs," and section 3, "Various Initiatives," report on a series of *aspirations*. This list of actions the commission hopes to accomplish includes no pledge to do so or a timeline for completion. The document says that the commission:

1. "*would like* to hold seminars on child protection leadership for the Curia to help them understand how serious this topic is for the life of the church";
2. *would like* to contribute instructional sessions for recently named bishops;
3. *proposes* to develop recommendations of policies to help seminaries screen candidates and develop human formation programs;
4. *hopes* that established best practices [unnamed] could be incorporated into the *Ratio* of seminary formation, and *hopes* to work with the head of security and papal bodyguard to develop child protection policies and reporting practices for the Vatican City State;
5. *hopes* to develop a definition of what it is to "fail to protect minors";
6. *would like* to design a day of prayer for the universal church comparable to the day of fasting observed for Syria;
7. *hopes* to address best practices for the outreach and care of perpetrators, their families, and their colleagues;
8. has *begun to reach out* to international Catholic funding programs to make child protection a priority, and has requested funds to train within the church;
9. "*wishes* to provide guidelines and best practices for the care and spiritual needs of victims and their families." (Emphases mine.)

This last, mentioned in passing and not resumed in an address otherwise focused on prevention, rather needs to become the axial center around which rotates everything else the church does as church in response to what has been called the "soul-murder" that is child sexual abuse.[10]

One can be faithfully critical of this response without personally criticizing O'Malley or the commission or the Curia standing behind them as persons. Even so, why would the head of this Pontifical Commission not employ the category of trauma, especially with the address's refrain of "best practices" but dearth of examples given?

Once we lean into the loss of personal self, there is no return to the *status quo ante*. We do well to consider unnoticed habits of shaming which are core to the traumatic experience and which communities perpetuate as a distancing mechanism to avoid the discomfort of encounter. Theologically, what are the features of trauma that need to be underscored to envision redemptive possibilities? What are the characteristics of traumatic wounding in need of redeeming? What are the root causes in us as persons and institutions driving the discomfort, given that we ourselves are dysfunctional and in need of redeeming? Yet more: Can we pivot away from the consideration of trauma as individual or isolated toward the contextualization of all traumatic wounding within cycles of history, where trauma is passed from generation to generation within families, institutions, states, and indeed global regions?[11] If so, we have moved away from traumatic experience considered as a mere personal challenge for some to a more honest recognition of the antecedent conditions and total impact within communities so affected. Trauma must be addressed as a *social* problem with concentric circles of interdependent influence and effects, exemplifying the truth of solidarity by drawing all into its orbit.[12] Trauma poses challenges to the church as the body of Christ precisely as a body, not merely to individuals.[13]

Alistair McFadyen, an Anglican theologian in the UK, contributed a constructive theological response in 2000 by focusing on the pathological dynamics that become internalized in the abused child. In his courage to focus on sites of trauma less as single events and more as a dynamic that repeats, McFadyen's pivot is of enormous pastoral significance. He suggests that sin-talk describes pathological dynamics arising in victims that foreclose their own integral development as persons. He summarizes in this way the chilling concrete "pathology" that can develop:

1. The abuse entails an abuse of trust and power which exploits age-related differentials, resulting in the distortion of the child's need for intimacy, affirmation, trust, and security.
2. Abuse is not best construed as acts with consequences but as an "expansive dynamic of distorted relationality" affecting all of the child's relationships.[14]
3. The core dynamic of abuse is "entrapment and isolation," neutering the victim's sense of agency.
4. Traumatic confusion concerning the nature of reality ensues.
5. A particular confusion is the incorporation of the child's own active agency in psychologically "accommodating" to the abuse and in keeping it secret.
6. Such abuse easily leads to the radical distortion of the very core of self-identity, which then becomes the means of transmission of the consequences of abuse into an "entire ecology of relating," even trans-generationally. These effects epitomize the meaning of "sin" as the loss of ability to will, the social situation of all sin, and the force of "inheritance" as a qualifier to sin.[15]

To redeem traumatic wounding first requires sustained conversation with trauma studies and with persons affected by traumatic experience. These conversations will help us name those distortions of life and well-being deeply lodged within persons and communities that stand in need of communal redemptive address. Although Shelly Rambo correctly refers to trauma as "a largely untheologized site," we can call to mind theologians who are contributing book-length publications to this area.[16] In addition to Reformed theologian Shelly Rambo and Anglican Alistair McFadyen, others include Anglican theologian Susan Shooter, Reformed theologians Serene Jones and Deborah van Deusen Hunsinger, Lutheran liturgical theologian Dirk Lange, and Catholic theologians Jennifer Beste, Elisabeth Vasko, and Julia Feder. These are—to the best of my knowledge at this writing—the theologians who have brought theological disciplines and construction to bear on traumatic experience.[17] They are truly impressive but small in number, whereas the problem to be addressed is ubiquitous and overwhelming by definition. One notices the missing demographic of male Catholic theologians. What are we doing? Our absence in this literature needs attention and may corroborate the worry that mainstream feminist theological principles have yet to gain satisfactory traction across the theological guild, with the strength of their inquiry into power, authority, representation, relationality, marginality, suffering, and mutuality being crucial to a theology of trauma and to the very recognition of its need.

I conclude with a brief consideration of Susan Shooter's ethnographic scholarship and suggest that it establishes the theological agenda and also the possibility of ecclesial authenticity, which is why the painstaking work of Shooter and others, not to mention survivor witness disclosed in PBS Frontline films such as *The Silence* and *Secrets of the Vatican*, is so important. Vulnerability to these forms of witness is a requisite first step.

From her interviews with nine women, Shooter gleans three concepts relevant for healing. We do well to honor and translate the wisdom of these women into communal best practices. The first concept displayed in the women—realization of "God's timeless presence"—helped the women heal past memories of abandonment and fear connected with the abuse while also helping to prepare them for difficulties ahead. Some respondents spoke of times when it seemed God was absent, but they spoke also of *acquiring* the understanding that God had been there even if they had not felt so at the time of the abuse.[18] From this concept we learn from survivors about being redeemed, namely, hope in the development of new understandings about their own traumatic experience so that intrusive memories and feelings of fear and abandonment might become reconfigured by a growing awareness of the loving intimacy of the God who always remained. Pastoral care does well to develop this form of hope where previously it was absent, with its clarification that God holds the wounded in unconditional positive regard before and beyond all harm, shame, and nonrecognition. This hope is spelled out in the words of Lydia: "I wouldn't want you to think this doesn't still hurt and I float over the top. No, things hurt and hurt and hurt, but they hurt with him and not without him."[19]

The second form of knowledge Shooter observes in the survivors she discusses is "transformation," and it builds on the understanding of God as permanently present and loving to survivors not by preventing violence but by providing spiritual resources to endure. One woman, Naomi, spoke of these spiritual resources in this way:

At the depths of the situation, I'd written [in my journal], OK God you're not going to bail us out, I'm sure you'll still be there for me when it's over. *When it's over.* I didn't say to him, be with me *in it*, because I hadn't learnt that. I remember saying right, I'll drown, that's it, I'll give up, the waters will go over my head, and if I am still alive at the end of this you can have what's left. But I did learn that he was walking along the bottom of the river with me, holding my hand.[20]

In Christian community, the assurance of God's loving presence cannot be merely taught or told, but Naomi's wisdom of "transformation" can be repeatedly and profoundly reinforced through habits of communal relating that bear all things by denying as lies any projections of shame on others who isolate, minimize, or otherwise disinvite relationship with survivors. Denying the lie includes providing pedagogical and spiritual opportunities for persons in community to see memories of their own traumatic experience transformed.

"Knowing ministry," the third form of knowledge Shooter gleans from her interviews, is the disclosure that transformation "inspires godly practice in the survivor's own ministry, that is to say, the survivor's pastoral relationship with others reflects God's healing relationship with her."[21] Crucially, Shooter claims that survivors who know personally of God's transformative presence are best positioned to serve others pastorally. "Any church which reflects this transforming action of God through its members—and leaders—is a sign of divine presence."[22] While this may be a devastating critique of the church as we know it, it may also summon the community toward what it might yet become if those with traumatic wounding are brought from the periphery to the center, and if those with institutional power choose willingly to empty or invert the power differential by facilitating and learning from the "knowing ministry" of others.

In light of this best practice of "knowing ministry," we can inquire about the role and contributions of Marie Collins and Peter Saunders, two members of the seventeen-member Pontifical Commission for the Protection of Minors who themselves are survivors of child sexual abuse. What is the impact of their witness on the commission's work? Sadly, Ms. Collins and Mr. Saunders have expressed frustration with the commission's lack of tangible progress, and this is shown in a public record. In February of 2016, Saunders was suspended from the Pontifical Commission when fifteen of his fellow members voted no confidence in his membership. The remaining member abstained. Mr. Saunders, who in England founded the National Association of People Abused in Childhood, notes that Pope Francis appointed each member of the commission and that he understands himself still to be a member until he hears otherwise from the pope.[23] His return to the commission remains an open question at the time of this writing. Ms. Collins resigned her position on the commission one year later, on March 1, 2017. In her statement printed in the *National Catholic Reporter*, Ms. Collins recalls her public remarks in 2014 on accepting the pope's invitation to join the commission, that if ever she discovered that what was happening behind closed doors conflicted with statements made to the public, she would not remain. With dismay she notes that the stumbling blocks placed before the commission include "lack of resources, inadequate structures around support staff, slowness for forward movement and cultural resistance. The most significant problem has been reluctance of some members of the Vatican Curia to implement the recommendations of the Commission despite their approval by the Pope."[24]

In a listening church, the presence on the commission of survivors like Mr. Saunders and Ms. Collins could provide the commission and the Curia reason to pivot from mere policies for prevention toward the recognition of the church as posttraumatic—as a "field hospital"—wherein Christians recognize their vulnerability as a matter of fact and choose it as a vocation, by taking responsibility to see and be seen, to witness and hear, to assist and be assisted, willingly and in gladness.[25] Doing all of this precisely when our lesser instincts would have us minimize religious violence in our midst, avert our eyes, or focus on penultimate goals like prevention, might require more than what the Pontifical Commission is currently doing, charged to be doing, or indeed prevented from doing. An honest appraisal of trauma requires nothing less than what McFadyen refers to as an "entire ecology of relating" that interrupts and begins to heal trauma's "expansive dynamic of distorted relationality," from which entire communities suffer, never just individuals.[26]

Notes

[1]Statement by H. Em. Cardinal Sean O'Malley, OFM Cap, at Consistory of February 12, 2015. http://www.vatican.va/. I am grateful to Julia Feder and Anselma Dolcich-Ashley for their formal responses to an early version of this chapter at the College Theology Society annual meeting.

[2]Shelly Rambo, "Spirit and Trauma," *Interpretation* 69, no. 1 (2015): 18.

[3]Deborah van Deusen Hunsinger, *Bearing the Unbearable* (Grand Rapids, MI: Eerdmans, 2016), 48–49, 52.

[4]Shelly Rambo, Introduction to *Post-Traumatic Public Theology*, ed. Stephanie N. Arel and Shelly Rambo (Cham, Switzerland: Palgrave Macmillan, 2016), 5.

[5]Edmund Chia, "Regensburg and Dialogue," *Studies in Interreligious Dialogue* 17, no. 1 (2007): 77.

[6]A notable exception is Martha Nussbaum, *The Clash Within: Democracy, Religious Violence, and India's Future* (Cambridge, MA: Belknap Press of Harvard University Press, 2007).

[7]Rambo, Introduction to *Posttraumatic Public Theology*, 3.

[8]In contrast to recent scholarship by members of the Center for Child Protection at the Pontifical Gregorian University (http://childprotection.unigre.it/), particularly Karlijn Demasure and Hans Zollner, SJ (also a member of the Pontifical Commission).

[9]"Papa Francisco Condena a Marcial Maciel," *Univision*, March 14, 2015. http://www.univision.com.

[10]Hunsinger, *Bearing the Unbearable*, 46.

[11]Rambo, "Spirit and Trauma," 10.

[12]Hunsinger, *Bearing the Unbearable*, 68.

[13]Serene Jones, *Trauma and Grace: Theology in a Ruptured World* (Louisville, KY: Westminster/John Knox Press, 2009), 31.

[14]Cf. Hunsinger, *Bearing the Unbearable*, 58; Rambo, "Spirit and Trauma," 10.

[15]Alistair McFadyen, *Bound to Sin: Abuse, Holocaust, and the Christian Doctrine of Sin* (Cambridge: Cambridge University Press, 2000), 78–79. For extended discussions of the clinical symptoms of trauma, see also Jones, *Trauma and Grace*, 13–18; Hunsinger, *Bearing the Unbearable*, 3–10, 149–55.

[16]Rambo, "Spirit and Trauma," 13.

[17]Susan Shooter, *How Survivors of Abuse Relate to God* (Aldershot: Ashgate, 2012); Shelly Rambo, *Spirit and Trauma* (Louisville, KY: Westminster/John Knox, 2010); Dirk Lange, *Trauma Recalled* (Minneapolis: Fortress, 2009); Jennifer Beste, *God and the Victim* (New York: Oxford University Press, 2007); Elisabeth T. Vasko, *Beyond Apathy* (Minneapolis: Fortress, 2015); Julia Feder, *Trauma and Salvation: A Theology of Healing* (Minneapolis: Fortress, forthcoming).

[18]Susan Shooter, "How Survivors of Abuse Relate to God: A Qualitative Study," in *The Faith Life of Women and Girls: Qualitative Research Perspectives,* ed. Nicola Slee, Fran Port, and Anne Phillips (Aldershot: Ashgate, 2013), 223–24.

[19]Ibid., 225.

[20]Ibid., 226.

[21]Ibid., 229.

[22]Ibid., 231.

[23]Elisabetta Povoledo and Laurie Goodstein, "Priest Abuse Victim Is Suspended from Vatican Panel," *New York Times*, February 6, 2016.

[24]Marie Collins, "Exclusive: Survivor Explains Decision to Leave Vatican's Abuse Commission," *National Catholic Reporter*, March 1, 2017.

[25]Adapted from Karl Barth, *Church Dogmatics*, III/2, *The Doctrine of Creation*, ed. G. W. Bromiley and T. F. Torrance (Edinburgh: T&T Clark, 1960), 250–67. Cf. John N. Sheveland, "Listening Church, Humbled Church," *Expository Times* 125, no. 11 (2014): 549–51.

[26]McFadyen, *Bound to Sin*, 78.

Part III

RESOURCES FOR RENEWAL WITHIN AMERICAN CATHOLICISM

The Church and Popular Movements

Signs of Renewal

Most Reverend Stephen E. Blaire

It is a delight to join with the College Theology Society at your 63rd Annual Convention. All of you have such an important mission working with our young people. The questions you are asking strike me as the right ones. Are we at a crossroads? Are we in crisis? Is it a time of renewal? Maybe it's all three.

I find in many of today's young people a genuine goodness, a hunger for meaning in their lives (while simultaneously questioning institutional responses), a great openness to making an integrated home for a diversity of cultures and yet an uncertainty about the relevance of traditional religious belief and practice. The more their Christian values are being deconstructed by those around them who live various secular ideologies, the more opportunity you have in your privileged positions as college theologians to help them construct a way of life that has deep meaning based on the inherent dignity of the human person rooted in the gospel. Above all they will find meaning in their lives when they come to encounter the living God in the person of Jesus Christ.

In responding to the three questions about crossroads, crisis, and renewal, I would like to draw on my recent experience with the World Popular Movements and with Pope Francis, with the hope that it might throw a little light from the church's social teaching on these thought-provoking questions.

Is the church in the United States at a crossroads? Yes. From a literal understanding of the term "crossroads," the church has always been at the intersection where the road of the world and the road of the gospel meet. If the gospel is to be incarnated in any culture, it must continue to encounter the reality and experience of people at the level of everyday life, as it always has. From a more idiomatic understanding of "crossroads," the church is at a point where it must make decisions as to how to move forward. Such decision-making has been part of the church's work from the very beginning. What is new is "how" the church moves forward in carrying out its mission from Jesus in the evangelization of the world in today's situation.

Is the church in crisis? Let me at this point call your attention to the written address from Pope Francis to the Regional World Meeting of Popular Movements in Modesto, California, in February, 2017. He wrote about the greatest areas of crisis in the world being related to "walls and fear" that challenge us to build "bridges and love."[1] He calls the "process of dehumanization" a "worsening crisis" that can be resolved only through people's involvement.[2] He then writes: "We should neither be paralyzed by fear nor shackled within the conflict. We have to acknowledge the danger but also the opportunity that every crisis brings in order to advance to a successful synthesis."[3]

Yes, the church has always been in crisis, but each crisis is not only a danger but an opportunity for the church to advance in carrying out its mission from Christ.

Is the church in renewal? If "renewal" is becoming "new again," I would say the church is always in renewal in the sense that it is always called to reform itself in its human dimension. We do this not only as individual members of the church but corporately as members of the Body of Christ. This sense of renewal runs throughout the documents of Vatican II.

I would like to draw your attention to three themes that appear in all of Pope Francis's addresses and messages to the World Meetings of Popular Movements: (1) working together, (2) changing structures, and (3) defending Mother Earth. They are words that speak to the church in its interaction with the world at the crossroads of faith and reality, confronting crises, and embracing challenges for renewal.

Pope Francis gave a personal address at the first three international meetings and sent a written message to the regional gathering in Modesto. The delegates who attended represented local and national as well as international popular movements; there were activists, community organizers, and human rights leaders from workers' groups and unions, indigenous peoples, social justice organizations, and social ministries of the church. Pope Francis described the delegates as "sowers of change, protagonists for social justice, and bold leaders of action."[4]

These meetings were different from other church or community gatherings because they were not organized by the church. While they were convened by the church (the first three by Pope Francis himself) and endorsed by the church, they were not meetings *of* the church. Representatives from the church participated and spoke along with others, but the meetings were run by community organizers and leaders of world popular movements for social justice. The church was present to listen and to accompany those experiencing exclusion, dehumanization, and the pain of poverty.

Working Together

In the pope's four messages he honors the people who organize for social justice, whether it be in community organizations, popular movements, local cooperatives, or neighborhood initiatives. He discounts neither government nor social organizations. In fact, he sees the popular ecclesial movements as working with them but not supplanted by them. He stresses that organizations cannot just be *for* the poor but must be *with* the poor and *of* the poor. Love for the poor, he reminds us, is at the center of the Gospel.[5]

Changing Structures

In the letter to the Modesto gathering he made it clear that he was speaking about "structural changes needed for a system that causes enormous suffering to the human family where the poor suffer exclusion and indifference."[6] In all four messages the system to be changed is described as one where the pursuit of money rules and the common good is neglected. Pope Francis proposed first of all "to put the economy at the service of peoples."[7] Such structural changes require that work for peace and justice rests on "the acceptance of 'interdependence' where people respect each other's culture, language, social processes and religious traditions."[8] Pope

Francis has suggested the image of the polyhedron (a solid formed by plane faces) where each group preserves its own identity within a plurality that reinforces unity.[9] Everything is integrated.

Defending Mother Earth

The third task is that of defending Mother Earth, which Pope Francis says may be the most important task facing us today. In his encyclical *Laudato Si'*, the pope reminded everyone that our "common home" is falling into disrepair due to exploitation. This harm is a spiritual degradation that has serious effects on the poor, diminishes the common good, and disrupts the integral ecology that respects the unique place of human beings in this world and our relationship to our surroundings.

So is American Catholicism at a crossroads? Yes, we are. The church is always at an intersection with the real world. We must decide how we are going to accompany people on the journey of life, how we are going to work for a just and peaceful world in a courageous manner, how we are going to stand for the dignity of every human person, and how we are going to promote the equality of all people in sharing the goods of the earth.

Is American Catholicism in crisis? Yes, we are. How do we preach and witness in today's world the God of mercy as opposed to the false and tyrannical god of financial gain? How do we walk with the poor and suffering humanity? How are we neighbor in our parishes, in our neighborhoods, in our nation and in the world? How do we carry out the mission of Jesus for healing and reconciliation?

Is it a time of renewal for the church? Yes, it is. When the church convenes people working for justice, when the church listens to the cries of the poor, when the church accompanies in faith and in love all who are suffering, these are signs of renewal. In union with Christ its head and in communion with one another the church as the people of God carries on the mission of Christ as an instrument for peace and justice in the world.

As college theology teachers, you are in a privileged position of education and formation with our young people. The way Pope Francis has convened the Popular Movements, listened to them, and accompanied them is a sign of renewal for us in the church and a model for us to follow.

Notes

[1]*Message of His Holiness Pope Francis on the Occasion of the World Meetings of Popular Movements* in Modesto, California (February 16–18, 2017). All texts cited here can be found at w2.vatican.va.

[2]Ibid.

[3]Ibid.

[4]*Address of Pope Francis to the Participants in the World Meeting of Popular Movements*, Old Synod Hall, October 28, 2014. Theme repeated in subsequent address, *Address of the Holy Father to the Participants in the Second World Meeting of Popular Movements*, Fexpocruz, Santa Cruz de la Sierra, Bolivia, July 9, 2015.

[5]Ibid.

[6]*Message of His Holiness Pope Francis on the Occasion of the World Meetings of Popular Movements*, Modesto, California.

[7]*Address of His Holiness Pope Francis to Participants in the Third World Meeting of Popular Movements*, Blessed Paul VI Audience Hall, November 5, 2016.

[8]Ibid.

[9]*Address of Pope Francis to the Participants in the World Meeting of Popular Movements*, Old Synod Hall, October 28, 2014.

After Americanism

Catholic Radicalism in the Age of Trump

Michael Baxter

Shortly after the US election on November 8, 2017, David Remnick of the *New Yorker* reported on how Obama and the outgoing White House staff were dealing with the reality of "president-elect Trump." The title of the article was "It Happened Here."[1]

The reference was to the novel by Sinclair Lewis *It Can't Happen Here*.[2] Published in 1935, it tells the story of a fascist takeover of the United States like the ones in Italy and Germany. The unlikely candidate who beats Roosevelt in the election of 1936 is Buzz Windrip, a populist authoritarian fashioned after Louisiana governor Huey Long. The unlikely hero is Doremus Jessup, editor of a small-town Vermont newspaper, who gradually perceives the real dangers of the Windrip presidency—the demagoguery, hyperpatriotism, consolidation of power, elimination of opposition, thuggery, murders, concentration camps—and takes action. He joins with other dissenters and publishes a seditious underground newspaper, *Vermont Vigilance,* exposing the corruptions and crimes of the American Corporate State and Patriotic Party. For this, Jessup is forced to flee to Canada, as the Windrip government dissolves into anarchy and the country faces a dark, uncertain future.

With the title of his *New Yorker* piece, Remnick suggested that the election of Trump had made this scenario a reality. This was one of many reflections on the renewed relevance of *It Can't Happen Here*, sales of which skyrocketed after the election. The same was true of books with similar themes: *The Origins of To-*

talitarianism by Hannah Arendt, *The Man in the High Castle* by Philip K. Dick, *The Plot against America* by Philip Roth, and *1984* by George Orwell. The popularity of these books, as well as the articles stressing their relevance in this Age of Trump, indicate that there is a specter haunting the United States: the specter of fascism.

In this essay, I bring this specter of fascism into conversation with the two traditions of Catholic social thought in the United States, Americanism and radicalism, by making two related arguments. First, I argue that the Age of Trump in US political life has revealed that the Americanist tradition has become exhausted as a moral and intellectual tradition, so that we are living "After Americanism." Second, I argue that the events associated with Trump and the threat of fascism "happening here" are better understood from within the countertradition of Catholic radicalism, which asserts that it *has* been happening here for quite some time.

1

"The Church in the Trump Era: Catholicism or Americanism?" These are the stark alternatives facing American Catholicism, according to Massimo Faggioli. The fact that a majority of American Catholics helped to put Trump in the White House—52 percent to 45 percent—is something "the Catholic Church will have to live with," and the Democratic Party's dismissive attitude toward the religious vote is partly to blame. But the real concern, says Faggioli, is the pro-Trump segment of the Catholic Church. "We are witnessing," he notes, "a return of what Church history students will remember as 'Americanism,' when in 1899 Pope Leo XIII accused the US Church of being too adaptive of American political culture." This reemergent "Americanism"—or "traditionalist-neoconservative Catholic Americanism," as he also calls it—is reasserting the union of the church with "Euro-North American" or "Western civilization" on the basis of "the belief that the United States is an exceptional nation charged with a special mission." This belief fits nicely with the neonationalist, anti-internationalist rhetoric of the 2016 presidential election. But, he argues, neoconservative, neo-Americanist elements within Catholicism contradict Pope Francis's "vision of the church and [the pope's] social-political message." Hence the future of Catholicism in the United States is riding on "the fundamental choice between being a Roman Catholic Church in America or being an Americanist Catholic Church."[3]

Faggioli's analysis of Catholicism in the Age of the Trump is, as I see it, half right. The choice he presents—Catholicism or Americanism—is on target. But his "Americanists" are only neo-conservatives, so that he fails to account for the liberal Americanists. But these others must be included in an attempt to connect present-day Americanism with the Americanist controversy of the late nineteenth century, for several reasons. For one thing, the leading Americanists at that time—Cardinal Gibbons, Archbishop Ireland, Bishop Keane of Catholic University, and Dennis O'Connell, their "agent" in Rome—took the liberal side in the controversial questions of the day. In fact, their opponents in "the Conservative Party," as it was called, accused them of "a spirit of false liberalism."[4] For another thing, these Americanists, drawing from the ideas of Orestes Brownson and Isaac Hecker, argued that the Catholic Church should endorse US democracy in order to lead the nations into the modern age. These themes were developed by Catholic thinkers throughout the twentieth century, most notably by John Courtney Murray, who transformed these Americanist ideas into a well-argued and compelling theological, philosophical, and political position. Murray's lifelong work of demonstrating the compatibility of Catholicism and liberal democracy led to his having a shaping hand in writing *Dignitatis Humanae*, Vatican II's Declaration on Religious Freedom. Finally, the leading historians of Catholicism in the United States—Thomas McAvoy, John Tracy Ellis, Jay Dolan, David O'Brien, John McGreevy—have narrated turn-of-the-century Americanism as a liberal movement that forged a rapprochement between, as McGreevy puts it, "Catholicism and American Freedom."[5]

In short, contra Faggioli, there are two versions of Americanism, a neoconservative and a liberal version of Americanism. These two versions of Americanism have been at war with each other for the past half century. We know the usual suspects. We know the usual labels: progressive versus orthodox Catholics, social justice versus pro-life Catholics, Francis versus John Paul II Catholics, and so on. As these Catholic culture wars wore on, each side promoted a form of cafeteria Catholicism that distorts the fullness of Catholic teaching. In philosophical terms, Catholics on each side operated as utilitarians, weighing the benefits and harms, the values and disvalues, to determine which partisan allegiance to adopt. Often these stances were justified by identifying a human and moral catastrophe to be averted, the dangers of which outweigh all other considerations, whether it be the catastrophe of abortion, climate change, war in the Middle East, or disintegration of the traditional family. Because each of these concerns is affirmed in Catholic teaching, it was plausible to identify a particular concern, or combination of concerns, as outweighing the alternative concerns and to justify one's politically partisan allegiance accordingly—a strategy we might call "catastrophic utilitarianism." So we have ended up not only with liberal and conservative Catholics, but also with Democratic and Republican Catholics. And because utilitarianism is notorious for providing no agreed-upon scale of value by which to weigh these competing political positions, there has been no way to resolve these moral and political conflicts. As a result, the decades-long political impasse and polarization among Catholics has only deepened.

What is happening within American Catholicism in this Age of Trump is that both political alternatives have lost moral plausibility. It is possible for a good Catholic, in good conscience, to vote for Donald Trump and to support policies of the Trump Administration on foreign policy, the economy, health care, immigration, or climate change. But a pro-Trump stance lacks plausibility within the context of Catholic teaching. Much the same would be true now with a Hillary Clinton Administration. A Catholic could support its policy on foreign affairs, taxes, health care, abortion rights, or Supreme Court justices. But the trade-offs make it less plausible to do so on the basis of Catholic teaching. The most telling sign that both partisan positions have lost plausibility is the defection of Catholics from the two main parties: the "never-trump" movement by conservatives such as George Weigel, Robert George, Rick Garnett, and others; and the defections from the Democratic Party in light of the demise of Pro-life Democrats in Congress and the aggressively pro-abortion stance articulated at the Democratic National convention of 2016, the latter of which spurred Timothy O'Malley to write about, in a sentiment shared by many Catholics, "The Week I Left the Democratic Party."[6]

In short, politically speaking, what "the Age of Trump" makes clear is that Catholics are not at home in the United States. The most compelling theorist of the Americanist tradition, whom liberals and conservatives identify as theirs, namely, John Courtney Murray, was well aware that "the American consensus" was tenuous and might be dissolved. "Perhaps one day," he wrote, "the noble, many-storeyed mansion of democracy will be dismantled, levelled to the dimensions of a flat majoritarianism, which is no mansion but a barn, perhaps even a toolshed in which the weapons of tyranny may be forged."[7] For Murray, this chilling prospect meant that we must redouble our efforts to reestablish the American consensus and its natural law basis; assert the principles of the limited state, separation of powers, consent of the governed; reclaim "the concept of conversation" so that our warring creeds clash intelligibly, producing genuine disagreements, which in his eyes were an achievement. And Murray knew what we were up against: individualism, elitism, manipulation of the masses by political operatives, the nihilism of the professoriat, a regime of technology, "barbarians in Brooks Brothers suits."[8] The American consensus is not so much a fact as a need, for Murray, something to be attained.[9]

But what if the consensus is not attainable? What if the populace does not constitute a politically mature "people," as Murray claimed about the US citizenry, but is composed instead of an "*imperita multitudo*, the illiterate masses," as he said of late-nineteenth-century Europe, a populace tending toward a misuse of liberty owing to ignorance, error, and vice?[10] What if the "American consensus" cannot be regained because it never was intact at the US founding in the first place? What if his agenda of regaining the nation's moral and intellectual foundations has in fact concealed the lack of any stable "American consensus"? What if this is also true of Murray's predecessors and successors in the Americanist tradition? But this line of questioning can only be pursued from within the alternative tradition of Catholic radicalism, to which I now turn.

2

Before and especially after the 2016 election, as I have already noted, people in the press, political pundits, and a good number of scholars observed the political dynamics of fascism in the Trump campaign, transition team, and White House. In doing so, they argued that Trump is fundamentally different from his predecessors, a decisive departure from US politics in the past.[11] But while this is true in certain respects, it is more important to note the continuities between Trump and what came before Trump.

Take, for example, the observation by Glen Greenwald that the Trump Administration is continuing the Obama Administration's policy on extrajudicial assassinations.[12] Or reports by Jeremy Scahill on the expansion of the War on Terror under Obama, with the use of drones for extrajudicial assassinations, carried out with presidential approval, and resulting in nearly 90 percent of those killed not being the intended targets.[13] Or the fact that the most deportations in US history were carried out under Obama in 2012 (although that may soon change).[14] Concerning the election, it has been reported that Trump's campaign was bankrolled by Robert Mercer, but the same reporter, Jane Meyer, found that the Koch Brothers helped the Romney campaign in 2012 and the Tea Party with their "dark money."[15] And dark money has also been used to fund the Democratic Party. Grover Norquist and the Koch Brothers have counterparts in Warren Buffett and George Soros.[16] Regarding race relations, Black Lives Matter began during the Obama years, in part out of disappointment with Obama, and it would not have ended if the last election had had a different outcome. These and other continuities remind us that the "Age of Trump" was not created by Trump alone.

Should we use the label "fascist" to describe these continuities? Admittedly, the word is misleading, as there are obvious disparities between the 1930s and the beginning of the twenty-first century. Still, the label fits, as Chris Hedges argues in *American Fascists*. Writing in 2006, Hedges takes aim at "the Christian Right" and its "war on America," recalling that James Luther Adams, his professor at the Harvard Divinity School, saw parallels between false claims to religious faith in this country and the rise of fascism in Germany.[17] We should note that Hedges identifies fascist dynamics a decade before the Age of Trump. But we can go back even further by citing a very different critic. In 1995, Pope John Paul II, in his encyclical *Evangelium Vitae*, warned that a government protecting supposed rights to abortion and euthanasia risks becoming a "tyrant state," and in two earlier encyclicals, he noted the potential, even within a democracy, of an "open or thinly disguised totalitarianism."[18] Indeed, as early as 1982, parallels were drawn between the de-personalization of the Jews in the Holocaust and the de-personalization of the "fetus" in the practice of abortion.[19]

What this juxtaposition of waging imperial wars and legalized killing of the unborn shows is that fascism in the United States is a bipartisan phenomenon. It was evident during the Nixon years, not only with Watergate, but also with US policy in Vietnam, especially the back-channel dealings between Henry Kissinger and the North Vietnamese before the 1968 election (note the parallel to Trump). It was evident during the Kennedy and Johnson years regarding Vietnam as well. And it was evident during the Truman and Eisenhower years, with the creation of the "Deep State." Does the name "fascist" describe CIA "operations" during the Cold War? Installing the Shah of Iran in 1953; undermining of the Arbenz government in Guatemala in 1954; the Bay of Pigs in 1961; the coup in Chile in 1973; the US-sponsored atrocities committed in El Salvador in the 1970s and 1980s? Whatever name one prefers, this dark history, narrated well by Howard Zinn in *A People's History of the United States*, should instill in us deep skepticism concerning the central idea of Americanism, in both conservative and liberal versions, that we in the United States are citizens of a "providential nation."[20]

Among Catholics in the United States, this skepticism is nowhere better exemplified than by Dorothy Day. Her credentials for opposing fascist regimes are clear. In an early issue of the *Catholic Worker* (November 1933), Day addressed anti-Semitism in Germany and the United States.[21] In May 1934, the paper reported that the Catholic Church in Germany was "fighting a battle against the quiet insidious persecution of Hitler's brownshirts."[22] In 1935, she decried the Italian invasion of Ethiopia.[23] Again in 1935, she protested Nazi anti-Semitic policies by picketing at the German consulate and the *SS Bremen*.[24] In 1936, she took a neutral stand on the Spanish Civil War, criticizing Franco as well as the Republicans, for which she was roundly criticized by both sides.[25] Generally speaking, the *Catholic Worker*, as Nancy Roberts has observed, "eclipsed most—if not all—American publications, both religious and secular, in the speed and concern with which it disclosed the Jewish persecution."[26] As the fascist menace in Europe grew and the prospect of war loomed, Day confirmed the *Catholic Worker*'s pacifist stand, insisting that fascism could be defeated with weapons of the spirit.[27] During World War II, she persevered in this stand, rejecting fascism but also rejecting the war as a betrayal of Christ. Her condemnation of Truman's decision to drop the atomic bomb spoke of "our Japanese brothers, scattered, men, women, and children, to the four winds, over the seven seas."[28] Likewise, throughout the Cold War, she refused to line up against the "enemy," highlighting her youthful involvement in the Old Left, lauding the positive aspects of the revolution in Cuba in health care and education, and criticizing US imperialist designs.[29] In short, politically, Day stood in vigilant nonalignment before the triumvirate of Communism, Fascism, and Democracy.

This political nonalignment stemmed from Day's genuinely Catholic belief that all people are God's children, combined with her suspicion of any and all state ideology, including the ideology that presents the liberal democratic state as a guarantor of security, peace, freedom, and human rights. Her instincts were confirmed by Peter Maurin, who likewise refused to endorse communism, fascism, or democracy and adopted instead a personalist communitarian politics for realizing the common good as set forth in Catholic social teaching.[30] On this score, while it may be true (as Faggioli suggests) that the Second Vatican Council moved toward favoring constitutional democracy in its political teaching, it is also true (as he admits) that the council did *not* endorse any particular democracy, including US "democracy."[31] *This*, in church teaching—that is, *this* endorsement of a particular democracy—is a matter of prudential judgment, and it has been the prudential judgment of Dorothy Day, Peter Maurin, and others in the tradition of Catholic radicalism that such an endorsement should be withheld, owing to the absolutist, Leviathan-like character of the modern state, which must be held in check by the prior authority of the natural law and the teaching of Jesus Christ. Far better to give nothing more than a tentative, strictly conditioned tolerance of the political arrangement of any specific state.

This stance of political nonalignment does not mean that we refuse to engage the state or totally refrain from using what political tools may be at our disposal to work for justice. Dorothy Day engaged in state politics of her day, and we should do likewise in our day, fending for the rights of immigrants, workers, and the unborn; calling for religious freedom of Catholics in the military and of church institutions; decrying the use of torture and the warrantless surveillance of US citizens. But a stance of political nonalignment *does* mean that we are aware of the limits of such endeavors and of how the quest for political effectiveness can blind us to other concerns that our fellow citizens are all too ready to trade off. Moreover, it means we are ready to resist the state when the evils it sponsors call for our noncooperation, as in the new, Trump-era sanctuary movement, or in civil disobedience actions at drone bases, or in the refusal of pharmacists to fill prescriptions for abortifacient drugs. Such actions or refusals of actions fall within a tradition embodied by those we regard as exemplars, saints, and martyrs living in settings we readily associate with the word "fascism": Alfred Delp, Franz Jägerstätter, Dietrich Bonhoeffer, Edith Stein, Hans and Sophie Scholl, and many others. Finally, it means that we continue creating communal structures in which genuine justice and peace may be realized, building, as Peter Maurin put it, "a new society within the shell of the old."[32] If the Trump White House pursues its stated agenda of the "deconstruction of the administrative state," Catholics will need to redouble their efforts at what used to be called "social reconstruction."

My point is this: what the Age of Trump reveals about politics in the United States is what many in the tradition of Catholic radicalism have been saying for a long time now: that US politics is not a democracy but an oligarchy; that its "democratic" processes are controlled by political elites and party operatives beholden to the wealthiest of the wealthy; that the partisan divisions in this country are tearing apart the body of Christ; and that this is no coincidence, for the one thing that modern states—communist, fascist, or democratic—will not tolerate is a true church, one united by a Master Whose presence challenges any and all state authority.

This will not be an easy lesson to learn. For more than a century, Catholics in the United States have cherished the idea that ours is a "providential nation." Even now, many hold out the hope that the nation's citizenry will realize that (as many put it) "the new normal" for politics in this Age of Trump is not normal and that we will recover politics as usual. But the "old normal" of politics before Trump was not normal either. Now we live "after American-ism," in a setting within which we can more readily acknowledge that here we have no abiding city.

Notes

[1] David Remnick, "It Happened Here," *New Yorker*, November 28, 2016, 54.

[2] Sinclair Lewis, *It Can't Happen Here* (New York: Penguin, 2014).

[3] Massimo Faggioli, "The Church in the Trump Era: Catholicism or Americanism?" *La Croix International*, November 14, 2016. Quotations are taken from this online article. It should be noted that this early statistic on how Catholics voted in the presidential election has since been disputed. See Michael J. O'Laughlin, "New Data Suggest Clinton, Not Trump, Won Catholic Vote," *America*, April 6, 2017.

[4] William L. Portier, "Americanism," in *Dictionary of Christianity in America*, ed. Daniel Reid et al. (Downers Grove, IL: Intervarsity Press, 1990), 53–56.

[5] For the influence of Murray on these Americanist narratives, see Michael J. Baxter, "Writing History in a World without Ends: An Evangelical Catholic Critique of United States Catholic History," *Pro Ecclesia* 5 (1997): 440–69. See John T. McGreevy, *Catholicism and American Freedom* (New York: Norton, 2003). This essay does not analyze McGreevy's history, but the same basic critique applies.

[6] Robert George and George Weigel, "An Appeal to Our Fellow Catholics and to All Men and Women of Good Will," *National Review*, March 7, 2016, http://www.nationalreview.com; Richard Garnett, "Neither of the Above: A Conservative's Dilemma," *Commonweal*, September 15, 2016; Timothy P. O'Malley, "The Week I Left the Democratic Party," *Aleteia*, July 29, 2016.

[7] John Courtney Murray, *We Hold These Truths* (New York: Rowman & Littlefield, 2005), 56.

[8] Ibid., 23–39, 29.

[9] Ibid., 87–100.

[10] John Courtney Murray, "Leo XIII: Two Concepts of Government. II. Government and the Order of Culture," *Theological Studies* 15 (March 1954): 15.

[11] See, for example, Timothy Snyder, *On Tyranny: Twenty Lessons from the Twentieth Century* (New York: Tim Duggan Books, 2017).

[12] Glenn Greenwald, "Obama Killed a 16-Year-Old American in Yemen. Trump Just Killed His 8-Year-Old Sister," *The Intercept*, January 30, 2017, https://theintercept.com.

[13] Jeremy Scahill, *Dirty Wars: The World Is a Battlefield* (New York: Nation Books, 2013); Jeremy Scahill et al., *The Assassination Complex* (New York: Simon and Schuster, 2016).

[14] Serena Marshall, "Obama Has Deported More People Than Any Other President," *ABC News*, August 29, 2016, http://abcnews.go.com.

[15] Jane Mayer, "Trump's Money Man," *New Yorker*, March 27, 201, 34. Jane Mayer, *Dark Money: The Hidden History of the Billionaires behind the Rise of the Radical Right* (New York: Doubleday, 2016).

[16]Paul R. La Monica, "The Hillary Clinton Billionaires Club," CNN Money, August 2, 2016, http://money.cnn.com.

[17]Chris Hedges, *American Fascists: The Christian Right and the War on America* (New York: Free Press, 2006), 194–203.

[18]John Paul II, *Evangelium Vitae*, no. 20; *Veritatis Splendor*, no. 101; *Centesimus Annus*, no. 46.

[19]James T. Burtchaell, "Die Buben sind unser Unglück!: The Holocaust and Abortion," in *Rachel Weeping: The Case against Abortion* (San Francisco: Harper and Row, 1984), 141–238.

[20]Howard Zinn, *A People's History of the United States, 1492–Present*, rev. ed. (New York: HarperPerennial, 1995), 430, 432, 542, 577–78.

[21]Kate Hennessy, *Dorothy Day: The World Will Be Saved by Beauty* (New York: Scribner, 2016), 77.

[22]Quoted in Nancy Roberts, *Dorothy Day and the* Catholic Worker (Albany: State University of New York Press, 1984), 123.

[23]Mel Piehl, *Breaking Bread: The Catholic Worker and the Origin of Catholic Radicalism in America* (Philadelphia: Temple University Press, 1982), 192; Hennessy, *Dorothy Day*, 89.

[24]Hennessy, *Dorothy Day*, 112.

[25]Piehl, *Breaking Bread*, 123, 194–95.

[26]Roberts, *Dorothy Day and the* Catholic Worker, 122.

[27]Piehl, *Breaking Bread*, 194–98.

[28]Dorothy Day, *Dorothy Day: Selected Writings*, ed. Robert Ellsberg (Maryknoll, NY: Orbis Books, 2005), 261–70, 266.

[29]Dorothy Day, *The Long Loneliness* (New York: Harper and Brothers, 1952), 50–87, 96–99; Day, *Selected Writings*, 270–73, 147–50, 144–47; Dorothy Day, "Letter: Things Worth Fighting For?" in *Dorothy Day: Writings from Commonweal*, ed. Patrick Jordan (Collegeville, MN: Liturgical Press, 2002), 101–2.

[30]Day, *Long Loneliness*, 170. Peter Maurin, *Easy Essays* (Chicago: Franciscan Herald Press, 1977), 21, 75–77, 104–6, 111–12, 139–41, 167. On the common good, see 37, 44, 54–55, 132–33.

[31]Massimo Faggioli, *Catholicism and Citizenship* (Collegeville, MN: Liturgical Press, 2017), 46–66, especially 48–54.

[32]Day, *Long Loneliness*, 170.

The Communion of Saints in Life Writing

American Catholics Nancy Mairs and Mary Karr

Alison Downie

Dorothy Day is famously reputed to have said, "Don't call me a saint. I don't want to be dismissed that easily."[1] Decades later, this quip still resonates because of a prevalent North American assumption that the holiness of sainthood is so remote as to be irrelevant for contemporary life. In describing this problem, Elizabeth A. Johnson says that "the traditional symbol [of the communion of saints] has faded as a vital conduit of religious energy."[2] This great loss has diminished ways of recognizing, naming, experiencing, and celebrating the reality of graced holiness among us.

Johnson's study, *Friends of God and Prophets: A Feminist Theological Reading of the Communion of Saints*, rebuilds this vital conduit. In Johnson's ecofeminist reconstruction, sainthood includes yet reaches beyond individuals canonized by the church. For Johnson, sainthood is C/catholic, with both an upper- and a lowercase "c." It also extends beyond Christian affiliation and beyond the human to embrace the natural world. In Johnson's theology, the communion of saints names the dynamic presence of Creator Spirit within and among all those relational connections that empower and strengthen. The heart of this symbol, in Johnson's words, is "Holy Wisdom who makes the world sacred and connects people to each other as a great sea of support."[3] The symbol includes paradigmatic persons yet embraces an understanding of holiness not as a property of an individual but as gifted connection to the living God.

Johnson's theology of the communion of saints allows for recognizing, naming, and celebrating the power that so many readers experience at work in the life writing of acclaimed American Catholic authors Mary Karr and the recently deceased Nancy Mairs.[4] For purposes of this essay, I use the broad term *life writing*, which can include many genres, in order to discuss prose essays and memoir. Although each author is also a poet, in Karr's case an award-winning one, I limit discussion to their prose, for which each is well known. Mairs has written many collections of personal essays, and Karr has authored three best-selling memoirs as well as a book about the genre of memoir.

To analyze the powerful appeal of these authors, I first draw upon sociologist Arthur W. Frank's work in medical narrative ethics and the power of testimony in stories of illness, since each author's life story includes illness. Ultimately, however, I argue that the compelling power at work in Mairs's and Karr's life writing is not only ethical but profoundly sacramental. As each author offers the personal truth of her life to readers, mediated grace pours through these textual conduits, in their literary kenotic vulnerability. Their stories enact the truths they tell, demonstrating and thus opening up for readers who connect with their stories the real presence of transformative grace. Johnson's reconstruction of the symbol provides a way to recognize and celebrate the life writing of Mairs and Karr theologically, in terms of the communion of saints and so draw attention to graced holiness within the ordinariness of messy life.

Ethical Narrative Testimony

Arthur W. Frank develops what he calls a socio-narratology, an interdisciplinary approach to studying how story functions in people's lives.[5] Frank understands narrative as performative; no sharp line divides experience and story. He explains that "life and story imitate each other, ceaselessly and seamlessly, but neither enjoys either temporal or causal precedence."[6] His work on narratives of illness analyzes the processes and powers regarding who is authorized to tell stories of illness—medical experts, insurance companies, patients?

In the course of his extensive analysis, Frank describes three cultural/personal narrative patterns of illness that may all be present at different times in particular experiences of serious illness. Recognizing that some forms of suffering never come to story, Frank names this antinarrative experience the chaos story; in his terminology, chaos robs those suffering within it of the ability to reflect on or structure experience with narration, and there is no sense that this may ever be possible in some future moment. Chaos is living imprisonment in the raw, embodied immediacy of suffering.[7]

Frank argues that the story of illness that dominates North American culture is the restitution narrative. This narrative is really about health, because in this plot, illness is contained in an episode. Illness is a temporary interruption, a problem solved, after which life returns to normal. Frank cites advertisements for over-the-counter medicine as illustrative, in which illness does not result in any compromised performance or failure of duty and is resolved by the correct purchase.[8] In the restitution narrative, the threat of loss of control is quickly contained; existential questions are preempted in the return to normalcy.

Frank calls a third pattern the quest narrative, which he divides into three subcategories, one of which is memoir. In this pattern, illness brings loss of the point of view one lived in before becoming ill. As a result, "normal" life must be reevaluated. The essential quality of the quest narrative is the effort to develop a new point of view and, therefore, a fundamentally different life story; in this pattern, a person strives to make meaning out of experienced chaos.

As noted earlier, Frank intends this threefold heuristic to describe overlapping, recurring, and receding patterns. He says, "The quest narrative does not stand apart from the chaos narrative but bears witness to it."[9] In his view, such bearing witness is an ethical act, because "the witness offers testimony to a truth that is generally unrecognized or suppressed. People who tell stories of illness are witnesses, turning illness into moral responsibility."[10] In quest narratives, the storyteller demonstrates not only that change has occurred, but that it has occurred *because* of the person's response to suffering.[11] In addition, the ethical dimension of witness lies not only in who the person is becoming in response to suffering, but in what sharing that experience offers to others, whether this sharing occurs in face-to-face connection or through published story.

Whereas chaos robs the sufferer of narrativity, and restitution stories reinscribe the unexamined narrative of "normal" life, quest narratives tell of loss and reconstruction of voice. In quest narratives, Frank explains that "the teller not only recovers her voice; she becomes a witness to the conditions that rob others of their voices. When any person recovers his voice, many people begin to speak through that story."[12] Recovering voice is not simply returning to a previous voice, but regaining ability to narrate and narrating from a new point of view constructed out of lived chaos.

Since narratives are performative, Frank argues that stories of living well with illness are vitally needed in order to counter the culturally dominant narrative of restitution, which becomes oppressive when it is the only available or socially acceptable story. In this plot, illness is a problem that must be resolved so that life can get back on track. This narrative offers no plot for those whose illness is not cured, for those who do not return to being as good as new. In North American culture, the loss of control that any serious illness brings is shameful. Restitution narratives only have plotlines for regaining control, for those who "do not let illness get in the way." Quest narratives, however, witness to meaningful, good lives that encompass illness, courageously helping to make possible for others the experience to which these stories testify. Thus, such stories enact the truths they tell.

In his focus on physical illness, Frank frequently cites Nancy Mairs as a witness to living with multiple sclerosis. But Frank's work on narrative patterns and testimony is also useful for considering forms of mental illness to which Mairs and Karr bear witness as they make meaning in response to suffering. The process of coming into voice for both writers is inseparable from wrestling with loss of control, shame, and the effort of struggling into their personal truth. In addition to multiple sclerosis, Mairs writes about agoraphobia, depression, and attempted suicide. In the preface to her essay collection *Plaintext* she says,

> A few years ago I almost died by my own hand, and when I woke from that disagreeable event, I recognized for the first time that I was fully and solely responsible for my existence. . . . These essays enact that responsibility, however belatedly discovered, in the terms in which I can understand it: as a writer of my life.[13]

Mairs's writing is inseparable from enacting responsibility as she writes her life, including responses to her suffering in mental illness.

Although Karr also writes about mental illness in being hospitalized for depression and a near suicide attempt, the illness at the heart of her most recent memoir, *Lit*, is alcoholism. The narrative Karr tells in *Lit* is one of coming to terms with her alcoholism, a process that involves facing and dismantling many guises of fear, which, in hindsight she sees as having isolated her in many ways, including cutting her off from grace. Looking back, she writes, "You could say I needed God then, which notion would've gagged me like a maggot. But if you're a nonbeliever, replace the word *God* with *truth* or *mercy*. To kill truth to defend my fear was—in one way—to kill God."[14] In *Lit*, Karr loses the self-narrative inhabited while drinking and writes a new life story through gaining sobriety. In an interview, Karr explains, "Telling stories about yourself, whether on a therapist's couch, or in the arms of your beloved, or on paper, is one of the ways we become adults. We grow up by honing the narrative."[15] Karr tells her story of becoming sober and coming out of an episode of severe depression very much in terms of maturing, of developing a more insightful point of view, and narrating a new story of her life, in which gratitude blossoms into faith.

According to Frank's theory, both Mairs and Karr provide ethical witness to their truth in response to illness. An important distinction between these authors, however, is that for Karr, developing a new self-story includes a restitution plot, for although her marriage ends in divorce, illness recedes into her past, and depression becomes a resolved episode as she gains stability in sobriety. Karr's writing does not minimize the suffering of the chaos experience or romanticize the value of suffering, but she does tell a restitution narrative in that she leaves alcoholism and depression behind. Her story is also a quest narrative, however, in that for her, entering recovery leads her to the Catholic faith, a new point of view, and a new voice in which she tells her story of ongoing professional success as graced.

A restitution narrative is not possible for Mairs. In Frank's typology, her narrative is more purely a quest one. A theme of her life writing is living with ever-present and increasingly debilitating illness. For example, in *Remembering the Bone House*, she writes,

> "You can do whatever you put your mind to" is a watchword of rugged Americanism, and the incapacity to carry out an action is thus seen as a failure of will. In truth, however, you can't necessarily do whatever you put your body to. Some bodies, like mine, damaged by unfathomable processes of degeneration, just don't work. And there are no minds without bodies. None.[16]

In this and many other passages, Mairs directly critiques the oppressive nature of the culturally dominant restitution narrative as she witnesses to meaningful living with illness.

Although Frank's typology of illness narrative as ethical witness that enacts truth is helpful in understanding the compelling nature of their work, the life writing of Mairs and Karr is most fully appreciated theologically, through the lens of Johnson's reconstruction of the communion of saints. Frank's work offers a heuristic for describing the ethical responsibility demonstrated in these women's life writing. Yet breaking their lives open in narrative is sacramental in that Mairs and Karr extend a mediated grace to readers who connect with their stories.

Sinners as Saints

Undoubtedly, Mairs and Karr would recoil from my attempt to discuss them in the language of saints; each author ruthlessly presents herself as sinner, both implicitly and explicitly. In one of her most anthologized essays, using highly charged language which anticipates crip theory, Mairs writes, "I may be a cripple, but I'm only occasionally a loony and never a saint."[17] For her part, in *Lit*, while narrating an episode in which she loses her temper with her then-eighty-year-old mother, Karr writes, "And that's how I find my sinfulness in all its ugliness."[18] The language of both authors reflects the familiar but theologically inadequate North American sinner/saint binary that Johnson's theology dismantles.

Johnson critiques the way in which a hierarchical, patronage model of saints as influential intercessors quickly eclipsed an earlier, companionship model. As the patronage model gained ascendancy, saints became spiritual elites. The process of canonization became bureaucratic, and official saints were overwhelmingly "male, European, upper-class, and clerics."[19] The life stories of the many fewer canonized women have been written by patriarchal scripts about female holiness. Johnson writes:

> Instead of the empowerment that comes from knowing one is part of a struggling, creative, vital history of women with God, stories of the saints function as a means of ecclesiastical control. They sustain the status quo of male authority, foster spiritual elitism, and inculcate virtue that is unattractive and even oppressive to any woman whose goal is mature adult personhood.[20]

In her feminist reconstruction of the companionship model of the communion of saints, Johnson argues that the holiness or saintliness of this fellowship arises in the graced connection of the Spirit, not in individual traits, virtues, or achievements. She explains, "Holiness does not consist first and foremost in ethical or pious practices, nor does it imply innocence of experience or perfection of moral achievement."[21] Instead, holiness is relational, including all those responding to the Spirit "through lives that move in the direction of truth and love in the midst of ordinary time, seeking, even if often failing, to be faithful."[22]

Using Johnson's work, it becomes clear that discussing sinners as saints is necessary in order to recognize and affirm the transformative reality of grace in ordinary life. At stake in this reconstructed language of holiness and sainthood is greater access to the reality of grace in the messy here and now, especially for women, and for all those whose lives witness to a truth which, to echo Frank, is neglected or suppressed by culturally dominant life stories. Frank's theologically evocative work on narrative as ethical witness traces the contours of the empowering dynamism Johnson identifies as the communion of saints. Mairs and Karr offer textual conduits of grace not only by identifying themselves as sinners in need of it, but in the performativity of narrative life writing that demonstrates grace at work.

A shared quality of their life writing is frank, unflinching truth telling about their own shortcomings, weaknesses, and failures. Theologically, this functions as a form of kenotic vulnerability. Mairs and Karr speak out of and through multiple markers of stigma, refusing the silencing of shame, to write poignantly about loss of innocence, suffering, weakness, failure, and struggle. In addition to the illnesses already mentioned, Nancy Mairs's life writing also discusses her rape, marital infidelities, the experience of not finding mothering to be an instinctual joy, and the murder of her foster son. In her memoirs, Mary Karr wrestles with internalized classism in order to be able to write about, rather than hide, her rural Texan working-class roots, growing up with alcoholic parents, a mother who creates a great deal of chaos, and Karr's own sexual assault. These details are not the stories themselves but are the material of their truth telling, a complex theme each author addresses explicitly in numerous passages, recognizing her limitations while pledging her best effort to readers.

For example, Mairs says:

> I believe . . . that the proscriptions traditionally placed on a woman's speech foster feelings of shame that lead her to trivialize her own experience and prevent her from discovering the depth and complexity of her life. In defiance of the conventions of polite silence, I've spoken as plainly and truthfully as the squirms and wriggles of the human psyche will permit.[23]

In an essay on truth in personal life writing, Mairs also says, "There are no falsehoods in my writing, but there are secrets; and these, I suppose, twist the truth in ways I don't even recognize."[24] Mairs distinguishes between deception, privacy, and the selection writing memoir necessitates, pledging her limited best.

The memorable opening sentence of *Lit* reads: "Any way I tell this story is a lie."[25] Karr addresses truth telling head on throughout this memoir. For example, as she writes about the dissolution of her marriage, she says, "While I trust the stories I recall in broad outline, their interpretation through my old self is suspect. . . . When I reach to grasp a solid truth from that time, smoke pours through my fingers."[26] And in *The Art of Memoir* Karr writes, "No matter how self-aware you are, memoir wrenches at your insides precisely because it makes you battle with your very self—your neat analyses and tidy excuses."[27] Each author acknowledges the complexity of truth telling in life writing, offering her personal truth as necessarily limited and flawed, yet also her best effort in an ongoing process.

The life writing of Mairs and Karr demonstrates each author's process of taking responsibility in response to suffering in clear-eyed, though partial, truth telling, even as each explicitly counters the dominant North American narrative of the good life as individually achieved success, self-sufficiency, and control. It is socially dangerous to appear weak, not on track in one's life plan—in short, to be vulnerable. Mairs and Karr model grace-empowered resistance to the shame imposed by this culturally dominant narrative and, in so doing, offer ethical testimony to the truth of other life narratives. Ultimately, however, each author's personal truth telling in life narrative is best understood not only as ethical witness but as kenotic and sacramental, enacting the relational, graced power of the communion of saints. In sharing their desolations, struggles, and joys, Mairs and Karr empower and companion others. Their life writing witnesses to, thereby offering readers a textual conduit of, the real presence of grace in the ordinariness of messy life.

Notes

[1] James Martin, SJ, "Don't Call Me a Saint?" *America*, November 14, 2012.

[2] Elizabeth A. Johnson, *Friends of God and Prophets: A Feminist Theological Reading of the Communion of Saints* (New York: Continuum, 1998), 21.

[3] Ibid., 26–27.

[4] See Mairs's obituary in the December 7, 2016, *New York Times*, https://www.nytimes.com.

[5] Arthur W. Frank, *Letting Stories Breathe: A Socio-Narratology* (Chicago: University of Chicago Press, 2010).

[6] Ibid., 21.

[7] Arthur W. Frank, *The Wounded Storyteller: Body, Illness, and Ethics*, 2nd ed. (Chicago: University of Chicago Press, 2013), 98.

[8] Ibid., 80.

[9] Ibid., 182.

[10] Ibid., 137.

[11] Ibid., 128.

[12] Ibid., "Preface to the First Edition," xxi.

[13] Nancy Mairs, *Plaintext* (Tucson: University of Arizona Press, 1986), preface, xi.

[14] Mary Karr, *Lit* (New York: Harper Perennial P.S. edition, 2010), 184.

[15] Steve Ross, "A Conversation with Mary Karr," *Lit*, P.S. ed., 9.

[16] Nancy Mairs, *Remembering the Bone House: An Erotics of Place and Space* (Boston: Beacon Press, 1989), 147.

[17]Mairs, "On Being a Cripple," in *Plaintext*, 20. This essay by Mairs is cited, for example, in Alison Kafer, *Feminist, Queer, Crip* (Bloomington: Indiana University Press, 2013), 15.

[18]Karr, *Lit*, 380.

[19]Johnson, *Friends of God and Prophets*, 27.

[20]Ibid., 28.

[21]Elizabeth A. Johnson, "Friends of God and Prophets: Waking Up a Sleeping Symbol," in *Abounding in Kindness: Writings for the People of God* (Maryknoll, NY: Orbis Books, 2015), 266.

[22]Johnson, *Friends of God and Prophets*, 232.

[23]Mairs, *Remembering the Bone House*, preface to 1989 edition, xiii.

[24]Nancy Mairs, "Truth in Personal Narrative," in *Truth in Nonfiction: Essays,* ed. David Lazar (Iowa City: University of Iowa Press, 2009), 9.

[25]Karr, *Lit*, 1.

[26]Ibid., 88.

[27]Mary Karr, *The Art of Memoir* (New York: Harper Collins, 2015), "Preface: Welcome to My Chew Toy," xxi.

The Traditioned Word
in the Life of the Church

The Influence of the NABPR Region-at-Large/CTS
Partnership on the Second Baptist–Catholic
International Dialogue (2006–2010)

Steven R. Harmon

In 2006, I published a book titled *Towards Baptist Catholicity: Essays on Tradition and the Baptist Vision.* Two of its chapters originated in papers presented in sessions of the National Association of Baptist Professors of Religion (NABPR) Region-at-Large. The opening chapter of the book began with this:

> In 1996 a small group of Baptist theologians in the United States, the "Region-at-Large" of the National Association of Baptist Professors of Religion, began gathering as a program unit of the annual meeting of the College Theology Society, an organization of predominantly Roman Catholic college and university professors of theological and religious studies. This meeting has served as a forum for earnest discussions of the nature of Baptist identity, set in relief against the backdrop of parallel debates about Roman Catholic identity, as well as an occasion for mutual exploration of the catholicity to which both traditions are heirs.[1]

A decade later, in 2006, a joint commission representing the Baptist World Alliance (BWA) and the Catholic Church began a second series of international bilateral conversations that convened each year through 2010. This essay proposes that the partnership between the NABPR Region-at-Large and the College Theology Society had a demonstrable and substantial influence both on the course of this Baptist–Catholic ecumenical dialogue and on its joint report published in 2012 with the approval of the BWA General Council and the Congregation for the Doctrine of the Faith.[2]

The roots not only of the CTS/NABPR partnership, but also of the theological trajectory of its influence on the dialogue, are traceable to the relationship between the late Baptist theologian James Wm. McClendon Jr. and the Catholic theologian Terrence Tilley. In the section devoted to "Welcoming the Baptists" in Sandra Yocum's history of the first fifty years of the College Theology Society, she credits Tilley as "instrumental in forging the relationship with NABPR" in his roles as CTS convention director and president.[3] Tilley had reason to have more than a passing interest in welcoming the Baptists. The Catholic Tilley was the Baptist McClendon's former student twice over, first as an undergraduate at the University of San Francisco in the late 1960s and again as McClendon's doctoral student at the Graduate Theological Union.[4] In Tilley's dissertation on Ian Ramsey one can discern the shared influence of Wittgenstein, among other anticipations of common emphases in McClendon's and Tilley's subsequent work.[5] McClendon for his part was instrumental in initiating the process that led to the CTS/NABPR partnership. A report on the experiment published in the *CSSR Bulletin* provides this account:

> The process began during the NABPR session in 1993, when James McClendon of Fuller Theological Seminary appealed to members, asking that they reconsider the usual practice of meeting exclusively with the AAR/SBL. Instead, McClendon suggested that a joint meeting with the CTS might produce a collegial environment that is more suited to the practical challenges of teaching and less formed by the ideology that pervades the AAR/SBL. Thus the dialogue began between members of the societies that led to the unprecedented joint meeting.[6]

Some members of the CTS in addition to Tilley had considerable interest in McClendon's work. The NABPR Region-at-Large did not meet with CTS in 2001 at the University of Portland, having planned their only independent meeting to date to engage the theme "Baptists, Confessions, and Faith" immediately prior to the Cooperative Baptist Fellowship General Assembly in Atlanta in the wake of the controversial 2000 revision of the *Baptist Faith and Message* confessional statement by the Southern Baptist Convention. But CTS members engaged Baptist theology in Portland anyway, devoting a session of papers during that meeting to "The Theology of James McClendon."[7] Tilley's own ongoing appreciation for the new theological world McClendon opened for this Catholic theologian is expressed in his article "Why American Catholic Theologians Should Read 'Baptist' Theology."[8] A continuing legacy of this appreciation is seen in the way that the University of Dayton has become a hospitable academic home for emerging Baptist theologians to pursue their graduate studies in a Catholic context.[9]

With a different application in mind, Pope John Paul II insisted in *Ut Unum Sint* that such ecumenical dialogue "is not simply an exchange of ideas" but it is "always an 'exchange of gifts' " as well—an encounter between people.[10] And so these theological ideas have a socially embodied context. Joint commissions to an ecumenical dialogue do exchange ideas and craft agreed statements, but they also forge relationships with their dialogue partners. They eat together, worship together, see the sights in the locales of their dialogues together, and even engage in evening excursions to pubs. These relationships not only enrich what happens across the conference table during the dialogue; they become partnerships in the all-important process of ongoing ecumenical reception necessary for a dialogue to make a difference. They are also in themselves socially embodied instantiations of practiced Christian unity.

The social dimension of ecumenical dialogue applies also to the relationships between Baptist and Catholic theologians forged through their participation in the CTS/NABPR joint meetings. Though not an ecclesially sanctioned or formal dialogue, this partnership has functioned as an instrument of ecumenical encounter. It has played a role in the ecumenical formation of the Baptist participants, and surely this has been the experience of the Catholic scholars who have engaged and collaborated with them as well. Five members of the joint commission to the second series of Baptist–Catholic conversations had been participants in the College Theology Society annual conventions: among the members of the Catholic delegation, Sister Susan Wood, SCL, and Sister Sara Butler, MSBT; and among the Baptists, Curtis W. Freeman, Elizabeth Newman, and Steven R. Harmon. Many international bilateral dialogues proceed from series to series without much of a gap—the Catholic–Lutheran dialogue that began following the Second Vatican Council, for instance, has continued in successive phases for five decades—but the first series of Baptist–Catholic conversations that ended in 1988 was followed by an eighteen-year hiatus. The lack of socially embodied continuity in the dialogue commissions from the first to the second series meant that many members lacked significant experience in dialogue between the two communions at this level. Yet the two CTS members among the Catholic delegates were potentially aware of trajectories in Baptist theology that defied the stereotypes, and the Region-at-Large participants among the Baptist delegates brought with them some experience of engagement with Catholic theologians in the context of the partnership. They had also participated in Region-at-Large sessions that explored some themes addressed in the dialogue, one in particular, in ways that shaped their contributions to the dialogue and its report.

Themes explored in the separate NABPR Region-at-Large sessions, in joint sessions with CTS, and in CTS sessions with Baptist contributions have had varying degrees of relevance for issues addressed in the second Baptist–Catholic international bilateral. From the first meeting in 1996 through the years of the dialogue, some of the session themes were specific to Baptist studies. Others reflected broad and diverse interests shared by Baptist and Catholic participants in the theological academy: there were several joint sessions on Scriptural interpretation in the early years of the partnership, shared explorations of spiritual formation, and mutual attention to ethical issues. These discussions have their own ecumenical significance, even if not directly influential for the Baptist–Catholic dialogue. More directly relevant was a panel in the 1996 inaugural attempt at the CTS/NABPR partnership on the theme "Paths to catholicity: Ecumenical? Evangelical? baptist?" with McClendon, Freeman, and Dwight Moody as panelists.[11] McClendon and Freeman were also coauthors of the "Re-Envisioning Baptist Identity" statement conceived during that meeting and birthed the following year, which gave voice to a Baptist theological trajectory that made its mark on personalities and perspectives that shaped the course of the dialogue and its published report in un-endnoted ways that will be mentioned later in this essay.[12]

The most directly influential aspect of the CTS/NABPR partnership for the second series of Baptist–Catholic conversations, however, was the attention given by the Region-at-Large to tradition as theological category and source of authority. At the 2002 CTS conference at St. John's University in New York, Barry Harvey convened a joint CTS/NABPR panel discussion of Baptist patristics scholar D. H. Williams's book *Retrieving the Tradition and Renewing Evangelicalism* and Terrence Tilley's *Inventing Catholic Tradition*, with responses by Sandra Yocum from CTS and Mark Medley from the Region-at-Large, as well as from Williams and Tilley.[13] A revised version of Medley's presentation was published in *Perspectives in Religious Studies* under the title "Catholics, Baptists, and the Normativity of Tradition."[14] A brief summary of the article follows, as it plays a significant role in mediating the partnership's engagement with tradition to the dialogue.

Medley begins by engaging an article by Region-at-Large participant and "Re-envisioning Baptist Identity" coauthor Philip Thompson on early responses to that statement—in particular, Thompson's recommendation that Baptists move beyond their tradition of rejecting tradition "to discuss seriously the normativity of tradition."[15] Medley then documents the scant attention to tradition by Baptist theologians in a page-and-a-half-long discursive footnote, identifying Stanley Grenz and McClendon as the Baptist theologians who "offer the most constructive discussion of tradition."[16] But he urges Baptists to take this further: "to think seriously and constructively about tradition by engaging in ecumenical conversation with those who have reflected on tradition."[17] Medley suggests Tilley's Catholic account of tradition as an ideal starting place in light of Tilley's indebtedness to McClendon. He highlights especially Tilley's emphasis on practices as tradition, with his definition of practices taken straight from McClendon and developed in terms of Yves Congar's distinction between tradition as *traditia*, the things that are handed on, and *traditio*, the practice of handing on, with participation in the traditioning practices of worshiping communities guided by "rules" derived from good practice (at this point Tilley, like McClendon, is influenced by George Lindbeck).[18] Medley concludes that Tilley's Catholic account of tradition is one that can be taken up by Baptists in part because it moves beyond an understanding of tradition as a continuity of static doctrinal propositions to a more dynamic "retrospective" understanding of tradition as a critical, open-ended "looking back" to the Christian past in configuring continuity for present contexts. But it is also congenial to Baptist theological commitments because of an eschatological orientation that precludes elevating tradition to a position of "final authority," for, as Medley puts it, "throughout the ebb and flow of tradition's constancy and renewal the Spirit of God is at work bringing the people of God to a fuller participation in the Gospel."[19]

Medley's article was influential for a paper on Baptist understandings of authority presented in the North American phase of the international dialogue between the BWA and the Anglican Communion in September 2003, figuring prominently in that paper's articulation of a Baptist account of the function of tradition in a pattern of authority that opened up possibilities for ecumenical convergence not only with Anglican understandings of authority but other traditions that recognize the authority of tradition more explicitly.[20] The next year a paper was presented on tradition as a new horizon in Baptist theology at the 2004 CTS meeting, which engaged Medley to document a shift from the Baptist "tradition of rejecting tradition" to a more recent development characterized as "a noteworthy number of Baptist theologians [who] have joined Grenz and McClendon in urging their fellow Baptists to acknowledge the authority of tradition and to explore the implications of the catholic tradition for Baptist faith and practice."[21] The paper argued that "they constitute an identifiable movement in Baptist theology," for which Curtis Freeman's label of "catholic Baptists" was appropriated from an essay he published in 1994,[22] and developed a sevenfold typology of a catholic Baptist theology that included the explicit recognition of tradition as a source of authority. In illustrating this and the other marks of the catholic Baptist theological trajectory, the paper drew extensively on publications by Baptist theologians who have been participants at some point in the CTS/Region-at-Large meetings besides Medley: Philip Thompson, Barry Harvey, Beth Newman, Curtis Freeman, Ralph Wood, and D. H. Williams.[23] In revised form, both of these papers became chapters in *Towards Baptist Catholicity*.

The connections between these publications constitute an explicit link between the work of the Region-at-Large and the work of the Baptist–Catholic dialogue. The theme addressed in the first year's meeting of the second series of conversations was "The Authority of Christ in Scripture and Tradition." When the report from the dialogue was published under the title "The Word of God in the Life of the Church," the section of the report on Scripture, tradition, and authority noted that in the first series of conversations the relationship of Scripture and tradition was identified as a matter of difference needing further exploration.[24] But then it notes that when the Catholic and Baptist delegations met eighteen years later for a new series of conversations, participants were able to welcome two developments that surfaced during this new phase of dialogue: "a more appreciative assessment of the value of tradition and its relation to Scripture by the *Baptist* participants and a more critical approach to tradition in its relation to Scripture by the *Catholic* participants."[25] In a subsequent paragraph, the report elaborated the first of these new developments: Baptist participants were able "to express an appreciation for the value of tradition in the church's ongoing efforts to embody the teachings of the Scriptures in the present," while Catholic participants were able "to discern a convergence toward some sense of a shared tradition."[26] The endnote following that passage directs the reader to the first chapter of *Towards Baptist Catholicity* "for a useful summary of this trend." This chapter drew heavily on publications by members of the Region-at-Large in connection with the explicit recognition of tradition as a source of authority as a mark of "catholic Baptist" theological identity.

But the influence of the CTS/NABPR partnership on the dialogue and its report goes well beyond providing evidence of a trend among Baptist academic theologians. The Region-at-Large voices in the dialogue were able to help the joint commission to reflect on Baptist ecclesial practices in relation to Catholic practices in ways that led to the discernment of such convergences as these in the published report:

> Both Catholics and Baptists affirm a teaching authority in the church, but they conceive of it differently, the one finding it in the *magisterium* and the other in the local *congregation*.[27]

> The Bible can and should be read by individual Christians on their own. Yet this reading should not be isolated from interpretation by the community which is indwelt by the Spirit who inspired the Scriptures.[28]

> The Bible is the written embodiment of a living tradition (*paradosis*) which is handed down through the work of the Holy Spirit in the midst of the people of God.[29]

> There is a certain "coinherence" of Scripture and living tradition, in the sense of a mutual indwelling and interweaving of one in the other. They should not be considered as two separate and unrelated sources, but as two streams flowing together which issue from the same source, the self-revelation of the triune God in Christ.[30]

> We agree that conscience needs to be formed in order to hear the Word of God clearly.[31]

One can discern in these articulations of Baptist/Catholic convergences a NABPR Region-at-Large influence in terms not only of the authority of tradition, but also its communal practice as described in this affirmation from the "Re-envisioning Baptist Identity" statement coauthored by six participants in the Region-at-Large:

> *We affirm Bible Study in reading communities* rather than relying on private interpretation or supposed "scientific" objectivity. . . . We thus affirm an open and orderly process whereby faithful communities deliberate together over the Scriptures with sisters and brothers of the faith, excluding no light from any source. When all exercise their gifts and callings, when every voice is heard and weighed, when no one

is silenced or privileged, the Spirit leads communities to read wisely and to practice faithfully the direction of the gospel.[32]

Other influences on the dialogue by the Baptist delegation's NAB-PR Region-at-Large participants may be discerned in the report, especially by Newman in the section titled "Mary as a Model of Discipleship in the Communion of the Church" and Freeman in the section "The Ministry of Oversight and Unity in the Life of the Church," in addition to aspects of the section titled "The Authority of Christ in Scripture and Tradition" treated above.[33]

The CTS/NABPR partnership will likely continue to influence Baptist–Catholic dialogue at the international level. A third phase of the conversations between the BWA and the Catholic Church began in December 2017 and will continue through 2021, with some members (Newman and Harmon) of the joint commission formed for that work in part by their participation in the CTS/NABPR partnership.

Notes

[1]Steven R. Harmon, *Towards Baptist Catholicity: Essays on Tradition and the Baptist Vision*, Studies in Baptist History and Thought, vol. 27 (Milton Keynes, UK: Paternoster, 2006). Two of its chapters originated in papers presented in sessions of the National Association of Baptist Professors of Religion Region-at-Large. The initial chapter of the book (pp. 1–21) originated as a paper titled "Tradition as a New Horizon in Baptist Theology," which was presented at the 2004 meeting of the NABPR Region-at-Large during the Fiftieth Annual Convention of the College Theology Society at the Catholic University of America in Washington, DC, June 3–6, 2004; chapter 4, "Baptist Confessions of Faith and the Patristic Tradition" (*Towards Baptist Catholicity*, 71–87) had its origins in a paper on "Baptist Confessions of Faith and the Patristic Tradition" presented to the NABPR Region-at-Large Annual Meeting in Atlanta, Georgia, June 26–27, 2001.

[2]Baptist World Alliance and Catholic Church, "The Word of God in the Life of the Church: A Report of International Conversations between the Catholic Church and the Baptist World Alliance, 2006–2010," *American Baptist Quarterly* 31, no. 1 (Spring 2012): 28–122; published also in *Pontifical Council for Promoting Christian Unity Information Service* 142 (2013): 20–65, and on the Vatican web site (www.vatican.va).

[3]Sandra Yocum Mize, *Joining the Revolution in Theology: The College Theology Society, 1954–2004* (Lanham, MD: Sheed & Ward, 2007), 238–39.

[4]Terrence W. Tilley, "The Catholicity of a 'Baptist' Theologian," *Perspectives in Religious Studies* 40, no. 3 (Fall 2013): 303.

⁵Terrence W. Tilley, "On Being Tentative in Theology: The Thought of Ian T. Ramsey" (PhD diss., Graduate Theological Union, 1976).

⁶James Preston Byrd Jr. and Richard F. Wilson, "College Theology Society and National Association of Baptist Professors of Religion Share Meeting," *CSSR Bulletin* 25, nos. 1 and 2 (2006): 3–4.

⁷Program for the College Theology Society Forty-Seventh Annual Convention: Theology and Sacred Scripture, May 31–June 3, 2001, University of Portland, Portland, Oregon, p. 5 (College Theology Society Records, Box 19, Annual Conference Programs, 2000–2009, the American Catholic History Research Center and University Archives, the Catholic University of America, Washington, DC).

⁸Terrence W. Tilley, "Why American Catholic Theologians Should Read 'Baptist' Theology," *Horizons* 14, no. 1 (Spring 1987): 129–37.

⁹E.g., the dissertations written by the following Baptist graduates of the Doctor of Philosophy in Theology program at the University of Dayton: Aaron James, "Analogous Uses of Language, Eucharistic Identity, and the Baptist Vision" (2010); Derek C. Hatch, "E. Y. Mullins, George W. Truett, and a Baptist Theology of Nature and Grace" (2011); Jonathan A. Malone, "Changed, Set Apart, and Equal: A Study of Ordination in the Baptist Context" (2011); Andrew Donald Black, "A 'Vast Practical Embarrassment': John W. Nevin, the Mercersburg Theology, and the Church Question" (2013); Coleman Fannin, "From Churches in Cultural Captivity to the Church Incarnate in a Culture: Ecclesial Mediation after the Dissolution of the Southern Baptist Subculture" (2014); Jason A. Hentschel, "Evangelicals, Inerrancy, and the Quest for Certainty: Making Sense of Our Battles for the Bible" (2015).

¹⁰John Paul II, *Ut Unum Sint* ("On Commitment to Ecumenism"), May 25, 1995, no. 28 (www.vatican.va).

¹¹Program for the College Theology Society Forty-Second Annual Convention: Religious Intellectual Traditions in the USA, May 28–30, 1996, University of Dayton, Dayton, Ohio, 4.

¹²Mikael Broadway, Curtis W. Freeman, Barry Harvey, James Wm. McClendon Jr., Elizabeth Newman, and Phillip E. Thompson, "Re-Envisioning Baptist Identity: A Manifesto for Baptist Communities in North America," *Baptists Today* (June 1997), 8–10, and *Perspectives in Religious Studies* 24, no. 3 (Fall 1997): 303–10.

¹³Program for the College Theology Society Forty-Eighth Annual Convention: Christology: Yesterday, Today, and Tomorrow, May 30– June 2, 2002, St. John's University, Jamaica, New York, p. 19; D. H. Williams, *Retrieving the Tradition and Renewing Evangelicalism: A Primer for Suspicious Protestants* (Grand Rapids, MI: William B. Eerdmans, 1999); Terrence W. Tilley, *Inventing Catholic Tradition* (Maryknoll, NY: Orbis Books, 2000).

¹⁴Mark S. Medley, "Catholics, Baptists, and the Normativity of Tradition: A Review Essay," *Perspectives in Religious Studies* 28, no. 2 (Summer 2001): 119–29.

¹⁵Philip E. Thompson, "Re-envisioning Baptist Identity: Historical, Theological, and Liturgical Analysis," *Perspectives in Religious Studies* 27, no. 3 (Fall 2000): 287–302.

[16]Medley, "Catholics, Baptists, and the Normativity of Tradition," 119–20, n. 2.

[17]Ibid., 121.

[18]Ibid., 121–23; Tilley, *Inventing Catholic Tradition*, 53; James Wm. McClendon Jr., *Doctrine: Systematic Theology,* vol. 2 (Waco, TX: Baylor University Press, 2012), 28.

[19]Ibid., 128.

[20]Steven R. Harmon, "Baptist Understandings of Authority, with Special Reference to Baptists in North America," paper presented to the Anglican-Baptist International Commission—North American Phase, Acadia University, Wolfville, Nova Scotia, September 12, 2003; revised for publication, idem, "Baptist Understandings of Theological Authority: A North American Perspective," *International Journal for the Study of the Christian Church* 4, no. 1 (2004): 50–63.

[21]This paper became the basis for chapter 2 in Harmon, *Towards Baptist Catholicity*, 23–38.

[22]Curtis W. Freeman, "A Confession for Catholic Baptists," in *Ties That Bind: Life Together in the Baptist Vision*, ed. Gary Furr and Curtis W. Freeman (Macon, GA: Smyth & Helwys, 1994), 85.

[23]Harmon, "'Catholic Baptists' and the New Horizon of Tradition in Baptist Theology"; idem, *Towards Baptist Catholicity*, 1–21.

[24]Baptist World Alliance and Catholic Church, "The Word of God in the Life of the Church," no. 34.

[25]Ibid.

[26]Ibid., no. 55.

[27]Ibid., no. 36.

[28]Ibid., no. 48.

[29]Ibid., no. 56. The inclusion of *paradosis* was an echo of McClendon's appeal to that New Testament term in his affirmation of the coinherence of Scripture and tradition (McClendon, *Doctrine*, 469–70), introduced into the discussion of the dialogue commission through a paper I presented in Year 2 of the conversations: Steven R. Harmon, "*Dei Verbum* 9 in Baptist Perspective," paper presented to the bilateral conversations between the BWA Doctrine and Interchurch Cooperation Commission and the Pontifical Council for Promoting Christian Unity, Rome/Vatican City, December 2–8, 2007; revised as chapter 4 in idem, *Baptist Identity and the Ecumenical Future: Story, Tradition, and the Recovery of Community* (Waco, TX: Baylor University Press, 2016), 91–112.

[30]Baptist World Alliance and Catholic Church, "The Word of God in the Life of the Church," no. 58.

[31]Ibid., no. 69.

[32]Broadway, Freeman, Harvey, McClendon, Newman, and Thompson, "Re-Envisioning Baptist Identity," no. 1.

[33]See Baptist World Alliance and Catholic Church, "The Word of God in the Life of the Church," nos. 132–61; cf. Elizabeth Newman, "Mary in the Light of Scripture and the Early Church: A Baptist View," paper presented to the bilateral conversations between the BWA Doctrine and Interchurch

Cooperation Commission and the Pontifical Council for Promoting Christian Unity, Durham, North Carolina, December 14–20, 2008; and Baptist World Alliance and Catholic Church, "The Word of God in the Life of the Church," nos. 162–204; cf. Curtis W. Freeman, "Baptist Ecclesiology," paper presented to the bilateral conversations between the BWA Doctrine and Interchurch Cooperation Commission and the Pontifical Council for Promoting Christian Unity, Rome/Vatican City, December 13–19, 2009; as well as Baptist World Alliance and Catholic Church, "The Word of God in the Life of the Church," nos. 34–71.

A Spirituality of Resistance

Thomas Merton on the Violence
of Structural Racism in America

Daniel P. Horan, OFM

Racism was for Thomas Merton more than a series of discrete actions of prejudice or harm. Although he certainly recognized the reality of particular instances of physical, emotional, psychological, and spiritual violence deployed against individuals and communities of color, one of Merton's most notable (if often overlooked and underappreciated) contributions was his ability to recognize and name structural racism or what Bryan Massingale has called "the culture of racism" that permeates historical, cultural, and institutional realities throughout the United States. As Massingale explains, "Racism, at its core, is a set of meanings and values that inform the American way of life. It is a way of understanding and interpreting skin color differences so that white Americans enjoy a privileged social status with access to advantages and benefits to the detriment, disadvantage, and burden of person of color."[1] And Merton—a white, male, Euro-American, straight, ordained Catholic monk, who died in 1968—recognized and named this pervasive reality for what it is: a form of structural and systemic violence. As James Thomas Baker rightfully observed, "Merton believed that the most obvious and continuing sign of America's violence was the racism which had led to its greatest social crisis of the 1960s."[2] His contributions anticipate much of the contemporary developments of Critical Race Theory over the last thirty years and remain relevant in navigating many crises of faith and justice we face as church today.

This essay explores Merton's prophetic and prescient writing on racism in the American context. Despite his ostensibly isolated social location as a cloistered monk, Merton nevertheless scrutinized the "signs of the times in the light of the Gospel"[3] from a "surplus location" at one of the margins of mainstream American society.[4] The result of his writing from this unique social, geographic, and spiritual location was the production of several essays aimed at awakening his Christian sisters and brothers to recognize the violence of deep-seated structural racism and white supremacy.

What follows is organized in three parts. First, I survey Merton's writing on structural racism, white privilege, and violence. Second, I show how Merton's writings anticipate the work of Derrick Bell Jr., a legal theorist and early founder of Critical Race Theory, on the subject of "Interest Convergence." Finally, I close by noting how Merton's work contributes to articulating a "spirituality of resistance" aimed at disrupting the status quo and awakening white American Christians to their complicity with structural sin and their call to ongoing conversion.

Thomas Merton, Structural Racism, and White Privilege

I believe that Merton's awareness of the complexity of racism in the United States arose from the intersection of several factors converging in his unique position. One factor was his voracious reading, which put him in contact with writers such as W. E. B. Du Bois, James Baldwin, Martin Luther King Jr., and Malcolm X. A second factor was his work with Christian nonviolence movements, which put him in contact with, in addition to King, the Berrigan brothers, Dorothy Day, Jim Forest, John Howard Yoder, Ping Ferry, and others.[5] A third factor was the deeply mystical and contemplative discipline of prayer and reflection he cultivated especially as he embraced a more eremitical lifestyle in proportion to his social justice work. In this way, we might liken Merton to Howard Thurman, who, in the estimation of William Apel, was also a "mystic as prophet."[6]

Speaking as a white male in the context of American religious life and addressing an audience of similar composition, Merton noted his complicity in structural racism, demarcating it from discrete acts of racially based animus while also naming its inherently violent roots.

> There is, however, such a thing as collective responsibility, and collective guilt. This is not quite the same as personal responsibility and personal guilt, because it does not usually follow from a direct fully conscious act of choice. Few of us have actively and consciously *chosen* to oppress and mistreat the Negro. But nevertheless we have all more or less acquiesced in and consented to a state of affairs in which the Negro is treated unjustly, and in which his unjust treatment is directly or indirectly to the advantage of people like ourselves, people with whom we agree and collaborate, people with whom we are in fact identified.[7]

Merton added that "this kind of treatment is part of a whole subtle system of moral and psychological oppression which is essentially *violent*. Anyone who has such an attitude is then partly responsible for what is going on, and in that sense 'guilty.' "[8] The relationship between the particular and the collective as it concerns the violence of racism anticipates what scholars have said in subsequent decades.

Bryan Massingale affirms Merton's intuition that much of the violent and "subtle system of moral and psychological oppression" functions as "a largely unconscious or preconscious frame of perception, developed through cultural conditioning and instilled by socialization."[9] Massingale explains, "Racism's manifestations change, sometimes dramatically. But at its core, racism always involves the use of skin color differences for the purpose of assigning social rank or privilege."[10] The shifting manifestations of racism can lead people to dismiss its enduring and persistent reality, claiming that "improvement" is actually the eradication of racism in society. However, as Merton, Massingale, and others note, racism is only one side of the coin of this structural injustice. The other side is the privilege that is preserved and protected by racial injustice.

While many white women and men readily admit the reality of racial injustice as it disadvantages some, far fewer are able or willing to recognize their own advantages resulting from the very same system. For many whites the notion of white privilege appears theoretical, especially when the matrix of class, gender, and race come together in the lived realities of individuals. However, as Massingale notes, in the American context "white privilege is not an abstraction; it is real. White privilege is the range of unearned (and at times, unwanted) advantages that come simply from possession of an attribute our society prizes, namely, the status of being considered 'white.'"[11] Merton recognized the reality of white privilege, which arises from a society structured such that supremacy is bestowed on whites by virtue of law, custom, culture, and social systems. He takes particular aim at white Christians and their willful ignorance about white supremacy. "The actions and attitudes of white Christians all, without exception, contain a basic and axiomatic assumption of white superiority, even when the pleas of the Negro for equal rights are hailed with the greatest benevolence." Merton adds, "It is simply taken for granted that, since the white man is superior, the *Negro wants to become a white man.*"[12] In other words, in the structurally racist thinking of even those white women and men who, in principle, support civil rights, there is an insidious undercurrent of supremacy that governs what white society will accommodate, when it will accommodate, and for whom it will accommodate those rightfully demanding racial justice. I will say more about this in the next section, but suffice it to say that Merton's awareness of the violence of structural racism and white privilege allowed him to recognize the failures of white allies during the 1960s.

Recognizing the deep-seated and complex reality of structural racism in America, Merton was distinctive among white Catholic clergy in his time in acknowledging what black women and men knew for centuries: that racism is essentially a *white problem.* Merton wrote in his essay "Letters to a White Liberal" that the work of Martin Luther King Jr. and his fellow nonviolent activists was, in part, to help bring the social reality of the American context into white consciousness.

> The purpose of nonviolent protest, in its deepest and most spiritual dimensions then is to awaken the conscience of the white man to the awful reality of his injustice and of his sin, so that he will be able to see that the Negro problem is really

a *White* problem: the cancer of injustice and hate which is eating white society and is only partly manifested in racial segregation with all its consequences, *is rooted in the heart of the white man himself.*[13]

Although, for Merton, King's nonviolent protest was aimed at ushering in this awakening to racism and privilege, it did not succeed, even in the civil rights legislation that ostensibly advanced racial justice in America.

Merton and Interest Convergence Theory

The entire premise of Merton's essay "Letters to a White Liberal" was that those civil rights milestones lauded by white Christians in the North were insufficient in addressing the reality of structural racism in the United States. One primary reason is that white people have failed to acknowledge and therefore address the reality of white privilege and supremacy, which they, in fact, are uninterested in surrendering. As Merton put it strikingly, "We have been willing to grant the Negro rights on paper, even in the south. But the laws have been framed in such a way that in every case their execution has depended on the good will of white society, and the white man has not failed, when left to himself, to block, obstruct, or simply forget the necessary action without which the rights of the Negro cannot be enjoyed in fact."[14] From Merton's perspective, any liberties or rights extended to persons of color are done on the condition that the white supremacist American society maintains its status quo, affording no undue hardships for those who are currently privileged and remain in power.

Merton insisted that "as long as white society persists in clinging to its present condition and to its own image of itself as the only acceptable reality, then the problem will remain without reasonable solution, and there will inevitably be violence."[15] The remaining problem is that white women and men do not want anything to *actually* change, because the result would be another kind of society, a "new society," as Merton put it, and that society would not hold one race superior to another.[16]

Because of this dynamic, Merton actually sees the white northerners who are quick to join in the civil rights movement as not only inadvertently disingenuous, but actually counterproductive in advancing racial justice. He calls to task these "white liberals," many of whom are Christian leaders, for inserting themselves in a controlling position, seeking to set a tone and establish goals that at least do not demand they surrender their material, psychological, or social comforts and status. This is why Merton is incredulous when it comes to passing legislation like the Civil Rights Act of 1964. Merton writes: "The Negro is integrated by law into a society in which there really is no place for him—not that a place could not be made for him, if the white majority were capable of wanting him as a brother and a fellow-citizen."[17] Merton takes fellow white Christians to task for ostensibly supporting persons of color, but in fact seeking to control and undermine their righteous effort for true equality and justice. In a scathing rebuke, Merton names what he sees as the primacy of the white northern interests in controlling the civil rights efforts of black women and men:

> On the one hand, with your good will and your ideals, your fine hopes and your generous, but vague, love of mankind in the abstract and of rights enthroned on a juridical Olympus, you offer a certain encouragement to the Negro (and you do right, my only complaint being that you are not yet right enough) so that, abetted by you, he is emboldened to demand concessions. Though he knows you will not support all his demands, he is aware that you will be forced to support some of them in order to maintain your image of yourself as a liberal. He also knows, however, that your material comforts, your security, and your congenial relations with the establishment are much more important to you than your rather volatile idealism, and that when the game gets rough you will be quick to see your own interests menaced by his demands. And you will sell him down the river for the five hundredth time in order to protect yourself. For this reason, as well as to support your own self-esteem, you are very anxious to have a position of leadership and control in the Negro's fight for rights, in order to be able to apply the brakes when you feel it is necessary.[18]

White liberals are happy to support women and men of color, provided it is on their own terms and in a manner consonant with their interests.

What Merton identifies in writing anticipates what more than a decade later Derrick Bell will propose in a theory he calls "interest convergence."[19] Bell argued that "civil rights advances for blacks always seemed to coincide with changing economic conditions and the self-interest of white elites. Sympathy, mercy, and evolving standards of social decency and conscience amounted to little, if anything."[20] In other words, the commonsense reading of advances in civil rights arising from a recognition that injustices needed to be corrected—what Bell and other legal scholars call a "neutral principle" in this case—does not sufficiently account for why the changes actually took place at a given time and in a given manner.

To illustrate his thesis, Bell chose the Supreme Court decision *Brown v. Board of Education* (1954). He believed that, following nearly a century of black protest for equal rights, the *Brown* decision was decided in 1954 because of a "convergence of interests" according to which the interests of elite whites (politicians, business owners, etc.) converged with the long-standing interests of the oppressed. Bell identified three reasons for the decision according to this convergence: First, American politicians feared that legal segregation was weakening the credibility of American democracy internationally in the context of the Cold War; second, the decision would offer "much needed reassurance to American blacks that the precepts of equality and freedom so heralded during World War II might yet be given meaning at home";[21] and third, capitalists were concerned that the American South could never develop industry beyond its then-current rural plantation society as long as state-sponsored segregation remained intact.[22]

At the heart of Bell's theory lies a view that aligns well with Merton's intuition about why *real* change regarding the violence of racism in America remained so elusive. Given that white elites maintained control and the positions of governmental, social, and economic power, only concessions that did not threaten white privilege would ever be permitted. The alleviation of systemic oppression and structural racism in America would always be circumscribed and determined by unspoken rules that maintain white privilege and social supremacy. Bell describes the mechanism of this phenomenon well.

> Whites may agree in the abstract that blacks are citizens and are entitled to constitutional protection against racial discrimination, but few are willing to recognize that racial segregation is much more than a series of quaint customs that can be remedied effectively without altering the status of whites. The extent of this unwillingness is illustrated by the controversy over affirmative action programs, particularly those where identifiable whites must step aside for blacks they deem less qualified or less deserving. Whites simply cannot envision the personal responsibility and the potential sacrifice inherent in Professor [Charles] Black's conclusion that true equality for blacks will require the surrender of racism-granted privileges for whites.[23]

Merton was able to identify and name what critical race and legal theorists would later develop into a substantiated field of study that traces the relationship of the two-sided coin of structural racism and white privilege within the American context.[24] Whereas developments in Critical Race Theory in the decades after Merton's death lend clarifying language and structure to Merton's observations, analysis, and reflections, Merton's writing offers insight into the spiritual significance of this work for Christians.

Toward a Spirituality of Resistance

In a sense, Merton's entire written corpus can rightly be described as a reflection on lifelong conversion. Both his autobiographical texts and the more didactic efforts identify numerous opportunities for *metanoia*—a turning—away from sin, individualism, or the "false self" and toward reconciliation, communion, and the "true self." And this is the case in his writings on the violence of American racism, wherein he almost always draws a connection between what *Gaudium et Spes* would call the "signs of the times" and the Christian response these signs elicit. I am suggesting we can read Merton's Christian response as a nascent "spirituality of resistance" rooted in what he describes as a "theology of love" that is a theology of both revolution and resistance.[25]

Merton laments the "Christian failure in American racial justice" in his own time, noting that an increased awareness of what is happening in society brings out "the stark reality that our society itself is radically violent and that violence is built into its very structure."[26] What is the response of the Christian, especially the white Christian, supposed to be? I suggest Merton offers (at least) three points to be considered in forming a spirituality of resistance for white Christians in the American context.

First, he explains that the "job of the white Christian is then partly a job of diagnosis and criticism, a prophetic task of finding and identifying the injustice which is the cause of *all* violence, both white and black."[27] The exhortation is to resist simply resting in unexamined complicity and instead seek to uncover the injustice already at work in the system. Merton explains that this leaves Christians with a real choice: either to "find security and order by falling back on antique and basically feudal conceptions, or go forward into the unknown future, identifying [themselves] with the forces that will inevitably create a new society."[28] This is the revolutionary dimension that challenges Christians to move outside the cocoon of personal piety to embrace a spirituality of praxis and engagement.

Second, Merton encourages white Christians to *actually listen* to their black sisters and brothers. Again, the central conviction of his "Letters to a White Liberal" is that the seemingly benevolent "liberal" or Northern whites are in fact deploying control and influence that Bell would describe as interest convergence. For Merton, a spirituality of resistance calls white Christians in particular to step aside and recognize the prophetic voice of women and men of color. Their message, he believes, can be put in simple terms: "I would say that the message is this: white society has sinned in many ways. It has betrayed Christ by its injustices to races it considered 'inferior' and to countries which it colonized."[29] Merton adds: "What is demanded of us is not necessarily that we believe that the Negro has mysterious and magic answers in the realms of politics and social control, *but that his spiritual insight into our common crisis is something we must take seriously*."[30] The spirituality of resistance Merton imagines is not one in which the prophetic voice arises from the "white savior" within

American society, but one of humility and honest reflection that invites white Christians to embrace silence and openness. Merton concluded his "Letters to a White Liberal" with an instruction for what this might look like, invoking a familiar motif from the Gospels in the process:

> This is the "message" which the Negro is trying to give white America. I have spelled it out for myself, subject to correction, in order to see whether a white man is even capable of grasping the words, let alone believing them. For the rest, you have Moses and the Prophets: Martin Luther King, James Baldwin, and others. Read them and see for yourself what they are saying.[31]

The last point is essentially that white Christians should "get out of the way." Articulated in first person narrative, Merton concludes his essay "From Non-Violence to Black Power" with these lines:

> I for one remain *for* the Negro. I trust him, I recognize the overwhelming justice of his complaint, I confess I have no right whatever to get in his way, and that as a Christian I owe him support, not in his ranks but in my own, among the whites who refuse to trust him or hear him, and who want to destroy him.[32]

To move beyond uncritical interest convergence toward actual racial justice, white Christians need to follow rather than lead, listen rather than instruct, and support women and men of color on their own terms.

For Thomas Merton, racial justice can be imagined only when those who benefit from maintaining the status quo of inequality recognize structural racism and its complement of white privilege. Otherwise, progress is only ever advanced in circumscribed ways governed by the happenstance of interest convergence. As Christians, we are called by virtue of our baptism to work for peace and justice, which according to Merton means that white women and men in the American context have to move toward surrendering the unearned privilege and power granted by structural racism. Merton highlights that for white Christians this begins with incorporating into their spiritual practices a commitment to identifying injustice, listening to the women and men of color, and "getting out of the way" so that the agenda and mission of social change can be set by the hitherto oppressed and not by the oppressor.

Notes

[1]Bryan N. Massingale, *Racial Justice and the Catholic Church* (Maryknoll, NY: Orbis Books, 2010), 42.

[2]James Thomas Baker, *Thomas Merton: Social Critic* (Lexington: University Press of Kentucky, 1971), 99.

[3]Vatican II, *Gaudium et Spes*, no. 4.

[4]Here I am borrowing the notion of "surplus" from Joerg Rieger, whose interpretation of Jacques Lacan led him to pose this term as useful in postcolonial critique. See *Christ & Empire: From Paul to Postcolonial Times* (Minneapolis: Fortress Press, 2007), 9: "Such surplus is subversive because it cannot ultimately be controlled by the system. Surplus, in this context, can be anything that points beyond the status quo."

[5]For an excellent overview of Merton's role as an adviser to several key nonviolent activists in the 1960s, see Gordon Oyer, *Pursuing the Spiritual Roots of Protest: Merton, Berrigan, Yoder, and Muste at the Gethsemani Abbey Peacemakers Retreat* (Eugene, OR: Cascade Books, 2014).

[6]See William Apel, "Mystic as Prophet: The Deep Freedom of Thomas Merton and Howard Thurman," *Merton Annual* 16 (2003): 172–87.

[7]Thomas Merton, "The Hot Summer of Sixty-Seven," in *Faith and Violence: Christian Teaching and Christian Practice* (Notre Dame, IN: University of Notre Dame Press, 1968), 180–81.

[8]Ibid., 181.

[9]Massingale, *Racial Justice and the Catholic Church*, 26.

[10]Ibid., 36.

[11]Ibid., 41.

[12]Thomas Merton, "Letters to a White Liberal," in *Seeds of Destruction* (New York: Farrar, Straus and Giroux, 1964), 58.

[13]Ibid., 45–46.

[14]Ibid., 19.

[15]Ibid., 8.

[16]Ibid., 8–9.

[17]Thomas Merton, "Religion and Race in the United States," in *Faith and Violence*, 134.

[18]Merton, "Letters to a White Liberal," 33–34.

[19]See Derrick A. Bell Jr., "Serving Two Masters: Integration Ideals and Client Interests in School Desegregation Litigation," *Yale Law Journal* 85.470 (1976): 470–516.

[20]Richard Delgado and Jean Stefancic, *Critical Race Theory: An Introduction*, 2nd ed. (New York: New York University Press, 2012), 22.

[21]Derrick A. Bell Jr., "*Brown v. Board of Education* and the Interest-

Convergence Dilemma," *Harvard Law Review* 93.518 (1980): 524.

[22]Ibid., 525.

[23]Ibid., 522–23. The text Bell refers to here is Charles Black, "The Lawfulness of the Segregation Decisions," *Yale Law Journal* 69.421 (1960): 421–30.

[24]What Merton intuited and Bell later argued was confirmed beyond empiricism and theory in the work of, among others, the legal historian Mary L. Dudziak, *Cold War Civil Rights: Race and the Image of American Democracy* (Princeton, NJ: Princeton University Press, 2000).

[25]Thomas Merton, "Toward a Theology of Resistance," in *Faith and Violence*, 9.

[26]Merton, "Religion and Race in the United States," 144.

[27]Thomas Merton, "From Non-Violence to Black Power," in *Faith and Violence*, 129.

[28]Merton, "Religion and Race in the United States," 138–39.

[29]Merton, "Letters to a White Liberal," 66.

[30]Ibid., 69.

[31]Ibid., 70.

[32]Merton, "From Non-Violence to Black Power," 129.

Our Lady of Guadalupe

A Feminist, Performative Interpretation

Laura M. Taylor

With the inauguration of President Trump in January of 2017, debates about immigration and immigration reform captured headlines across the United States. In order to fulfill several of his key campaign promises, the newly elected president quickly signed an executive order that would initiate his sweeping crackdown on illegal immigration. This controversial order not only authorized US immigration authorities to expand and expedite their deportation priorities, but it also called for the construction and fortification of a sizable border wall between Mexico and the United States.[1] Rooted in the biblical call to "welcome the stranger," churches, universities, and cities across North America responded to these aggressive policies by declaring themselves sanctuaries.

This essay suggests that the borderlands between the United States and Mexico—the crossroads of *la frontera*—provide an important point of departure for contemporary theological conversations of crisis and renewal in American Catholicism. It asks what Our Lady of Guadalupe, "the Mother and Evangelizer of America," might say to North American Christians today. My argument takes place in three parts. First, I explore the historical, geographical, and political context of the borderlands between the United States and Mexico. Second, I highlight several theological themes in the tale of *la Virgen de Guadalupe*, outlining the importance of her message and manifestation to Juan Diego from a liberationist perspective. Finally, I lay the groundwork for a feminist, performative understanding of Our Lady of Guadalupe.

This understanding not only seeks to provide a preferential option for the "in-between" that speaks to the daily ordinary struggle of Latina/os to survive on the physical and metaphorical borders, but it also signals the irruption of God in the world, calling North American Christians to a posture of seeking justice for the most vulnerable and most marginalized in our midst.

The Borderlands

The present-day border between the United States and Mexico was, for the most part, officially established in 1848 with the Treaty of Guadalupe Hidalgo, which brought the Mexican–American war of 1846–48 to a close.[2] Due to its overwhelming military victory, the United States largely dictated the terms of the settlement, and, as a result, it acquired more than 500,000 square miles of Mexican territory, including a significant percentage of Mexico's population. The Mexican and indigenous peoples living north of the newly defined border literally became residents of a different country overnight.

Apart from those segments of the border delineated by the Rio Grande and Colorado Rivers, the 1,954-mile boundary between the United States and Mexico remained a line in the sand until the late 1990s, when the US government began constructing a series of large separation barriers from the landing mats of the first Gulf War. The purpose of the barricades was to dissuade migration and to channel all border crossings through official checkpoints. Despite this undertaking, the US–Mexico border remains one of the busiest land borders in the world, with an estimated 300 million official and unofficial crossings each year.

Additionally, the border also marks one of the few places in the world where a highly developed country and a developing nation come together.[3] As feminist philosopher and cultural theorist Gloria Anzaldúa observes, this asymmetrical meeting point has inflicted "*una herida abierta* where the Third World grates against the first and bleeds."[4] Consequently, many North Americans have come to imagine their Mexican neighbors as freeloaders, menaces to the economic fabric of the United States, and in the words of Louis Léon, "the economically ravaged neighbor banging anxiously at the back door of prosperity longing for the opportunity to enter."[5]

In recent headlines, Mexican immigrants have been predominantly characterized as criminals, rapists, drug smugglers, and threats to national security. These alarmist representations, marked by illegality, have been compounded by the sharp escalation in border control and security. Under President Trump, US Immigration and Customs Enforcement (ICE) has been authorized to expand their deportation priorities to include even those persons charged with minor offenses, such as traffic infractions. Moreover, a recent report suggests that the mass prosecution of undocumented border crossers has become so much the norm over the last two decades that it now one of the driving forces of mass incarceration in the United States today.[6]

In *Border Games*, Peter Andreas points out that those persons who criticize this border enforcement as ineffective or costly overlook the ritualistic and performative elements that are embraced by its proponents. The criminalization of undocumented immigrants, coupled with the policing of the border, has enabled the United States to assert its authority by creating a dividing line that distinguishes the safe from the unsafe, the insider from the outsider, and those who are thought to be deserving of social benefits (including citizenship) from those who are not.[7]

This imposed distinction between "us" and "them" has in turn given rise to anti-immigrant sentiment and hate crimes in the United States. As Miguel De La Torre observes:

> Regardless of if the Hispanics were part of the land prior to the founding of the United States or if they crossed a border in the past century or the past few days, all Hispanics are usually seen as not belonging, part of an immigration problem. Those living in the borderlands are forced to defend and prove their very existence and worth to the dominant Euro-American culture.[8]

Seen as not fully American, and therefore, not fully human, it is assumed that immigrants should not be in the United States at all, much less warrant fair treatment.

More worrisome still are the men and women who risk their lives to cross over the border between Mexico and the United States. They are the ultimate outsiders, whose systematic exclusion renders them insignificant, invisible, and even disposable. Judith Butler's work *Precarious Life: The Power of Mourning and Violence* poses two important questions that address this drastic kind of identity trouble—namely, "Who counts as human? Whose lives count as lives?" The answers to these questions, Butler contends, are beholden to a "differential allocation of grievability," which implies that some lives are worth mourning and need to be protected at all costs, whereas other lives matter less, if at all.[9] The thousands of migrant deaths along the US–Mexico border, along with the unidentified remains of border crossers skeletonized in the desert, make up an astonishing example of those persons who are considered disposable and fundamentally ungrievable. As De La Torre observes, these brown bodies are collateral damage of US immigration policies. He writes, "Not since the days of Jim Crow has the US government maintained a policy that systematically brings death to a group of people based on their race or ethnicity."[10]

The ways of valuing and devaluing life that govern our thinking and acting are not simply sociopolitical questions but also theological ones. The good news of the Gospel suggests that Jesus came so that all can have life and have it abundantly (Jn 10:10). Thus, as Christians, we must not only recognize the vulnerable and marginal in our midst, but we must respond to their suffering by defending the rights of those who are disproportionately vulnerable. Our Lady of Guadalupe's boundary-challenging commitments offer us one way forward.

The Tale of Guadalupe

Known as the "undocumented Virgin," *La Morenita* has long accompanied Mexicans on their treacherous journey across the border, whether on baseball caps, articles of clothing, food wrappers, prayer cards, or medals held close to their bodies. For Mexican immigrants, her story not only provides a lifeline to their culture and spirituality, but it also represents a source of transformation, hope, and healing for the marginalized and oppressed.

The tale of Guadalupe began in 1531 on a sacred mountain in Tepeyac where an apparition of the Virgin Mary is said to have occured to an Indian by the name of Juan Diego in a land recently colonized by the Spanish Empire.[11] Adorned in the garb and symbols of the Aztec peoples, Guadalupe instructed Juan Diego to go to the bishop of Mexico and convey her desire to build a hermitage. In this sanctuary, she said, "I will show and give to all my people all my love, my compassion, my help and my protection. . . . There I will hear their laments and remedy and cure all their miseries, misfortunes, and sorrows."[12]

Because the bishop was reluctant to believe the words of a poor *campesino*, Juan returned to Tepeyac and pleaded with Mary to send someone more powerful than he so that the bishop might be persuaded. Assuring him that he was the right person for the task, Mary sent Juan Diego back to the bishop, who again turned down his request, this time asking him for a visible sign.

In the meantime, Juan Diego's uncle fell ill. Upon hearing the news, Mary assured Juan Diego that his uncle had already been healed. In order to dispel his anxiety and fear she said, "Am I not here, your mother? Are you not under my shadow and my protection? . . . Are you not in the hollow of my mantle where I cross my arms? Who else do you need?"[13] She then gave him a sign to bring back to the bishop—beautiful out-of-season flowers, which she placed carefully in his mantle. When Juan Diego unfolded his tilma to show the flowers to the bishop, the image of Guadalupe appeared on his cloak. According to the story, all who saw the image were converted, and they began the construction of her sanctuary on the hill in Tepeyac, where her sacred image remains on the tilma of Juan Diego to this day.

Centuries later, Virgilio Elizondo would describe this tale as a "major moment in God's saving plan for humanity."[14] In what follows, I want to highlight three key points from Guadalupe's story that illustrate her transformative, liberating, and life-giving role as relevant for North American Christians today.

First, the Guadalupe event can be read as a narrative of resistance against the totalizing powers in society. As US Latina theologian Jeanette Rodriguez reminds us, the significance of Guadalupe's story cannot be understood apart from the near death and destruction of the Aztec people brought about by the Spanish conquest and colonization of Mexico in the sixteenth century.[15] At a time when the very humanity of the Indians was being debated by the church and the empire, a resistance movement began on a mountain in Tepeyac with two unlikely heroes—a brown-skinned Virgin and a "simple conquered Indian from the *barriada.*"[16] Guadalupe's presentation of the gospel message in the language and symbols of the conquered people (as opposed to those of the colonizers) affirmed the full humanity and dignity of the marginalized.[17] Thus, with the self-worth imparted to him by the Virgin, Juan Diego confronted the oppressive colonialist powers, becoming an agent of historical change.[18]

Second, Guadalupe's story can be interpreted as the birth of *mestizo* Christianity. By her very nature, Guadalupe crosses over the boundaries of cultures, nations, races, languages, and religions. Elizondo recalls the pivotal moment in his young life when a *mestizo* priest, Father Aguilera, explained to him that it is "in and through [Guadalupe] that the Iberian soul had united with the ancient Mexican soul to give rise to the *mestizo* soul of Mexico."[19] As Gloria Anzaldúa notes, *Guadalupana*'s intermixture affirms "[the] ambiguity that Chicanos-*mexicanos*, people of mixed race, people who have Indian blood, people who cross cultures, by necessity possess."[20] Yet Guadalupe is more than a symbol of multi-belonging and multi-subjectivity, she is also understood to be a divine revelation. Roberto Goizueta notes, the "divine is here revealed in—of all things!—a mestizo Virgin, a woman of mixed blood, La Morenita. . . . She is the Beauty of the mestizo, of the poor, a beauty rejected by the conquerors."[21]

Finally, in Guadalupe's story we witness the divine's preferential option for the poor. Throughout the story, the Virgin reveals the gratuitousness of God's love by standing with Juan Diego and by extension all those who are suffering and marginalized. She flips the script from the center to the margins in both her appearance to a poor *campesino* rather than the bishop (the symbol of Spanish power) and in her call to build a sanctuary located on the periphery rather than in the wealthy city-center. Through this sanctuary, Guadalupe herself will become a refuge, showing her love and compassion to *all* the inhabitants of the land, and inaugurating the kin-dom of God at the margins.[22] Elizondo writes: "Guadalupe's significance is the voice of the masses calling upon the elite to leave their economic, social, political, and religious thrones of pseudo-security and work with them—within the *mov-*

imientos de la base—in transforming society into a more human place for everyone."[23]

Feminist Retrieval

For many Mexican and Mexican American women, however, Guadalupe has been an ambiguous figure. On the one hand, androcentric interpretations of the narrative and symbols of *Guadalupana* have been used to sanction and reify the traditionally feminine and maternal codes of silence, submissiveness, chastity, passivity, and self-sacrifice that have been harmful to women, yet fundamental to the patriarchal social order in both the church and society.[24] On the other hand, she has been an important symbol of empowerment for Mexican and Mexican American women who are able to see themselves reflected in her image—as a Mexican, as a woman, and as a mother.

Although important work has been done by feminist theologians on both sides of this divide, I want to move the discourse in a different direction by laying the groundwork for a feminist, performative interpretation of the Guadalupe story based on the work of Judith Butler. This interpretation not only speaks to the daily ordinary struggle of Latina/os to survive on the physical and metaphorical borders, but it also seeks to provide a preferential option for the "in-between," calling North Americans to action.

Judith Butler is perhaps best known for her revolutionary understanding of identity, which claims that the categories of sex and gender are constituted through language and discourse and are therefore neither "naturally" nor "causally" related. She argues that people commonly thought of as biologically female are not automatically born with feminine-identified traits, but are "gendered" or "girled" over time through their performance of a received set of norms that associate a specific set of meanings or behavior with the female genitalia.[25]

According to Butler, the appearance of one's gender as "natural" is sustained only through dutiful repetition of specific gender norms. As a result, it is subject to slippage or resignification if these norms are repeated differently (or not at all). Take, for example, cross-dressing or dressing in drag. Butler illustrates that this act involves the appropriation of a gender norm traditionally associated with one sex by a member of the opposite sex.[26] A man in drag inevitably draws attention to the disjunction between his "male" body and the "female" gender he is performing, particularly when "he" makes a "better" "she" than most biologically identified females. By subverting and denaturalizing the link between sex and gender, such performative acts call into question the very assumptions on which heteronormative societies operate.

Likewise, I propose that when Our Lady of Guadalupe is viewed as Mary in Aztec drag, she undermines and resignifies the traditional colonialist models of Mary, revealing the kyriarchal and hegemonic norms upon which they were founded. This interpretation brings to the fore two important dimensions. First, the initial shock associated with this revelation illustrates the way in which certain bodies failed to matter in the Spanish and Christian Empire, except as salvific beneficiaries, and even this was considered up for debate. Second, her presence as a *mestiza* destabilizes the empire's singular, rigid constructions of belonging and exclusion, such as male/female and Anglo/Hispanic. Thus, in her border-crossing capacity, Guadalupe affirms the multiplicity and hybridity of all our identities.

Accordingly, a performative interpretation of Guadalupe enables feminists to loosen the patriarchal stronghold on her image, while simultaneously accounting for the ways in which she has been and continues to be a source of empowerment for women. Moreover, it brings to the fore the way women already do re-member and re-cite Guadalupe in communal performances that call for social and political change and affirm the full humanity and dignity of all people.

Take, for example, Chicana artist Ester Hernandez's depiction of Guadalupe as a kickboxer in her 1971 etching "Virgin of Guadalupe Defending the Rights of Chicanos" or Yolanda Lopez's triptych of Guadalupe in which she depicts three generations of women portraying Guadalupe—herself, her mother, and her grandmother. In each of these pieces, the artist interweaves the Guadalupe narrative with the everyday lives and struggles of Chicanas.[27] Summarizing the significance of Yolanda Lopez's work, Guillermo Gómez-Peña said, "[Guadalupe] was no longer just standing motionless with praying hands and an aloof gaze.

She actually walked, she showed up in demonstrations and strikes.
. . . She could even sit down and take a break, abandon temporarily her holy diorama and jog, or let a working-class woman
temporarily take her place."[28]

Given these artistic recitations, how might feminist, performative understandings of Our Lady of Guadalupe speak to North
American Christians today? More specifically, how might Guadalupe enable us to continue to speak of a God of life and love in
a reality characterized by the numerous premature and innocent
deaths of undocumented immigrants who are fleeing economic
and political conditions that make life in their homeland unsus-
tainable?

First, I contend, we must recognize that it is the least among
us, the undocumented immigrant, who is God dwelling in our
midst. Like the parable of the sheep and the goats (Mt 25: 31–46),
Guadalupe's story reminds us that God chooses the oppressed in
history and makes them the principal means of salvation. The
brown-skinned Virgin does not appear to the power players of the
day, but rather she appears to the most marginalized in the land,
who are suffering under the rule of the powerful, reminding them
that they are created in God's image and therefore have inherent
dignity and intrinsic worth. She stands with them against the injustices of their day, and she informs them that it is only through
their courage and action that God's grace will be manifest.

Second, I argue, we must remember Guadalupe by being sanctuary. In her story, we not only become bystanders to the slaughter
of the indigenous by the colonizers, but we also experience a call
to action. We must create communities of resistance that disrupt
and dislodge the dominant norms that criminalize and dehuman-
ize immigrants, and we must begin to re(as)semble the beloved
kin-dom free from border walls. In effect, we are called to be a
place of refuge as ample, expansive, and compassionate as the one
Guadalupe envisioned.

To do so, I believe, we must practice a "preferential option for
the in-between"—an option for those persons who constantly live
on the border (whether racial, economic, cultural, sexual, linguistic, and so on). Like Guadalupe, we must flip the script from center
to margin and stand with the immigrants and refugees who arrive
in our country, the indigenous throughout the Americas who are

working to obtain their legitimate rights to their sacred lands and water, and the black and brown bodies struggling for justice in the face of police violence. In so doing, we are called to recognize our own complicities and to break down the barriers that separate the privileged from the disenfranchised, the powerful from the marginalized, the significant from the disposable. Guadalupe has no ungrievable lives. Neither should we.

The lived story of Our Lady of Guadalupe reminds us to consider what we have seen, take counsel on what actions to take, and embody her liberating message. "Does not Wisdom call / And does not understanding raise her voice? / On the heights, beside the way / At the *crossroads* she takes her stand (Prov 8:1–2)."[29]

We know Guadalupe's story. We have seen her face. Now we must act. Our Lady of Guadalupe, pray for us.

Notes

[1] Executive Order 13767 of January 25, 2017, Border Security and Immigration Enforcement Improvements, *Code of Federal Regulations,* title 3 (2017), https://www.whitehouse.gov.

[2] In 1853–54 the United States would acquire an additional 29,970-square-mile portion of Mexico as part of the Gadsden Purchase. This land, which later became part of present-day New Mexico and Arizona, slightly altered the southern border between the United States and Mexico and provided the land necessary to build a transcontinental railroad across the southern United States.

[3] Other examples of such inequitable borders include, but are not limited to, the Demilitarized Zone dividing North and South Korea and the contested boundaries between Israel and Palestine.

[4] Gloria Anzaldúa, *Borderlands/La Frontera: The New Mestiza*, 2nd ed. (San Francisco: Aunt Lute Books, 1999), 25.

[5] Louis León, "Metaphor and Place: The US–Mexico Border as Center and Periphery in the Interpretation of Religion," *Journal of the American Academy of Religion* 67, no. 3 (1999): 543.

[6] Judith A. Greene, Bethany Carson, and Andrea Black, *Indefensible: A Decade of Mass Incarceration of Migrants Prosecuted for Crossing the Border*, Justice Strategies and Grassroots Leadership (July 2016), https://grassrootsleadership.org.

[7] See Peter Andreas, *Border Games: Policing the US-Mexico Divide* (Ithaca, NY: Cornell University Press, 2009).

[8] Miguel De La Torre, "Living on the Borders," *Ecumenical Review* 59, no. 2–3 (April/July 2007): 215.

[9] See Judith Butler, *Precarious Life: The Power of Mourning and Violence* (New York: Verso, 2005).

[10]Miguel A. De La Torre, "On Becoming a Hispanic in the US Borderlands," in *Across Borders: Latin Perspectives in the Americas Reshaping Religion, Theology, and Life*, ed. Joerg Rieger (Plymouth, UK: Lexington Books, 2005), 105.

[11]The quotes in this version are from the *Nican Mopohua*, originally written in 1649 in Nahuatl, by Luis Lasso del la Vega, and translated by Virgilio Elizondo. See Virgilio Elizondo, *Guadalupe: Mother of the New Creation* (Maryknoll, NY: Orbis Books, 1997), 5–22.

[12]Ibid., 8.

[13]Ibid., 16.

[14]Ibid.

[15]See Jeanette Rodriguez, *Our Lady of Guadalupe: Faith and Empowerment among Mexican-American Women* (Austin: University of Texas Press, 1994).

[16]Elizondo, "The Virgin of Guadalupe as a Cultural Icon," in *Quoting God: How Media Shape Ideas about Religion and Culture* (Waco, TX: Baylor University Press, 2005), 205.

[17]Elizondo, *Guadalupe: Mother of the New Creation*, 53.

[18]For this reason, Guadalupe became a popular symbol of rebellion and liberation for the Mexican War of Independence and the United Farm Workers movement led by Cesar Chavez.

[19]Virgilio Elizondo, "Transformation of Borders: Mestizaje and the Future of Humanity," in *Beyond Borders: Writings of Virgilio Elizondo and Friends*, ed. Timothy M. Matovina (Eugene, OR: Wipf & Stock, 2009), 178–79.

[20]Anzaldúa, *Borderlands/La Frontera: The New Mestiza*, 52.

[21]Roberto S. Goizueta, "US Hispanic Popular Catholicism as Theopoetics," in *Hispanic/Latino Theology: Challenge and Promise*, ed. Ada María Isasi-Díaz and Fernando Segovia (Minneapolis: Fortress Press, 1996), 282–83.

[22]Elizondo, *Guadalupe: Mother of the New Creation*, 72.

[23]Elizondo, "Virgin of Guadalupe as a Cultural Icon," 207.

[24]In their book *The María Paradox*, Rosa Gil and Carmen Inoa Vázquez describe this view of Guadalupe as *marianismo*. See Rosa Gil and Carmen Inoa Vázquez, *The María Paradox: How Latinas Can Merge Old World Traditions with New World Self-Esteem* (New York: G. P. Putnam's Sons, 1996).

[25]Judith Butler, *Gender Trouble: Feminism and the Subversion of Identity* (New York: Routledge, 1990).

[26]Ibid., 137–40.

[27]For a theological meditation on Lopez's triptych of Guadalupe, see Nancy Pineda Madrid, "Holy Guadalupe . . . Shameful Malinche? Excavating the Problem of 'Female Dualism,' Doing Theological Spade Work," *Listening: Journal of Religion and Culture* 44, no. 2 (Spring 2009): 71–87.

[28]Guillermo Gómez-Peña, "The Two Guadalupes," in *Goddess of the Americas/ La Diosa de las Americas: Writings on the Virgin of Guadalupe*, ed. Ana Castillo (New York: Riverhead Books, 1996), 180–81.

[29]Emphasis mine.

American Catholicism, Sacramentality, and Care for Creation

Resources for a Local Ecological Ethic

Mathew Verghese

As the College Theology Society turns its attention to American Catholicism in the twenty-first century through the lens of the question "Crossroads, Crisis, or Renewal?" an issue that comes to the fore is the church's response to climate change and ecological injustice. Indeed, with the promulgation of Pope Francis's encyclical *Laudato Si'*, the public and ecclesial imagination has grappled with the growing ecological crisis like never before. However, if we view the reception of the encyclical through the lens of a key theme of *Laudato Si'*—that of collegiality—we will see that the roots of the conversation go back farther into the country's imagination. This essay argues that Francis's implicit emphasis on collegiality in *Laudato Si'* illuminates both a past and a future of American Catholic action and advocacy for environmental justice that emphasizes local engagement and knowledge.

Starting in 1975 and advancing to the present, from Appalachia to the Pacific Northwest, New Mexico to New England, Alaska to the Midwest, regional groups of Catholic bishops, in dialogue with their local communities, have articulated responses to the various struggles and gifts of their local environments.[1] This dynamic and challenging tradition of listening, teaching, and advocacy has created fertile grounds for reception of *Laudato Si'* in the United States of America, particularly in the Appalachian Region. In this view, the church in the United States exemplifies a promising, although not perfect, past and future for implementing more just care for the environment.

Synodality, Collegiality, and Locality

Scholars have recently pointed to the significance of a speech that Pope Francis gave in October of 2015 to commemorate the fiftieth anniversary of the establishment of the Synod of Bishops.[2] Francis makes his vision clear: "The world in which we live . . . demands that the Church strengthen cooperation in all areas of her mission. It is precisely this path of synodality which God expects of the Church of the third millennium."[3] To this end, Francis envisions renewal of synodality at three levels: in the particular churches, in ecclesiastical provinces and conferences of bishops, and in the college of bishops united "*cum Petro et sub Petro*." Francis offers a motivating rationale behind this ecclesial renewal in *Evangelii Gaudium*: "The renewal of structures demanded by pastoral conversion can only be understood in this light: as part of an effort to make them more mission-oriented. . . . I invite everyone to be bold and creative in this task of rethinking the goals, structures, style and methods of evangelization in their respective communities."[4] The urgent tone and appeals for renewal resonate strongly with the tone and style of *Laudato Si'*.

Francis's commitment to collegiality was central to the widespread distribution of his ecological message. Gerard O'Connell notes that Francis cited sixteen regional bishops' conferences and sent a copy of the encyclical to every diocesan bishop along with a handwritten note. The note "was particularly significant since it contained an explicit reference to No. 22 of Vatican II's 'Dogmatic Constitution on the Church,' which speaks about collegiality."[5] This method of communication, along with his citations of the regional conferences, speaks to the juxtaposition of collegiality to Francis's concern for the environment. The references to local realities such as coral reefs and the needs of *campesinos* in *Laudato Si'* are highlighted by the inclusion of the voices of those who minister to the people and the geographical features in the local context. We can see how "these regional letters gave universal principles a regional focus, suggesting a sense of place for their implementation."[6]

Summary of Regional Bishops' Documents
on the Environment

The tradition of regional groups of bishops reflecting on the local exigencies of their people and environment exemplifies the type of ecclesial renewal for which Francis calls. Starting in 1975 with the Appalachian bishops' *This Land Is Home to Me,* a unique style and focus, perhaps a genre, of church reflection on environmental issues brought Catholic social thought and the sacramental imagination to bear on cries for justice in particular areas of the country. Here, I seek to call attention to these documents in the light of the imperatives of *Laudato Si'* before diving more deeply into the documents released by the Appalachian bishops.

Following *This Land Is Home to Me,* in the genealogy of these documents, is the Midwest bishops' 1980 *Strangers and Guests.* The bishops speak in a way that echoes the diagnosis of *Laudato Si'*, albeit with a local flair: "We are witnessing profound and disturbing changes in rural America. Land ownership is being restructured, agricultural production is becoming more heavily industrialized and concentrated in fewer hands and the earth all too frequently is being subjected to harmful farming, mining and development practices."[7] Branching out from this diagnosis, this document stands out among this tradition as one of the most concrete as it takes stands on specific legal, financial, agricultural, zoning, and economic principles. The claims to the positions are grounded in the biblical narrative and in Catholic social teaching. For what it emphasizes in concrete recommendations, however, the document speaks less from a robustly developed sense of a sacramental principle.

While a shorter and less extensive document, the Alaskan bishops' letter "A Catholic Perspective on Subsistence: Our Responsibility toward Alaska's Bounty and Our Human Family" is just as, if not more, concrete.[8] The bishops bring the breadth and depth of Catholic Social Teaching to bear, in an illuminating way, on the debate on Indigenous subsistence rights in Alaska. This debate occurs at the intersections of federal treaties, claims to states' rights, the local situations of impoverished peoples, and the investments of various local parties. Such an approach clearly demands that

Catholic Social Teaching be familiar with the local social, political, and cultural milieu. In making explicit the demands of one principle of CST, solidarity, to affirm Indigenous culture in an active political discussion, the Alaskan bishops make good on the call of *Laudato Si'* "to show special care for Indigenous communities and their cultural traditions," for "they are not merely one minority among others, but should be the principal dialogue partners, especially when large projects affecting their land are proposed."[9] Indeed, this emphasis on complex intertwining of culture, subsistence, and land is central to the bishops' application of the tradition. Without being able to assess the impact of the bishops' reflections and exhortations on the debate in Alaska, we can at least appreciate that they were engaged, listening, and prophetic in the spirit of *Laudato Si'*.

Some documents from this tradition focus less on specific details and more on articulating a robust framework for dealing with a wider variety of issues. While documents from the bishops of the Boston region and from the bishops of New Mexico emphasize issues historically important to their regions (family fisheries and water access, respectively), their focus is on making clear the principled commitments of the church in these regional contexts. For example, the New Mexico bishops articulate a need to claim humanity's vocation to be stewards of the earth's goods with renewed urgency.[10] Similarly, the Boston bishops speak of the sacramental nature of their local environment: "The New England landscape, which is so blessed with forests and lakes, seashore and mountains, is not merely an economic resource, but a window into the beauty of God revealed in what God has made."[11] Set in a familiar environmental context, these principles have the potential to resonate in new and profound ways.

One of the most well known documents from this tradition strikes a balance between the critically engaged and sacramental framing approaches. The bishops of the Columbia River Watershed offer a reflection on environmental justice that is framed itself by the metaphor of its central subject: the river.[12] The bishops speak of the rivers of our moment, rivers through our memory, the rivers in our vision, and the rivers of our responsibility. Through this sacramental narrative frame, they are able to bring into focus the multiple concrete activities that make the river a central object of reflection (such as fishing, industry, and recreation). One can detect in this work, and all of those described above, a strong resonance with key themes of *Laudato Si'*: hearing the cry of the poor and the cry of the earth by attending to the importance of local knowledge and history. These themes are rooted especially deeply in the Appalachian communities from which the two most famous pastoral letters emerged.

Progress and Challenges in Appalachia

Taken as a whole, the two documents, *This Land Is Home to Me* (1975) and *At Home in the Web of Life* (1995), make up an extended conversation between the bishops and the wider population of the region. Referred to sometimes as "people's pastorals," the documents emerged from many listening sessions with groups from all sectors of society.[13] From these sessions, the issues of coal, culture, civic and political participation, dependence, land ownership, work, health, sustainability, the environment, and poverty came to the fore. The focus on these integral issues, as well as the emphasis on listening, already evoke key themes from *Laudato Si'*, forty and twenty years before its promulgation.

What the bishops heard was a lament from the people. The free-flowing prose of *This Land* narrates a history that has a relationship with coal at its center: "The coal-based industry created many jobs, and brought great progress to our country, but it brought other things, too, among them oppression for the mountains."[14] It speaks of how "'development' often brings little to the poor or to the workers" and speaks out against "the anonymous character of economic interests."[15] Contributing to this narrative, *At Home* attests to ways that "large super-stores . . . coal companies . . . the waste of consumer society . . . new prisons . . . appear to be trying to turn Appalachia into a social and natural dumping ground, exploited in a post-industrial way which threatens the very web of life."[16] Where the Columbia River Watershed document often proceeded in a more even-handed tone, the bishops of Appalachia name structural and corporate sin plainly and call for conversion in a way that seeks to cause its readers to "become painfully aware, to dare to turn what is happening to the world into our own personal suffering and thus to discover what each of us can do about it."[17]

If a balance does exist, it is in discerning "that the cry of the poor is also a message of hope."[18] When new editions of the documents were released in 2007, John Rausch, director of the Catholic Committee of Appalachia, notes the ways in which they had effects in their communities:

> Just as the first pastoral called forth the founding of the only monastery in eastern Kentucky at Mt. Tabor and sparked creative ministries in health care, addiction counseling, education, economic development, family violence assistance and environmental work, so today more than 35 years later it reissues the call for justice. Just as the second pastoral questioned frivolous consumption in society and challenged the church to emphasize sustainable values, so today readers must face the urgency of global warming, poor air quality and threatened water sources.[19]

Giving voice to those who were oppressed in the region brought about change, perhaps not in all of the structural ways needed, but certainly in ways that progressed toward just ends. From these conversations the writers of *This Land* put out calls for "citizen control . . . Centers of Reflection and Prayer . . . Centers of Popular Culture . . . attention to the presence of powerful multinational corporations now within our region . . . a multinational labor movement" as well as attention to various other aspects of mining, land acquisition, energy use, cooperatives, and visions of the church.[20] Many of these calls turned into realities in the decades that followed.

Another key development in *At Home* is a localized sacramental imagination. Its elaboration is complementary to the emphasis on sacramentality in *Laudato Si'*, and pushes beyond the encyclical in its ability to draw on local memories of both beauty and pain in relation to the land. One area in which this shift to a sacramental lens is particularly striking is in the letter's discussion of some central symbols of Appalachia: forests, mines, and the work of people. Against a vision of forests as raw material, mines as pits, and people as cheap labor, the letter offers a sacramentalized reading of these realities. Instead, "the mountain forests are sacred cathedrals," "empty mines are sacred wombs of Earth," and "the people are God's co-creators, called to form sustainable communities."[21] This robust focus on the sacramentality of the region offers a challenge to a purely instrumentalized vision, by way of an indicting juxtaposition. The ways in which this vision plays out in the bishops' reflections are significant, as it situates the lives and work of all in Appalachia in a dignifying and empowering horizon wherein one's homeland becomes a locus for the work of Almighty God to take place.

The missions of small local organizations and businesses testify to the enduring legacy of the people's pastorals.[22] The presence of these groups resonates with an important call from *Laudato Si'*: "Society is also enriched by a countless array of organizations which work to promote the common good and to defend the environment, whether natural or urban. . . . Around these community actions, relationships develop or are recovered and a new social fabric emerges."[23]

These avenues are also cultivated by the work of individuals such as the Jesuit Michael Woods. Father Woods is based at the Appalachian Institute, an organization at Wheeling Jesuit University whose origin lies in *This Land Is Home to Me*. Woods writes about his work through Grow Ohio Valley (GOV) in downtown Wheeling in a way that makes clear the way his work builds on both the Appalachian bishops and *Laudato Si'*: "GOV reclaims abandoned city lots, grows good healthy food, and seeks to make it accessible to all, especially those in the struggling Ohio Valley, part of the depressed Rust Belt."[24] Woods focuses on the ways that both his work as a farmhand with GOV, the hands-on healthy eating education programs run by GOV, and his teaching enact the principles of Catholic environmental teaching and push them further by grounding them in a specific practice: food. His citations employ the emphasis in *Laudato Si'* on "integral ecology" to show that he is consciously changing his local community into a more environmentally just one through his work. As the bishops in *At Home* say, "Small amounts of capital often go a long way."[25]

Despite the important steps being made in agriculture and through small groups, big capital still exerts most of the power in the region, as significant work remains to be done in the realms of coal and land ownership, from both cultural and structural perspectives. Brian Roewe quotes Franciscan Sister Robbie Pentecost, a thirty-year veteran minister in the region, to capture the ambivalence of Appalachian residents in their reception of *Laudato Si'*: "In an area long swayed by coal company talking points (or fearful of challenging them), and one where 'Catholic' is sometimes seen as a negative term, it's rocky ground for planting. 'They don't have a sense of what's possible, and so think it is the only thing and decide to stay with what you know.' "[26] Statements like this are part of a wider trend of cultural inertia that Roewe traces, even as the prospects of coal become bleaker.

Another structural obstacle is the ownership of land in Appalachia. The major "Appalachia Land Ownership Survey" sought to ascertain the owners and value of land across Appalachia. Elizabeth Payne writes: "In 1981, the group released its findings in a multi-volume 1,800-page report. They found that 40 percent of the property and 70 percent of the mineral rights in Appalachian counties sampled were owned by corporations, and of the land owned by individuals, less than half was owned by 'local individuals.' "[27] While certainly leaving us in need of updated data, the study emphasizes what has been true of coal in the region for decades: the benefits of the land are funneled elsewhere while the instability and waste of extraction remain. As the bishops of Appalachia wrote in *This Land Is Home to Me*: "There is a saying in the region that coal is king. That's not exactly right. The kings are those who control big coal, and the profit and power which come with it. Many of these kings don't live in the region."[28]

In this dire, yet not bereft of hope, situation, Bishop John Stowe, recently installed bishop of the Diocese of Lexington, Kentucky, took a series of pastoral visits to coal strips within his diocese at the start of his episcopate. Brian Roewe remarks on how Bishop Stowe also preached consistently during this time on the messages of *Laudato Si'* in his homilies at rural parishes, carefully crafting his message to address the local context. Bishop Stowe reflects that he views his coalfield trips as "in line with the listening sessions undertaken by past Appalachian bishops who authored *This Land Is Home to Me* and *At Home in the Web of Life*."[29] In this bishop's mission, standing on a coalfield, we have the intersection of past and present, the application of past and present wisdom from both the global and local church to the challenges of his people. By fostering images like these, the reciprocal enrichment of local environmental engagement and the tradition of the church's social teaching forges a way forward into twenty-first-century America.

Notes

[1]I focus on the role of the bishops as bridge figures between the work of all local ministers and articulation of the social tradition in these local contexts and for the whole church. For an example of the work on the ground that went into these letters in the Appalachian context, see Carlye Burket-Thatcher, "'The Mountains Shall Yield Peace for the People and the Hills Justice': The Bishops' Pastoral Letter on Powerlessness 'This Land Is Home to Me,' 1950–1980," (PhD diss., University of Kentucky, 2011), 193–249. Additionally, the United States Conference of Catholic Bishops has produced three major texts related to the environment: "Reflections on the Energy Crisis" (1981), "Renewing the Earth: An Invitation to Reflection and Action on Environment in Light of Catholic Social Teaching" (1991), and "Global Climate Change: A Plea for Dialogue, Prudence, and the Common Good" (2001), at www.usccb.org. Due to space constraints, I focus on the more local documents here.

[2]See Richard Gaillardetz, "A More Pastoral Magisterium: Papal Authority in the Francis Era," *Commonweal*, January 27, 2017, 18–21; Massimo Faggioli, "Are the Bishops Up to the Pope's Challenge to Build a Synodal Church?" *La Croix International*, at https://international.la-croix.com.

[3]Pope Francis, "Address of His Holiness Pope Francis: Ceremony Commemorating the 50th Anniversary of the Institution of the Synod of Bishops," www.vatican.va. See also Francis, *Evangelii Gaudium*, no. 27–33, www.vatican.va. In these opening sections, I mean collegiality and synodality to be two not entirely distinguishable movements of Pope Francis's intention for mission-centered decentralization.

[4]Francis, *Evangelii Gaudium*, nos. 27, 33.

[5]Gerard O'Connell, "Francis Pushes Collegiality," *America*, July 20, 2015, 27. *Opposing Viewpoints in Context*, at www.americamagazine.org under the title, "Francis Leads Less Like a Monarch, More Like a Fellow Bishop."

[6]John Hart, *What Are They Saying about Environmental Theology?* (New York: Paulist Press, 2004), 38. This insight from Hart finds a kindred sentiment in *Laudato Si'*, no. 84.

[7]Midwestern Catholic Bishops, *Strangers and Guests* (Sioux Falls, SD: Heartland Project, 1980), no. 1. This paragraph aligns well with *Laudato Si'*, no. 134 (Francis is quoting an Argentine bishops' conference here).

[8]Catholic Bishops of Alaska, "A Catholic Perspective on Subsistence: Our Responsibility toward Alaska's Bounty and Our Human Family," *Origins* 31, no. 45 (April 25, 2002): 745–52.

[9]*Laudato Si'*, no. 146.

[10]See Catholic Bishops of New Mexico, "Reclaiming the Vocation to Care for the Earth," *Origins* 28, no. 4 (1998): 63–64.

[11]Catholic Bishops of Boston Province, "And God Saw That It Was Good: A Pastoral Letter of the Bishops of the Boston Province," *Origins* 30, no. 20 (2000): 318–20.

[12]*The Columbia River Watershed: Caring for Creation and the Common Good: An International Pastoral Letter by the Catholic Bishops of the Region*, 2001.

[13]For example, see introductory letter from Bishop R. Daniel Conlon in Catholic Bishops of Appalachia, *This Land Is Home to Me* (1975) and *At Home in the Web of Life* (1995) (Martin, KY: Catholic Committee of Appalachia, 2007), 3.

[14]*This Land*, 14.

[15]Ibid., 20, 28.

[16]*At Home*, 62–63.

[17]*Laudato Si'*, no. 19.

[18]*This Land*, 10.

[19]Ibid., 4.

[20]See ibid., 32–37.

[21]*At Home*, 46. See also Pope Francis's quotation of Patriarch Bartholomew in *Laudato Si'*, no. 9. For exceptionally beautiful examples of a rooted sacramentality in Appalachia, see Lucas Briola, "Sustainable Communities and Eucharistic Communities: *Laudato Si'*, Northern Appalachia, and Redemptive Recovery," *Journal of Moral Theology* 2, Special Issue 1 (2017): 28–32.

[22]For examples, see the mission statement of Bethlehem Farm, a Catholic Worker–inspired farm in West Virginia, available at www.bethlehemfarm.net; and the history of the Appalachian Institute of Wheeling Jesuit University, www.wju.edu/ai.

[23]*Laudato Si'*, no. 232. See also *At Home*, 42.

[24]Michael Woods, "God, Too, Has a Hand in the Soil," unpublished version of earlier published article, shared via personal communication on April 20, 2017. See also Woods's in-depth study of the confluence of the liturgical and agricultural movements in *Cultivating Soil and Soul: Twentieth-Century Catholic Agrarians Embrace the Liturgical Movement* (Collegeville, MN: Pueblo Books, 2009), for remarkable insights into the variety of local communities' environmental action.

[25]*At Home*, 84.

[26]Brian Roewe, "What's Happening after Coal?" *National Catholic Reporter*, November 6, 2015, 1, 10–11.

[27]Elizabeth E. Payne, "Owning the Mountains: Appalachia's History of Corporate Control," *Appalachian Voices*, http://appvoices.org.

[28]*This Land*, 14.

[29]Roewe, "What's Happening?" 11–12.

Contributors

Frederick Christian Bauerschmidt is a professor of theology at Loyola University Maryland and a permanent deacon of the Archdiocese of Baltimore. His most recent publications include *Catholic Theology: An Introduction*, with James Buckley (Oxford: Wiley Publishers, 2017) and *Thomas Aquinas: Faith, Reason and Following Christ* (Oxford University Press, 2013).

Michael Baxter teaches religious studies and Catholic studies at Regis University in Denver. He has published articles in *Communio, Pro Ecclesia, The Thomist,* and *Nova et Vetera* and is completing a book of essays titled *No Abiding City: Radicalism against Americanism in Catholic Social Ethics* to be published by Cascade Press.

Most Reverend Stephen E. Blaire is the Bishop of Stockton, California. As a member of the US Conference of Catholic Bishops, he has served as chairman of the Pastoral Practices Committee and the Committee on Domestic Justice, Peace, and Human Development.

William A. Clark, SJ, is an associate professor of religious studies, College of the Holy Cross (Worcester, Massachusetts), where he teaches courses in Catholic doctrine, church community, and Christian prayer. Among his published works are *A Voice of Their Own: The Authority of the Local Parish* (Liturgical Press, 2005), and the co-edited volume *Collaborative Parish Leadership: Contexts, Models, Theology* (Lexington, 2016).

Jessica Coblentz is an assistant professor of theology and religious studies at Saint Mary's College of California and a 2017–19 Louisville Institute Postdoctoral Fellow. She's at work on a monograph that proposes a Christian theology of depression. Her other research focuses on feminist theologies and Catholic higher education. She earned her PhD in systematic theology from Boston College in 2017.

Dana L. Dillon teaches at Providence College, where she holds a joint appointment in the department of theology and the department of public and community service studies. Her research and teaching focus on virtue ethics, Catholic social thought, political theology, liberation theology, race, dialogue, and inclusion.

Mary Doak (PhD, University of Chicago) is a professor of theology at the University of San Diego. Her publications include *Divine Harmony: Seeking Community in a Broken World* (Paulist, 2017); *Translating Religion* (Orbis Books, 2013; The Annual Volume of the College Theology Society, 2012), co-edited with Anita Houck; and *Reclaiming Narrative for Public Theology* (SUNY, 2004); as well as various articles on public theology, eschatology, and ecclesiology.

Alison Downie is an associate professor in the religious studies department at Indiana University of Pennsylvania, and affiliated faculty in the women's and gender studies and sustainability studies programs. She has published in *Feminist Theology* and *Teaching Theology and Religion*. Her current research is in feminist disability theology.

Curtis W. Freeman is a research professor of theology and director of the Baptist House of Studies at Duke University Divinity School. His books include *Contesting Catholicity* and *Undomesticated Dissent*. He is co-editor of the *American Baptist Quarterly* and is a member of the Doctrine and Christian Unity Commission of the Baptist World Alliance.

Timothy R. Gabrielli is an associate professor of theology at Seton Hill University in Greensburg, Pennsylvania. He is the author of *Confirmation: How a Sacrament of God's Grace Became All about Us* (Liturgical, 2013) and *One in Christ: Virgil Michel, Louis-Marie Chauvet and Mystical Body Theology* (Liturgical, 2017). He is co-editor of *Weaving the American Catholic Tapestry* (Wipf & Stock, 2017).

Anthony J. Godzieba is a professor of theology and religious studies at Villanova University and editor emeritus of *Horizons: The Journal of the College Theology Society*. He is the author of *Bernhard Welte's Fundamental Theological Approach to Christology* (Lang, 1994) and is co-editor with Brad Hinze of *Beyond Dogmatism and Innocence: Hermeneutic, Critique, and Catholic Theology* (Liturgical, 2017).

Steven R. Harmon is an associate professor of historical theology in the School of Divinity at Gardner-Webb University in Boiling Springs, North Carolina. He is the author of *Baptist Identity and the Ecumenical Future: Story, Tradition, and the Recovery of Community* (Baylor University Press, 2016) and is co-secretary of the joint commission to the Baptist–Catholic international bilateral dialogue, Phase III (2017–21).

Derek C. Hatch is an associate professor of Christian studies at Howard Payne University in Brownwood, Texas. He is the co-editor of *Gathering Together: Baptists at Work in Worship* (Wipf & Stock, 2013) and *Weaving the American Catholic Tapestry* (Wipf & Stock, 2017). He is also the author of *Thinking with the Church: Toward a Renewal of Baptist Theology* (Cascade, 2018).

Daniel P. Horan, OFM, PhD, is a Franciscan Friar, an assistant professor of systematic theology at the Catholic Theological Union (Chicago), and the author of several books, including the award-winning *The Franciscan Heart of Thomas Merton: A New Look at the Spiritual Influence on His Life, Thought, and Writing* (2014). His latest book is *All God's Creatures: A Theology of Creation* (2018).

Katharine Mahon teaches in the department of theology as a visiting assistant professional specialist at the University of Notre Dame. She earned her PhD in theology specializing in liturgical studies at the University of Notre Dame in 2016.

Timothy Matovina is a professor of theology and chair of the theology department at the University of Notre Dame. He works in the area of theology and culture, with specialization in US Catholicism and Latino/a theology. Recent publications include *Latino Catholicism: Transformation in America's Largest Church* (Princeton University Press, 2014) and the forthcoming *Engaging a New World: Theologies of Guadalupe from the Era of Conquest to Pope Francis.*

Nicholas Mayrand is the director of faith formation and mission for the Diocese of Wheeling-Charleston. He is also a PhD candidate in theology at the University of Dayton. His dissertation research focuses on the "rise of the nones" and the challenging theological vision of Ivan Illich.

Margaret McGuinness is a professor of religion and theology at

La Salle University, Philadelphia. She is the author of *Neighbors and Missionaries: A History of the Sisters of Our Lady of Christian Doctrine* (Fordham University Press, 2012) and *Called to Serve: A History of Nuns in America* (New York University Press, 2013), and co-editor, with James T. Fisher, of *A Catholic Studies Reader* (Fordham University Press, 2011).

Paul G. Monson is an assistant professor of church history at Sacred Heart Seminary and School of Theology in Hales Corners, Wisconsin. He studied historical theology at Marquette University with a dissertation on transatlantic monasticism. His research focuses on the relationship between evangelization, history, and culture in American Catholicism, with a distinct transnational lens.

Benjamin T. Peters is an associate professor of theology at the University of Saint Joseph in Connecticut. He is the author of *Called to Be Saints: John Hugo, the Catholic Worker, and a Theology of Radical Christianity* (Marquette University Press, 2016).

William L. Portier is the Mary Ann Spearin Chair of Catholic Theology and the director of the PhD program at the University of Dayton. He served as president of the College Theology Society from 2014 to 2017. His most recent publication is *Every Catholic an Apostle: A Life of Thomas A. Judge, CM, 1868–1933* (Catholic University of America Press, 2017).

Nicholas Rademacher is an associate professor of religious studies and the coordinator of the social justice minor at Cabrini University in Radnor, Pennsylvania. His scholarship concentrates on traditions of American Catholic radicalism and socially engaged pedagogy. He is co-editor of *American Catholic Studies*. His book *Paul Hanly Furfey: Priest, Scientist, Social Reformer* was published by Fordham University Press in 2017.

Mary M. Doyle Roche is an associate professor of religious studies at the College of the Holy Cross in Worcester, Massachusetts. She is the author of *Children, Consumerism, and the Common Good* (Lexington, 2009) and *Schools of Solidarity: Families and Catholic Social Teaching* (Liturgical, 2015).

John N. Sheveland (PhD, Boston College) is a professor of religious studies at Gonzaga University in Spokane, Washington. He serves on the board of directors of the Society of Buddhist–Christian Studies and on the steering committee of the Interreligious and Interfaith Studies Group of the American Academy of Religion, and is the author of *Piety and Responsibility* (Ashgate/Routledge, 2011).

Laura M. Taylor is an assistant professor of theology at the College of St. Benedict and St. John's University in Central Minnesota. Her teaching and research interests include feminist and liberation theologies, theories of race, class, and gender, and contemporary Catholic systematic theology.

Mathew Verghese is a doctoral student at Villanova University, where his studies focus on liturgy and environmental ethics. He is interested in how the church takes up the things of creation both in and beyond liturgical celebration. He also has a background in psychology and counseling and hopes to contribute to discussions concerning theology and science as well as pastoral care.

Patricia Wittberg, SC, is a Sister of Charity of Cincinnati, Ohio. She holds a PhD in sociology from the University of Chicago and has written extensively on the sociology of the Catholic Church and Catholic religious orders. Currently, she is a research associate at the Center for Applied Research in the Apostolate at Georgetown University.

Sandra Yocum, PhD, is the University Professor of Faith and Culture at the University of Dayton. Her publications include *American Catholic Traditions: Resources for Renewal* (Orbis Books, 1997; The Annual Volume of the College Theology Society, 1996), co-edited with William Portier; *Joining the Revolution in Theology: The College Theology Society, 1954–2004* (Sheed and Ward, 2007); and *Clergy Sexual Abuse: Social Science Perspectives*, co-edited with Claire M. Renzetti (Northeastern, 2013); as well as journal articles and book chapters.